Reminiscences of an Old Timer

Recital of the Actual Events, Incidents, Trials of a Pioneer, Hunter, Miner and Scout of the Pacific Northwest, ...Indian Wars, Anecdotes, etc.

By Colonel George Hunter

PANTIANOS
CLASSICS

Published by Pantianos Classics

ISBN-13: 978-1-78987-583-6

First published in 1887

Yours Truly,

Colonel George Hunter

Contents

Dedication

To My Aged Father,

WILLIAM HUNTER

A Pioneer of the Northwest, a member of the Brotherhood which especially encouraged me in placing before the public the story of my life; a man who, at seventy-eight years of age, still proves to be a loving husband, a kind father, and a square and charitable Brother — this book is respectfully dedicated by

THE AUTHOR

Introduction

Reader, do not for a moment imagine that in these pages you will discover any literary gems, brilliant word paintings, or imaginary legends; but rather the plain unvarnished story of the life, incidents and adventures of a blunt, uneducated man, who has "roughed it" in the great Northwest from boyhood, and writes from memory only.

Preface

In the compilation of the narrative contained in this work, the author has told in graphic language the history of his early youth and subsequent incidents that partake of more than ordinary interest. Colonel George Hunter, one of the band of pioneers whose advance to the slopes of the Pacific paved the way for the tide of emigration, has passed through a series of those hair-breadth escapes and adventures so incidental to Western life. At the solicitation of numerous friends the task of collating his reminiscences have been undertaken, and, although the present work does not pretend to any high literary effort, its contents can scarcely fail to be interesting, especially to those who have become identified with the events described.

The incidents relating to the migration of the Hunter family across the plains in 1852 will awaken many memories; the earnest endeavors of young Hunter to obtain work, showing the indomitable spirit in the youth, that afterwards developed in the man, are minutely described.

Mining life in Shasta City district is vividly portrayed, and the arrival of the first white woman at the camp is described with a minute detail that shows how welcome such a *rara avis* was in those days. Chapter Five contains a stirring tale of the Rogue River Indian War of 1853, and the author, who participated with honor in that and other campaigns, details in plain language the horrible mutilations and cruelties practiced upon the dead by the Indians. The conduct of the war against these Rogue River Indians was given to the noted veteran, General Joe Lane, and a high compliment is paid to Oregon's "friend" for services rendered then and up to the time of his death.

As a sequence to the narrative it follows that the hunting of grizzlies and other noble game is accurately described in these pages, and the exciting accounts of the chase and its results prove that Colonel Hunter was no mean nimrod.

A contrast between the aspect of the Umatilla "Meadows" in 1855 and its present appearance is admirably portrayed, and it must indeed be a source of gratification to the old pioneer to witness the improvements that have been made in the land in which he took so deep an interest.

The events which led to the massacre of the worthy missionary, Dr. Whitman, to whom the credit belongs of saving Oregon and Washington Territory to the Union, are given in Chapter Eight, and the supposed causes which led to his death are discussed.

The lack of emigration and transportation retarded the development of the Walla Walla Valley, and Colonel Hunter after abandoning mining in the Shasta City district went to Shoalwater Bay, engaging in the oyster business and occasional hunting trips.

The colonel was appointed sheriff of Pacific County about this time, and graphically describes his first arrest and how his prisoner escaped by jumping from the steamer that was conveying him to jail.

In 1861 the Civil War broke out, Hunter and his wife's relatives ranging on the Union side, being strong "Douglass Democrats." He bravely defended the honor of the flag in an attempt to lower it by some rebel sympathizers, and shortly afterwards resumed his old vocation of mining on the upper Columbia.

Wandering through the country, from Boise City to Snake River, the author became sick west of Salt Lake City, where, afraid to trust himself in the hands of the Mormon doctor, he was taken care of by the doctor at Camp Douglass and speedily regained his health under the kind attentions of a Mormon family.

In conjunction with a partner Colonel Hunter then carried the mails from Salt Lake to Virginia City, via East Bannack, and in this service again encountered the hostility of his old enemies, the Indians.

But the old gold fever was still strong and, when news of the strike at Kootenia in British Columbia came, our pioneer went with a party to seek a fortune. The enforcement of the rigid mining laws on British territory are narrated, and an illustration given of the respect shown by miners to their regulations.

In 1865 Hunter left Kootenia for Walla Walla, traversing the Pen d'Oreille to the Spokane, over the Snake River, and on to Walla Walla. That town, in 1863, was a "lively" place, and our pioneer soon had his hands filled with the task of regulating the bands of road-agents and Indians who were stopping travelers and robbing stages. Vigilance committees were organized in which he took a prominent part, and the disturbers were soon "cleaned out" of the country.

In 1877 the Nez Perces war commenced and Colonel Hunter tendered his services to General O. O. Howard, which were thankfully accepted. From the general he received the most considerate and kind attention, being in close attendance upon that distinguished officer throughout the campaign. The details of the outrages and practices of the Indians are given in full, and horrible indeed they are when narrated by an eyewitness of the scenes.

The war being over Colonel Hunter returned to his home to receive care and nursing at the hands of his wife, and upon recovering removed his family to Grange City. At a "pow-wow" with the Indians, where he acted as interpreter to General Howard, Colonel Hunter was elected their chief.

The remainder of the volume is taken up in describing the many events of the years that followed the discovery of gold in the Columbia basin, and a humorous description of the author's first dabble in politics is given.

Becoming a member of the "Grange" Colonel Hunter entered into the warehousing business and still continues in that pursuit. In 1880 he was elected to serve in the Washington Territory Legislature, and his experiences and labors as a law maker proved that he served his constituents with honor.

It is now Colonel Hunter's intention to travel East in order to disseminate information about the great Northwest country of the Pacific Coast, a country which he helped to build up and for which he predicts a glorious future.

In conclusion I may add that the present volume is well worthy of perusal, not only to those whose interests are in that portion of the country described, but also to the class of readers who may be desirous of gaining some ideas of that vast and productive portion of the Union which, though scantily populated at the present time, is destined to become the home of a great and wealthy people.

Gideon P. Woodward,
Manager Historical Pub. Co.

My First Friend and Teacher

Chapter One

My name is George Hunter. I was born near Goshen, in Claremont County, Ohio, on the 20th day of December, 1835.

My father's name is William He is of the old Virginia stock, of revolutionary Hunters, and, as I am informed, a distant relative of *Adam the First.*

My mother was a Meek; a second cousin of the renowned free trapper and Oregon pioneer General Joseph L. Meek, who used to declare that he "first came to this country when Mount Hood was but a hole in the ground."

From my childhood I was pronounced very different from most boys. I preferred rambling through the tangled woods and bushy swamps, gathering nuts and sweet roots, catching birds, squirrels and insects, while accompanied by a large and faithful mastiff dog, in whom my parents placed implicit confidence; they knew that old "Lion" would protect me and never leave me alone in the woods, and as I write this my heart thumps hard, while memory reverts to the scenes of my childhood and recalls the times when, lost and bewildered in those woods, I would always find my home, by following that noble brute as he trotted ahead of me, saying, by his actions, "follow me, Georgie, I know the way."

To my infantile associations with that faithful friend I attribute much of my success, in training and educating wild horses and other animals, in later years.

From infancy I have always abhorred the restraints of a school-room, and sought a wild and roving life, only educating myself mechanically as occasion required, to fill the positions which emergency, fortune, or friends, placed me in.

One reason being that, until I was sixteen years of age, I was puny and delicate and required out-door exercise.

During the winter of 1849, my father caught the "California Gold Fever," and started with his family, consisting of mother, four sons and four daughters — of which I was the third in age (of the children, I mean) for the new *Eldorado.*

Loss of stock from the murrain necessitated his stopping in Iowa, from whence my two elder brothers went up the Mississippi to "try their luck," steam-boating and lead-mining.

Being so young and frail, father thought I would be an incumbrance to them, so he kept me near our new home, which he had entered with his "Mexican Land Warrant."

Being a good blacksmith, he constructed a large breaking-plow, with wheels to guide it, and having secured the use of an ox-team "on the shares," I earned for my father, during that year's breaking-season, a yoke of oxen and two good cows, and for myself a good rifle and a year's outfit of clothing, while father had to forward money to my brothers for them to come home on.

In the spring of 1852 my father rigged up two teams of six yoke of cattle each, and we started across the plains for Oregon, driving a dozen cows along.

Our wagon-boxes were decked over, so that we could sleep in them as well as in the tents that we hauled for that purpose. We had a six months' supply of provisions and clothing.

A young man named John Haligan, an Irishman, who had been educated for the priesthood, but on account of ill health had abandoned that intention and become a country schoolteacher, "engaged passage" with us, thinking that the trip would be beneficial to him. He was small and delicate, and one of the best men I ever knew. More of him hereafter.

At Kanesville, near Council Bluffs, on the Missouri river, we joined an emigrant train of about fifty wagons, loaded with men, women and children, and the necessary outfit of arms, ammunition, clothing, provisions, etc., for the tedious seven-months' journey over the parched plains, burning sands and arid wastes intervening between us and the "promised land," which journey is now accomplished in a palace-car in ninety-six hours.

For protection against the numerous bands of marauding and hostile Indians that infested the route in those days, we organized, *a la* military, choosing one Smith, of Bonaparte, Iowa, as captain of the train. We also chose sub-officers to serve under him, and from among our able-bodied men and boys was formed relays for guard, picket and herd duty.

Of the dangers, trials, privations, hardships, heart-rendings and sufferings endured by those who crossed the plains in early days, very much has been said and written, but not enough; nor am I capable of conveying with tongue or pen any adequate idea of the ordeals those plucky people necessarily underwent.

The thousands of lonely mounds yet to be seen along the old emigrant roads — on mountain, desert and plain — without monument, headstone, paling, or anything else to call attention to them, except, perchance, a few rocks that were piled over them to prevent the wolves from exhuming their treasures, are the only monuments to the memory of the many who in those days fearlessly faced the setting sun, and "fell by the wayside."

After a thorough inspection of all the teams, wagons, arms and stores, as a precautionary measure against possible hindrance, we were ferried over the Missouri on a steamboat that was brought there for the purpose, and soon found ourselves actually started on the toilsome journey, and away from civilization.

As the saying went "everybody came to Oregon in '52," and there being an almost continuous string of teams and loose stock on the road, for a distance of 500 miles, we soon had to drive our cattle a mile or two from the road for feed. The water became impure, and much sickness prevailed along the line; finally the cholera broke out among the people in a malignant form and the majority of those attacked were soon buried. Our captain and many others of our own train fell a prey to this disease and were left by the roadside under a few shovelfuls of earth and some rocks. The burial services were primitive and brief and no coffins were used.

In the case of our captain, an aged pioneer who was beloved by the whole party, when he was attacked we encamped on a low bottom near the Platte, and I was beside him during his few remaining terrible hours. I shall never forget that cold, foggy and dismal night, when the stillness was only broken by the groans of the other sick and dying, and the howling of the myriads of prairie wolves around us, who seemed intuitively to know that flesh must be left there.

Next day we dug a shallow grave, baled out as much of the water as we could and wrapping the remains of the noble man in a blanket and a feather bed, we held them down in the water till the earth and stones were piled above them, then leading away his two sorrowing sons we moved on westward, leaving him to his solitary sleep far away from friends or kindreds, in a desolate and uninhabited region. For weeks we were scarcely out of sight of one or more burial parties.

It was said that if there was any devil in a man the plains would bring it out, and I am sure they would have tried the patience of a more saintly person than the devil is usually given credit for having.

In our train was a family named Kent, consisting of a man, wife, son and several daughters.

This family was stricken with the cholera; and to keep them with the train, I volunteered to drive one of their teams.

After the son "Ben" got well Kent prevailed on my father to allow me to continue driving till the rest of the family recovered. This "Ben" was a burly, red-headed scamp, two years older than myself and equal to two of me in size. He was the most disagreeable fellow it was ever my ill luck to meet with. He was continually raising the deuce with his sick sister and mother, quarreling with his father, and fighting his team. Finally, his oxen became so unruly from his abuse, that he couldn't manage them at all, and he traded teams with me, and afterward would trade first one yoke of oxen then another. To all of this I had to submit or be in a continuous quarrel, which I didn't relish owing to his size. But one morning he overdid the thing by trying to take an ox-bow out of my hand when I was yoking up.

He declared he would "have that bow," and he "staid with it" till he "*got it bad*" right over his head, and I am of the opinion that he would have *got it worse* if my father had not caught hold of me in time to prevent a repetition of the *giving* business.

Father, thinking that if the Kents could fight they were able to drive their own teams, called me back to his own wagons, and it was remarked that that ox-bow had either reduced Ben's bump of combativeness, or developed that of caution.

One thing is certain, I knew him in the West for years after and he never attempted to take anything away from me again.

Soon after this incident our train "split up" near Ft. Laramie. Passing on, we found ourselves in company with a family named McFarland who were also from Iowa. This family consisted of a sprightly girl of about fifteen summers, named Helen; her father a good-natured fellow, and her stepmother who was a "holy terror." One day we reached a stretch of country that was void of water, and our guide-books being imperfect, we were led into the error of not filling our water casks. After traveling eight or ten hours, we all became intensely thirsty, and, being a good walker, I volunteered to go ahead, fill the canteens and return to meet the rest!

Returning with the water, I met Helen, in company with my sister and our friend Haligan, some distance in advance of the train; giving them some water, I went on to meet the others, *Helen taking my arm.* Meeting my father's team first, I was supplying the family with some water, when Mrs. Mc. came up, and, seeing Helen's hand on my arm, she struck at her with a stick she carried. Seeing the motion, I stepped in front of Helen, and received a smart whack over the shoulder.

Mc., the papa, seeing the act, jumped from his wagon, and gave Mrs. Mc. a *lift in the eye,* saying: "Is this the way you treat a boy who goes ahead and brings back water to keep us from choking?" Mrs. Mc. declared she would teach Helen "better than to be so familiar with *young men.*" (This was the first time I was ever accused of being more than a boy.) The knockdown became general between the two, and, finally, my father *took a hand;* "that settled it," and there was another "split up" in the train.

Our family, being left alone with our teams, day after day we toiled on, leaving here an ox and there a cow, from the effects of poor grass and alkali water. Finally, we had to leave a wagon; and when we reached old Fort Hall, on Snake River, we found ourselves with but three yoke of poor oxen and a wagon.

To lighten ourselves, we were compelled to throw away provisions, until we had scarcely sufficient left to last us three weeks.

At this time we were all with the wagon except one of my brothers, who had gone ahead with another family. Believing two men were enough to care for the team, Haligan and myself concluded to go on ahead; thus, working a saving of the provisions, and, if possible, send help back to meet the rest. So, while father was out with us after the cattle one morning, we told him of our resolution, and he, realizing the necessity of such a movement, gave his permission; and then and there we bade him good-bye, and commenced the weary journey of nearly a thousand miles on foot, without provisions or money, and myself very poorly clad. I dared not return to the wagon, knowing that my mother would not allow me to start on such a trip; and, as will hereafter appear, that was the last time that I saw any of the family for more than two years.

One ox left on the John Days Mountain

Day after day we plodded along, getting a bite to eat here and there, as luck would favor us; and, on one occasion, traveling four days and nights without eating a mouthful.

On many a cold night did we pull bunch-grass, and, piling it up, burn it, then lie down on the warm place, and thus get a little sleep.

At John Days river we met a supply train, that had been fitted out in the Willamette Valley, and started out to the relief of distressed emigrants. They gave us a little flour to go on with but would give us nothing to return to the wagon with, for as they very justly said, all they had was needed by those in distress behind us.

In the latter part of November, we reached the Dalles of the Columbia, where we found a Catholic priest by the name of Mesplie, he couldn't speak a word of English, but Haligan, being a fine French scholar, explained to him our situation, and he immediately prepared for us what I thought was the best meal of victuals of which I ever partook.

Father Mesplie prevailed on Haligan to remain there, and teach him the English language; thus I was left to wander alone, in a strange and uncivilized land.

This priest gave me some provisions, and in company with some friendly Dalles Indians, I struck across the country, to the Tych (or Indian) valley, to intercept my folks. After stopping a few days with these Indians, I learned that my father with the family, had passed there some days before my arrival, in company with one Belknap. I afterwards learned that my father had struggled along till he found himself and family on the top of the John Day mountain at 10 o'clock at night with only one yoke of poor steers, and mother very sick. Here one of the remaining cattle fell dead in the yoke. My elder brother having left them on account of scarcity of food; my father and oldest sister rolled the dead ox out of the road, and he taking one end of the yoke, my sister took the steer by the horns, and thus they managed to roll the wagon down the long, steep, and rocky hill to the John Days river. The reader may form a faint idea of the trials of that family when he pictures to himself a worn out man with his 15-year-old daughter, being pulled, pushed, jerked and dragged, bruised and bleeding, down a two-mile hill in the dark; steering a wagon, in which lies a sick mother and small children that are crying for bread.

The next day a Mr. Belknap came along with a team of fat cattle; he had started to meet some friends, that he expected that season, but learned they had not started that year. Father hired him and his team to take the wagon and family across the Cascade mountains and into Willamette valley, which they reached in safety, and finally settled near Corvallis which was then called "Marysville."

My mind being easy regarding the rest of the family and fearing that the snow was too deep for me to cross the Cascades by the "Barlow Route" I returned to the Dalles, got some more provisions from the priest, and started down the Columbia river on the trails.

(I will here state that some of the emigrants sent their wagons and families down the river on flat boats, or barges, to the Upper Cascades, and drove their stock down these trails.)

Although I had been having the chills and fever, which always affects my head (probably my weakest member; fever always affected our whole family in the same way — their heads I mean), I pushed on "afoot and alone." The trail was at that time a "rough and rugged road to travel." Towards the night of my first day out, when on the summit of a spur of the mountains over which the trail led, I had a chill and being tired out I selected a convenient log, collected wood, made a good fire, and sat me down to pass a long and weary night, with wild animals howling around me. To say that this was a "lonely vigil" is drawing it mild, for remember I was but sixteen years old. But it probably required these lessons to prepare me for the rough and somewhat eventful life I have since passed through. Suffice it to say, that night like all others came to an end.

It had snowed continually, and in the morning I found myself wet and cold and but little refreshed by my night's *entertainment.* The snow was now so deep that it required my utmost skill to follow the trail. About noon, on getting back to the river, I found two men in charge of a few oxen they were trying to drive down. The owner's name was Adams. They had been out a long time, and were out of "grub." Adams proposed that I should help them drive the cattle, promising to give me five dollars on our arrival at the Cascades, if I would do so. I told him I had the chills, and could hardly walk, much less drive cattle; but he said I could keep the trail, and keep up the hind ones, while he and his man did the rest, and the five dollars would pay my fare from the Cascades to Portland. So I divided my provisions with them and helped them drive the cattle. Arriving at the Cascades, I asked Adams for my five dollars. He said he didn't think I had earned anything. I said I had told him I wasn't able to do much, but would do all I was able to; that he and his man had eaten all the provisions that the priest had given me, and tried to reason with him, but to no purpose. He being a powerful man and I a sick boy, of course he had the brute force on his side, and knowing this, I turned from him with probably the first "cuss words" of my life on my lips. It was probably well for both of us that I had nothing with me that would *make us equal.* I cautioned him to look out for me, if we ever met on anything like an equal footing — which the reader will see that we did later on.

Walking across the portage to the lower cascades, I saw a man (whom I afterward learned was the mate) in charge of a gang of men who were carrying pieces of "knocked-down" wagons aboard of a small steamboat that was running between there and Portland. I "braced up" and told him that I had no money, was worn out and sick, and asked him if I couldn't work my passage to Portland.

After he had taken a look at me, he said I could have passage, if I would help put the freight on board. I at once "tackled" a wagon-reach, and tried to carry it on board; but, in my weak condition, it was sometimes boy and sometimes wagon-reach. Finally, a voice from the deck above asked: "What's that boy trying to do?" — (this from the captain). The mate answered: "He is sick, worn out, and broke, and wants to work his way to Portland." The captain said: "Send him up here." I went up to him, caring but little what became of me. The captain, seeing my condition, and being a big, warm-hearted, Western man, caused me to sit down and tell my story. After listening to me, he called the steward, and said: "Take this boy and take care of him;" then, turning to me, he said: "I guess my men can load this boat without your help." "But," said I, "I am give out, and can't walk much further, and this is my only chance to get to some place where I can rest and get work;" then, while tears trickled down his swarthy cheeks, he said: "God bless us, boy! — do you think I would put you ashore?" And he again said to the steward: "Take him and feed him, and put him to bed; that's the place for that boy."

I need not say that his orders were obeyed to the letter; and, after satisfying my weak stomach, I was shown a good mattress and blankets, upon which I laid my tired and worn body, and, with thoughts of soon meeting my father, mother, sisters and brothers, I soon fell into a deep sleep, which continued till we reached Portland, when the captain had me awakened, and said to me: "Wait till the other passengers land, and I'll see that you have a place to stop for the night, and until you can find something to do" (this was about midnight). He placed me in charge of a colored man named Francis, who kept a boarding-house, making the necessary explanations, etc. I accompanied my new-found friend (who had a big, white heart, *if it was* covered with a black skin), bidding the captain a feeling good-night! (I regret that I have forgotten the name of that generous-hearted captain; also, that I have never had the pleasure of meeting him since.)

Chapter Two

I remained with Mr. Francis over night, had breakfast and felt better. Finding that there were fifty strong emigrants for *every work* to be had in Portland (which was then but a village), I "struck out" through the timber on the Lafayette road, hoping to obtain work, and eventually find my folks. I had not traveled more than ten or twelve miles when a chill came on me, and when the fever raised, that follows a chill, I laid down by the road. When I got able to resume my journey I was confused and took the *wrong end of the road*. Passing a house near a swale, I asked an elderly woman who was out near the road, how far it was to Lafayette, she said: "you are not going toward Lafayette, but to Portland;" and she asked me if I had not passed there some time previous, I replied that I thought not, that I had come from Portland, and was on my way up the valley. She said "you are going toward Portland now, and it was you that passed here some time since, are you sick?" I told her I had been having the chills, and was then just getting over one.

She said: "I thought you were not well when you passed here before, and had a mind to call to you." I thanked her, and turned to proceed in the right direction, when she said: "No, no! You must come right in, and have something to eat, and take a rest. My husband will be home soon from Oregon City, and, as he is quite a doctor, he will cure you." On telling her that I had no money, and was looking for something to do to earn a living till I could find my people, she said: "Poor boy! — you can't work or travel when you are sick; so, come right in and get well, and we will find you work when you are able to do anything." So I stopped with her; and I must say that my *own mother could not have been more kind* to me than was this noble woman. Her husband came home in due time, and gave me the necessary medicines. (The name of this family was Merrill.) I staid there ten or twelve days.

After a day or two, I found that Mr. Merrill had quite "a patch" of potatoes, and that he wanted them dug. So I dug, ate, and chilled; ate, chilled, and dug by turns, till the chills and fever were broken up, then I *dug* and *ate*. At digging I got tired, but at eating I could have put in the *entire day,* if my stomach would have permitted; at any rate, I "put in my best licks" as long as any of the family were at the table, and quit just as hungry as I commenced. Finally, the old lady told me to come in and get a lunch between meals, as she knew that emigrants never got enough to eat during the first few months after crossing the plains.

Potatoes being dug (and *"grub" running short*), I left this pleasant family and started on up the valley, making a few rails here and doing odd jobs there to pay my board. From place to place I trudged on through the Willamette Valley and Umpquas, hearing nothing of my father or the family. At last I got in with a pack-train, and worked my way to Jacksonville, in Rogue River Valley. From there I footed it up the valley and over the Siskiyou Mountains to Yreka, in Siskiyou County, California, arriving there on the last of December, 1852, just as it began snowing. The snow had soon fallen so deep that for six or seven weeks pack-trains could not cross the mountains. This new mining camp (Yreka) was poorly provided with supplies — in fact, there was scarcely enough provisions, except beef, to last two weeks. Here I stopped some weeks, living on. "beef straight" *without salt.* Salt sold at a dollar an ounce, and then only upon a certificate from a doctor in cases of chronic diarrhoea.

Here I fell in with an uncle, by the name of Martin Fisher; he having married my father's eldest sister. Fisher was one of the most powerful men I ever knew, being over six feet in height and well proportioned. He was an old frontiersman of the Western Atlantic States, a great hunter, and a bold daring man. Uncle and I made our home with an emigrant family, while here, who were as poor as ourselves, and beef the only provision to be had for love or money; and if there had been ever so much "grub" in camp, our "stock in trade" would have been composed largely of *love,* for we were confoundedly short of the metallic substance.

Off for a Rabbit Hunt

We hearing there was any amount of game at the head of Shasta valley, near the foot of Mt. Shasta, some forty miles distant, procured guns and ammunition, and in company with our emigrant friend, started for the hunting grounds. Our friend had a couple of small mules on which we carried our blankets. He went about twenty-five miles with us, then returned to his family after we had arranged with him to come out in a few days after our venison and other game. He could easily find us, as we would *keep up a smoke* after the first day or two.

There was little or no snow in this valley, till we reached the juniper timber at its head. These junipers are a species of the cedar, and as they stand, from a distance, much resemble our old orchards "back in the States." The boughs crowning their low tops, form a perfect thatch, so thick that the hardest rain storms scarcely penetrate through, to the sandy soil beneath.

Upon reaching these friendly junipers, we spread our blankets under the one that would afford us the best shelter.

The snow here was about ten inches deep. Fisher said "you build a fire and arrange camp, and I'll look around and see if there are any deer near by." He struck out, and I commenced gathering dry twigs to start a fire, thinking we would have to pass a hungry night, for we had nothing with us to eat, depending entirely on our guns to supply our wants.

While I was thus occupied, a jack rabbit jumped up some twenty steps distant. To pick up my rifle was but the work of a second, and as its sharp crack rang out, assuring me that here at least was "supper for two," a score or more of his kind, bobbed up their mule-like ears, seeming to say, "get your breakfast as well;" acting on this suggestion, I soon had three or four of the long-eared gents stretched out before the fire, which was now burning famously.

These rabbits are very large, weighing from eight to twenty pounds. Our mode of cooking them was to roast them, by hanging them on short sticks before the fire. While I was engaged in this pleasant duty, thinking I certainly would "have the brag" on my uncle when he returned, I heard his gun fire. "There," thought I, "more rabbit!" (The reader will see that by this time I had *rabbit on the brain*.) Again and again Fisher's gun spoke, and, knowing him to be a "dead shot," at each report would think, "more rabbit;" for I had rabbit so firmly fixed on my mind, that nothing else could have found room to enter it, especially while the fragrant smell of the cooking one filled my nostrils — appealing to my empty stomach.

Imagine my surprise, when my uncle came in a few minutes later, carrying a fine deer, and told me he had two more lying a few hundred yards out, assuring me that deer were plenty here, and that they were not wild, as they had probably never before been hunted with guns. We soon carried in the other two deer, and by the time Fisher had dressed his deer, my rabbit was cooked to perfection. After supper we laid our tired bodies under the juniper, and were soon in the "land of nod," dreaming of family, friends, deer and "jasack rabbits." Next morning we went out and killed several fine deer, as we did on each succeeding day.

Coming into camp one evening, three or four days after our arrival, we observed a dense smoke curling above the trees some distance away. This assured us that our friend had come out and was trying to find our whereabouts. We gathered a lot of green juniper-boughs and placed them on the fire, which made a dense smoke, and within an hour we heard his welcome shout. He had seen our signal, and hastened to join us. When he saw the amount of game we had hanging around our camp, he was more than pleased.

We spent a pleasant night together, and in the morning packed his mules with venison and started him back to his family, he promising to return within a week, unless the snow went off the mountains so that pack trains could come in. Our luck continued good, and when he came to us the second time, believing we had sufficient venison to last till pack trains could cross the mountains, we returned with him to Yreka.

Hearing that there was no snow in the Sacramento valley, and that there were plenty of provisions at Shasta city (an older mining camp) near the head of that valley, some hundred and twenty-five or fifty miles distant from Yreka and across two ranges of mountains, Fisher and I determined to try for "Shasta city, warm weather and grub;" so, leaving Yreka "we hoofed it" through Scotts valley to the foot of Scotts mountain where we found about fifty miners, who had been trying from day to day to break a trail over the mountain and had succeeded as far as the summit, but feared to go further as there they sunk to their waists in snow, and, knowing that it was still deeper on the south side and the mountain much steeper, if they should fail to get through they couldn't get back again. Upon inquiry we learned that it was only sixteen miles across to the "Mountain House" on the other side, and of this distance the trail was broken for seven or eight miles. Fisher determined to try it so I concluded to cast my lot with him, as also did an old miner called "Grizzly," (I never knew any other name for him); I was called "Buckeye" for some years, because I came from Ohio. Nearly all the miners, hunters and scouts were nicknamed, or went by their first names, as "Jack" or "Bill" with other *embellishments* added to suit friends or enemies as occasion presented itself, in the early and venturesome mining days, and the settling up of the Pacific States and Territories.

Snow-shoes and their use were not known to the miners in those days. But, early one morning we three, led by Fisher, started up the mountain, reaching the summit about 11 o'clock. Thus far the trail was partly broken; but now came the "tug of war." For me to say how deep the snow was would be out of the question, as we never touched bottom.

We found that the parties who had thus far broken the trail had gone a short distance down the mountain, became scared, and struggled back, having to throw away their blankets and clothing. I unrolled a bundle of these blankets, and found a case of ivory-handled razors. These I stuck in my pocket. Fisher, seeing this, asked: "What are you going to do with those razors?" (Bear in mind, I had no beard then.) I replied: "I am going to cut the throat of the first man that gives out or says 'go back.'" Little did I imagine what was before us when I said this.

After resting a few moments, we boldly pushed on, "injun file," Fisher leading, "Grizzly" next, and "Buckeye" following. We, like the others, soon found it necessary to throw away our blankets and clothing, and reduce ourselves to "light marching order," for we were sinking to our armpits in the snow at every move. Within an hour I took the lead, as I was but a boy, and the lightest of the party. The others weighed over two hundred each. For the rest of the day we rolled and pushed ourselves down the mountain.

At night we tried to build a fire, wood being plenty; but our matches were wet from melted snow; so we had to travel on, or freeze. On down the mountain we went, till we struck Trinity river, which, like all other mountain streams, ran like a mill-tail.

The mountain spurs frequently came to the water's edge, and, as we couldn't climb over them, we were forced to wade the river. We joined hands, so that if one slipped, the others could support him, and into the water we went. It came up to our hips, and was *by no means warm*. Three times during that night, we were forced to wade that stream, for we could only walk on level or descending ground.

About 10 o'clock the next day we came to the long looked-for house; but lo! the snow had *broken its back,* and only the gable-end protruded, warning us that we had not yet reached a place of rest or refreshment, both of which we so sorely needed.

We afterward learned that the proprietors of this house had retreated down the river some sixteen miles, to "Verry's ranch," earlier during the storm, their provisions having given out.

During all of this time we had nothing to eat, and for weeks previous had lived on *poor beef* "straight," which accounts, to some extent, for the slow time we made. To say the least, the sight of that broken and snow-covered house was a gloomy one, indeed.

As none of us had ever traveled the trail before, we knew not how far we yet had to walk before finding a place of rest and help. One thing was as sure as fate: *to stop meant death.* So after a few minutes' look at the wreck, we resumed our weary tramp, wet, cold and hungry. In this mountain valley the snow was about eight feet deep, and had commenced melting, so that every gulch formed a small lake on reaching the level bottom land; hence, for the rest of the day, we had it snow, ice and water, snow, water and ice, and night coming on, we had it duplicated.

About eight o'clock the next morning, after wading some hundreds of yards through snow, water and ice, Fisher and "Grizzly" laid down by a tree and said it was of "no use," they were "give out," and couldn't go a foot further. God knows, we had had weary work for many hours past. I scolded, begged, and probably swore some, to get them to try it a little further, but of no use; move they would not. To say that this was a time to try a boy's soul, would be putting it mild.

There I stood in snow six feet deep, surrounded by mountains, in a strange land, not knowing how far I was from help, with two given-out comrades — one a beloved uncle — after having breasted the snow, ice and water for fifty-odd hours without anything to eat.

Even now it makes my heart tremble as I look back and think of myself as I stood there, scolding, begging and swearing by turns, to get these loved comrades again to their feet. At last I had to move on or freeze myself; so, with tears trickling down my cheeks, I started on alone. After getting some hundreds of yards away, and being about to pass out of sight, I turned to take a last look at them. This look was too much for me, and I returned to them. As I was approaching, I caught uncle Fisher's eye (he had become somewhat rested), and thought of the razors I found on the mountain, and of what I had said at the time. I jerked the case out of my pocket, pulled one of the razors out of it, and with as fierce a look as I could assume, I stepped up to Fisher, flourishing the razor.

This joke proved too much for him; with a sickly laugh he staggered to his feet, and helped me get "Grizzly" up and force him along; we hadn't made more than four hundred yards further than I had been, when I saw a smoke curling up from among the trees. This welcome sight caused me to raise a joyous yell which was answered, and in a few moments I saw twenty or thirty men coming as fast as they could to meet us. Seeing us staggering, (if the road had been sixty yards wide we couldn't have stayed in it, frozen and benumbed as we were), they took hold of us and assisted us as though we were babies, pouring in a stream of questions, "Where'e ye from?" "How long have ye been on the trip?" "Are ye froze?" "Is Yreka an' all them northern camps snowed in an' starved to death?" All these questions I had to answer, as my comrades were too far gone to make intelligent answers.

I was apparently all right, till the warm air from the house struck me as the door was opened, then I gave way and fell as one dead. Being young and light they held my feet and hands in snow water till the frost was extracted (as I was afterwards told), thus probably preventing me from being a cripple for life, for my hands and feet were badly frozen, as were those of both the others, but they being such large men were not so easily managed. "Grizzly" had both his legs amputated just below the knees, and Fisher went home as I afterwards learned a cripple for life.

When I came to myself, my hands and feet were bundled up in cloths.

Some two weeks afterwards I started on to Shasta city j in company with the packers who had been snowed in at Verry's ranch, leaving Fisher and "Grizzly" to come on when able. Fisher returned home to Iowa as soon as he got able. I never heard exactly what became of "Grizzly," only that he got well, minus his feet.

There were some two hundred mules, laden with general merchandise and provisions for Yreka, frozen to death or starved at Verry's ranch, leaving their owners with *aparajos* and cargoes cooped up for weeks as above described.

As the snow melted off, with warm winds, these packers and miners started for Weaverville, French Gulch and other places, I in their company, with hands and feet bundled up in rags and pieces of blankets.

My feet and hands were very raw yet, but I managed to make six, eight, or ten miles a day, until at last one evening I reached Shasta city.

Chapter Three

Shasta city in the spring of '53, was surrounded by flourishing mining camps. On my arrival there, I sought out a hotel called the "Kossuth House," which was kept by a Dutchman. Approaching the proprietor, I told him I had no money, but wanted supper, bed and breakfast. Without looking up he said, there had been so many emigrants there broke during the last fall and winter that he couldn't keep any more. This was about my first experience in bumming.

I was leaving the house when a man that was sitting by the stove about as full of whisky as an owl, stepped forward, and catching me by the arm roughly said: "What's the matter with your hands and feet, that they are bundled up so." I wasn't in a humor to be "shook around," so I replied "froze," and tried to "shake loose" from him, when he said "hold, pardy, don't cork yourself," and led me to a chair. Seating me he proceeded to undo the wraps from one of my feet; taking a hasty look he, tenderly as he could in his condition, tied it up again asking, "is your other foot and hands like that?" I replied "much the same, and now if your curiosity is satisfied I will move on." "Not much, Mary Ann," said he, laying his hand heavily on my shoulder.

He then went to the bar and asked the proprietor what his bill was; being told he pulled out a purse of dust and had the amount weighed out. Then turning to the others in the room he said, "fellers did you see this boy's foot?" They all said "yes." He then said, "any man that would eat a meal or take a drink with a s__ of a b___ that has refused a meal to a boy in that fix ought to go straight to hell or poor diggings!"

All agreed, paid their bills and left the house. This man was a gambler and miner named Jack Moore; nearly all the miners in those days were addicted to "sporting."

Moore asked me where I was from, I replied "Yreka." "Are you one of the three that broke the trail over Scotts mountain?" "Yes, I'm the boy 'Buckeye,'" (the news of our trip had been received there and published). He said "bully boy, come along with me and we'll find some grub, you bet your sweet life." Tired and worn out as I was I saw that I had "fell upon my feet," as this man

Moore was well dressed, and every body seemed to respect him. I followed him to the "Empire Hotel" kept by an old sea captain and ex-prize fighter named Sam Francis. Moore went into the bar-room and said "Sam, can you give me and *my boy* board and room?" Then, turning, he told those assembled my story and my reception at the "Kossuth House."

Sam said, "bet yer life, Moore, best in the house, if you'll let me have half of Buckeye."

This being settled to the satisfaction of Moore and Francis, I was taken to a room and fed. A doctor was called in, who dressed my feet and hands, and looked to my welfare until my recovery.

By these two big-hearted men, Moore and Francis, I was cared for and fed, and in every way made as much of, as though I had been a brother.

I mention this as an incident of California life, and the warm-heartedness of those "rough and ready" pioneers.

When I got well, I was furnished with a letter to a friend of Moore, on "Jackass Flat," where I went, and through his management got a good claim, out of which I had the good fortune to make in a few weeks $1,600 for my share. After settling with Moore's friend, I returned to Shasta city and tried to settle with Moore and Francis, or pay them, but every time I offered to divide or pay them, they would take a drink, and before ten o'clock they couldn't have told gold-dust from Chile beans. Next morning, seeing they would not take anything from me, I started back to Yreka, and to hunt up the rest of our family, as I had plenty of money with which to do so; but at Yreka I fell in with three young men, Dan Allen, Joe Draper and Jim Carwile, whom I had known in Iowa.

The last-named party we called "Augur Jim," because he slept in a *twist,* with his head and heels together. He told me he had seen my father in the Willamette valley, and that the folks were all well, but father thought I was dead from starvation on the plains.

After consulting with these friends, I concluded to stop at or near Yreka until I could get an answer to a letter from my uncle, Samuel Meek, of Ohio (which would take about a year), believing that my father would write to him, giving his address in Oregon, and he in turn would send it to me.

So, in company with the three, I engaged in prospecting on Humbug creek, near Yreka, I furnishing the funds, they the experience. But at the end of a few months, *I had the experience,* and none of us the *funds.*

At last I received a letter from Ohio, telling of father's family and their address, which made my mind easy on their account.

About this time we were joined by a man named Scarbrough, and we finally struck very "good pay" on Old Humbug Creek. Here we worked till the water gave out in the fall, when we went prospecting on a smaller stream over the mountain about ten miles away. Striking a small prospect, we named this "Young Humbug," and a flat near by we called "Bark House."

A grizzly bear in camp – A "tearing" climb

We had to pack our provisions over the mountain on our backs, which called one or more of us over to Old Humbug every few days for supplies. We usually carried fifty or sixty pounds to the man.

Our temporary camp we built facing a log, by driving two forked sticks into the ground some fifteen feet apart, laying a pole across them, shedding one side with fir poles and thatching over them with fir boughs. This made a good shelter.

We had brought some fresh beef with us on our first trip, and, after forming our camp, hung it up in a tree near by. The next morning we found the tree all right minus the beef. After a short investigation, we found by footprints in the soft sand that the robbery was committed by a large grizzly. A few days later some of our company, going over to Humbug and returning with supplies, brought some beef with them and hung it in the same tree, but a little higher. Dan Allen and myself concluded to watch for the return of the bold robber; and, after putting out our camp-fire, we took our rifles and revolvers, wrapped a blanket around us, and laid down by the log in front of the camp, "Augur Jim," Draper, and Scarbrough going to bed in the brush tent, saying to us that we had also better go to bed in the tent, as it was not at all likely that the grizzly would return. We thought different, and our judgment proved correct.

After arranging our mode of attack, in case he should return, we laid down to rest, Allen keeping watch. I being young, soon fell sound asleep. Some time in the night I was woke up by Allen shaking me and whispering in my ear: "Wake up Buckeye, he's here." After I succeeded in getting my eyes open I saw by the light of the bright moon the Grizzly upon his hind legs, rearing up against the tree trying to reach the beef. On taking a look at him, and as I had heard of their strength and ferocity when attacked, (he being an immense brute — looking the size of an ordinary smoke house,) I became somewhat "shakey" and felt my valor oozing out at my fingers' ends. I whispered to Allen "shall we shoot him?" He said, "yes, of course." With fear and trembling, I leveled my gun across the log as Allen had already done. Upon his touching my foot, we fired together. The bear was probably twenty feet from us. At the crack of the guns he gave an angry "snort." (This noise resembles the "snort" of a horse when at play he stops running, throws his head high in the air, and forces the breath from his lungs through his nostrils, so producing a sound similar to the angry snort of a grizzly.) As the sound of the guns and "snort" of bear died out, we heard a smashing behind us and back of our brush tent. My first thought was "another grizzly." Grasping my revolver and whirling around I saw Jo Draper scrambling up a small white fir tree that stood just behind our tent. When I first saw him he was fully fifteen feet up the tree and making time that would not have disgraced an Ohio grey squirrel. As the grizzly had disappeared, we all turned our attention to Draper, in the tree. Just imagine a man climbing a tree, in shirt and drawers, said tree a perfect thistle of small, sharp dead limbs, hard to describe to any one that has never seen one of our white firs. On Jo's again reaching the ground he somewhat resembled the map of Mexico, after that country had been interviewed by Generals Taylor and Scott.

To say that we slept more that night would be preposterous, and only an old-timer can fully realize the comical remarks of first one and then another, accompanied by peals of laughter that made the surrounding mountains ring with our merriment at Draper's expense. One would say: "Jo where's the rest of your drawers," another "Jo I have an extra shirt, you can have it," and again "there is plenty of balsam on your tree for your scratches." Some of the party allowed that a rag-picker would make a "stake" if he only could get to Draper's fir tree.

Next morning we followed the trail of the grizzly which was easily traced by the blood; we found him dead some miles below the camp.

This was one of the largest grizzly bears I ever saw and would have weighed fully 1,500 pounds.

After working a short time on this creek, the prospect being poor, we returned to Old Humbug and "divided up," I selling out to Carwile, Draper and Allen. I then went in partnership with a young man by the name of Len Study, and commenced prospecting a high bar on the north fork, by running a drift or tunnel.

We had been at work six weeks or two months without raising a color, and, as the bed-rock raised toward the mountain, we were of the opinion that there was no "pay" in the bar. As we had left our blankets at Round Town, Study said to me one morning, "If you will go and get our blankets to-day, I will run the drift a few feet further, and if the bed-rock keeps raising, we will move to some other place to prospect." So I started down the creek for the blankets, some ten miles distant.

On my return about 4 o'clock in the afternoon as I came within hearing, I heard Study whistling. This being the *first whistle* I had heard from him for a month, it naturally excited my curiosity to know what had put him in such fine spirits.

On reaching the cabin I found Study busy preparing supper, and asked him what had put him in such good humor? He showed me seven or eight dollars in specimens, which he said he had panned out of dirt taken from the drift that evening, and that he had no doubt but we had "struck it," and in the near future we would be rich and respectable.

After much talk and speculation as to the probable richness of the strike, we wrapped ourselves in our blankets and were soon dreaming of rich diggings, big nuggets, home and relatives.

In my dreams that night I had from my claim amassed an immense fortune, returned to my poor relatives, and by every way possible strove to impress upon their dull minds that I was a *superior being*, made of very different *mud*, and that my blood was bluer, and even my hair had assumed a finer texture (since I had made a raise) than could be found among any of my brothers, sisters, cousins, second-cousins, or, in fact, among any of the tribes that had been honored by an alliance with *Buckeye, the man of brains,* whose *gigantic intellect* had enabled him to carry blankets while his partner struck a bonanza.

But, alas! I awoke at the sound of Study's voice: "Buckeye! beefsteak and coffee, smoking hot!"

After breakfast we repaired to the drift, and during the day run it back four or five feet by seven feet in width, running off the top dirt down to the cement or pay. This latter we cleaned to the bed-rock, which we found formed a deep crevice or channel, it being some three or four feet lower than the other portion of the rock. The bed-rock was soft slate, and easily dug up for six or eight inches in depth.

After we had cleaned as deep as we thought necessary, I took a pan of the soft, shell rock, and panned it out. Getting several dollars, we dug it deeper, and until we were satisfied there was no more gold.

We dumped the dirt over a steep bank into the bed of the creek, where we had our long torn and rocker set. A *long tom* was used for washing the dirt, as was a rocker; the former was made the same as sluices — that is, three planks nailed together, forming a trough two inches wider at one end than the other; the last box bulged at* the lower end to two or three times its former width, and was sloped similar to a sled-runner; the last four feet were bottomed with sheet-iron, punched thickly with half-inch holes. Under this was placed what was called a "riffle-box," the same width of the one above, and six or eight feet long. Across its bottom was fastened slats that would form riffles when the box was placed at the proper angle. These riffles would catch and retain all heavy substances, such as gold, black sand, etc., while the lighter sand and pebbles would pass over and into the tail-race.

This is as near as I can describe a primitive "long torn," used in early mining days.

The sluice-box soon took its place, as it was found that the punched iron and riffle-box were superfluous, and only adding labor, as riffles placed in the sluices answered every purpose, and would save more gold, *fine* and *coarse,* and required less labor to handle them.

But to our clean-up for the day, it did not require more than an hour to wash the dirt drifted that day.

That evening, upon our panning out the rifflebox, and putting it with *nuggets* picked up while cleaning the bed-rock, and out of the sluices, upon weighing all, we found we had taken out of the drift that day over $900. The largest nugget found weighed $279. This was the largest nugget and out of the richest pocket ever found on the bar.

That night Study's whistle rang out more joyous than ever. We were soon in our blankets, and again dreaming of happy homes, pretty girls and sweet babies. The early dawn of the next morning found us at work in our drift. We soon found that this crevice (an old channel) was, where we struck it, not more than five feet wide. As soon as we were assured of this fact, we turned our drift at right angles up the bar. For a week or so we run this drift, trying to follow the channel, taking out from two to twelve ounces per day. (This dust was worth $19 to $20 per ounce, but we always reckoned it at $16 per ounce in those days).

As we proceeded up the bar, the channel or "pay-streak" widened out, and paid less to the foot. Within two weeks we got clear off the "pay," and were some weeks in finding it again. Having found it, we continued on good "pay," and after some time we commenced "breasting" and "timbering." We had breasted out a space about twenty by thirty feet, I drifting and Study wheeling. (He had to run his wheel-barrow down the drift some fifty feet, then turn at a right angle, and go to the creek-bank or front edge of the bar).

One day, while I was working in the back part of the drift, and just after Study had passed out, the caps on the timbers gave way, and as the dirt above was loose and full of large boulders, it soon caved in, bringing the grass-roots from thirty feet above. At the first crack of the timbers, I sprang back to the furthest part of my drift, knowing I could not run out, as it was caving between me and the outlet or mouth of the drift. To sit down with my back to the solid bank, and put out my candle, so as not to consume the fresh air, was my first thought. But I soon had fresh air enough, for as the dirt and rock came tumbling all around me from above, I could soon gaze up and out at the mountains above; but, alas! I was covered to my waist with dirt and rock, which held me like a vice a large rock had fallen on to the dirt above and slid down the slope made by the cave, till it finally rested against my breast. Study, hearing the noise made by the breaking timbers, ran into the main drift and up to where it was caving, then seeing that he could not get to me, he ran out again, and, hearing my shouts for help, which sounded from above him, he was soon gazing down upon me from the top of the bar, while I sat wedged in by dirt and rock. Seeing that he could not do anything alone in time to save my life, he ran swiftly down to the next claim and soon returned with a dozen hardy miners, who made a hasty survey of my situation, then cut some logs and pushed them down at the edge or side of the sloping dirt. Two of them cautiously slid down and got one of these short logs across in front of me, with one end resting against either of the solid banks, thus forming a breastwork in front of me, to prevent the dirt from sliding down and covering me completely up. Then more men came down, and. working the rocks away from my breast, commenced sinking logs in front of me. They added logs and dug for some hours before they succeeded in releasing me from my perilous position.

I had often heard the expression, "a mighty tight squeeze," but I never realized its full force before that day. I had received several bruises. from which I did not recover sufficiently to resume work for some time; and for years afterward I suffered more or less from these bruises.

The boys would probably have allowed me to remain buried, but being of a religious turn of mind, they concluded it would be best to save me till a minister could be found, to say a few "appropriate words" to wring the hearts of my relatives and friends, which hearts would be already broken and bleeding.

Chapter Four

Humbug society was exclusive— exclusively male. There was not a white woman or child on the creek at the time of which I am writing, nor had there been.

We used to amuse ourselves by assembling in some one of the little towns, to-wit: The Forks, Round Town, Howlets, Free Town or Jacksons, and listening to speeches — we had some well-educated young lawyers among us — also by singing, etc., sometimes making up original songs on local and other topics.

The following are some verses which were sung at one of our meetings.

"AN ODE TO HUMBUG."

"Ye miners attend, I will sing you a song,
  My brothers, my fellows, bold, dauntless and strong!
  Who develop gold's fountains, and send it in streams
  Through the world, that all mankind may bask in its beams.
  Others boast about "freedom," yet, who is so free,
  So full of wild notions, so wandering as we?
  For we work and we rest, and we sit at our ease,
  We rise up and lie down — do just as we please.

"All the banks of the city with "papers" abound,
  Their "checks" maybe forged, or their "issues" unsound;
  We have banks, but the cashiers will not run away,
  Leaving drafts all unpaid, and "the devil to pay" —
  For our steel picks are "checks," and the "Oro" we pull,
  And our "long toms" and "rockers" receipt them in full.
  Mother Earth is our bed, with her carpets of green,
  Our pillow some rock, which the rain has washed clean.

"We have rifles, revolvers, no locks, bolts or bars,
  For our coverings the sky with her beautiful stars.
  Should the wild red man's arrow whizz near us in sleep,
  We start all at once, though our slumbers be deep;
  We muster, we rally! and soon make him feel
  That the arms of a white man are "thunder and steel."
  So, early next morning we watch the sun rise —
  Come, get up, my brave fellows! our path we despise.

"We climb the bold rocks, where your railroad's a fool, —
  It is not worth the hoof of my sure-footed mule. —

32

Even *Humbug* — a name that all classes despised —
Has now altered its meaning, and highly is prized.
Ask the girls of Yreka, who will say half their joys,
Yes, and more, is afforded by bold Humbug boys.

"Now, exult, my brave fellows! the time's drawing near,
When our arms will encircle our bright-blushing "dears;"
We'll kiss them, protect them from danger and cold,
And fill up their aprons with oceans of gold.
Oh, what do we toil for, if it is not for this —
A bright home, a sweet smile, a hug and a kiss?
It's a true miner's motto — so, come, brothers, come!
The harder we dig, we'll the sooner get home."

These were offered by "Buckeye."

The winter of 1853 closed in on us, and the snow fell deep in those mountains.

Study and I were "drifting" under a high bar when, returning to our cabin one night, we found sitting in front of our door *two Indian girls*. (The snow was then five or six feet deep on the creek, and much deeper on the mountains.) These girls were aged about ten and fifteen years respectively, as well as we could judge. But there being no Indians nearer than Klamath, some thirty miles away, and as neither Study nor myself could understand their language, we were at a loss to know what they wanted, or where they came from. Finally, after considerable sign-making, we learned that they were starving and nearly perishing with the cold, and that they wanted to stop with us for the night. We took them in, warmed and fed them, and gave them blankets to sleep in. They had staid with us three or four days, when one night while we were cooking supper, six or eight Indians appeared at our door, looking somewhat sullen. The youngest girl, upon hearing them speak, went to the head man and talked to him in a rapid manner. At last the Indians looked pleased, shook hands with Study and I, and signified a wish to stay over night with us, which we allowed them to do.

I found that one of them was a young chief named "William," and that he could talk a little English. By words and signs I learned that these girls had been sent out in company with some older squaws for some deer that the Indians had killed, and that these two, getting separated from the other squaws, became lost, and in wandering about, had crossed the divide, and come down Humbug to our cabin.

Some time during the next spring, as some of the miners were passing down the creek, they discovered wearing apparel hanging on the bushes near a cabin, that *indicated the presence of a woman and child*. The news spread rapidly from the head to the mouth of the creek, and the next Sunday there appeared before that cabin no less than a hundred miners, dressed in their gorgeous woolen shirts and patched pants. (It was not uncommon in

Miners of 1852

those days to see an old miner passing through our towns with a pick, shovel and pan on his back, and as you gazed at his retreating form, you would read, *"Albany Mills Superfine, 50 lbs."* in large letters, on the patch on the seat of his pants.) These miners had selected a spokesman for the occasion in the person of "Old Uncle Gilbert." The boys surrounded the cabin, and "Uncle Gilbert," mounting a convenient stump, loudly hailed the inmates of the cabin. A gentleman — all miners were *gentlemen* in those days — making his appearance, "Uncle Gil" thus addressed him:

"Honored Sir. — Do not for a moment be alarmed at this demonstration, for I assure you these gentlemen are quiet, peaceable miners, who were *once* partially civilized. Many of us have been in the mines one, two or three years, without having had the pleasure of gazing upon a woman or a child.

"A day or two ago, in passing here, some of us noticed, hanging upon those bushes, garments, that denoted the presence of a woman and child — that is to say, unless we have forgotten the garments worn in our childhood, and those of our mothers and sisters. Upon being informed of the suspicions of the brothers regarding this cabin and its inmates, we at once called a mass-meeting, and resolved to proceed as a committee of the whole, to investigate, being reassured by the wisest of us, that *our mothers were women,* and that, singular as it may appear to you, *we were once children*.

"Now, my dear sir, allow rue in behalf of my fellow-miners and myself, to tender to you and yours a hearty welcome to Humbug and the surrounding camps.

"Be assured that we congratulate ourselves on this most welcome addition to our community, believing it will prove a benefit to each of us, inasmuch as it will remind us of *home and mother.*

"My dear sir, you can be assured that your wife and child will be sacred objects to us, and while they cast their lots among us rough and somewhat uncouth miners, will be as safe from insult or danger as they would be within the limits of the capital of our country, surrounded by an army of police.

"Again, we bid you welcome to Humbug, and may God bless you, your wife and child."

At the close of this address, the gentleman brought to the door a most beautiful woman and child and responded to "Uncle Gil's" remarks in a most happy manner.

Then went up such a ringing shout as was never before heard in those rough and craggy mountains, and we imagined that old "Mount Craggy" gave back a joyous smile as it certainly never bore a more imposing appearance than it assumed as it towered above us, on this, the day of the welcome of the first white woman and child to old Humbug.

On one of my visits to Yreka I was prevailed upon by an acquaintance to make a trip or two with H. P. French's Saddle-express train. On our return one trip we camped on a bottom, well up on the Sacramento river. We had several passengers, and some express matter. The "Digger" (or Pitt river)

Indians would steal horses and mules, run them into the hills and kill and eat them, and frequently they would attack small parties on the trails. So it was our custom, when traveling through this country, to keep a guard with our stock at night.

This night French watched until one or two o'clock, when he woke me up; we had tied our mules to some trees that stood around our camp and fringed a small bottom that was covered with rye-grass which was nearly the height of a man.

Taking a shotgun, I sleepily went to a tree and took my stand to watch for the rest of the night. The moon was shining brightly, and the wind came in spurts.

Soon after taking my stand I glanced over the bottom, when I thought I *saw a "Digger" raise his head,* but a short distance from me, and then sink down. This woke me up thoroughly, and I watched closely; soon again he raised and, as it appeared to me, took a hasty look and sank down again. This was kept up at short intervals till I fancied I could see his long black hair when he raised. I watched this performance till I was sure that I could see his features. At last I determined to put a stop to his coming into camp — as he seemed to be coming nearer every time he raised up — so raising my gun, on *his* again making *his* appearance, I let drive a barrel of buck-shot at *him*. All was clear to me before the echo died out. I, in my sleepy condition, had seen a black stump in the grass, which was nearly as high as the grass, and at each, spurt the wind blew the grass down, and thus exposed the top of the stump. When the wind died down the grass would straighten up again and hide the stump from sight; this being repeated every few minutes, I had gazed at it till my imagination had led me to shoot at it.

When French and some of our passengers rushed up I was sitting by the tree, laughing heartily at my scare. They asked what was the matter, and I told them I had shot a Digger! They asked where? I said "there," (pointing to the stump.) Just then the wind blew the grass down, and as the grass straightened up in a moment, hiding the stump, French jerked out his pistol as he said "What are you laughing at you fool? It is a Digger;" and he was about to fire when I said, "Hold on French! I have killed that stump myself." But it was some time before any of them would believe it was only a stump, it appeared so natural. Finally we went out to it, and found that I had peppered it pretty well with buck-shot.

I had failed to make a good Digger, but succeeded in being relieved from guard duty, as one of the passengers took my post, laughingly saying he thought he could kill as many stumps as I had. I didn't demur, as I much pre-ferred my blankets to standing by a tree, watching for Diggers, when I was liable to get an arrow, for my reward, as many a more watchful man had while standing guard on these trails.

We had with us a young man by the name of Crosbie, a finely educated lawyer.

I mention him, as his name will appear later in these reminiscences, and to more fully portray early mining life in California and the kind of material the early pioneers and miners were composed of.

The Fourth of July coming around many of us assembled at "Round Town." After toasting each other we induced Watson, (the hotel man) to give us a supper worthy of the occasion, then selected Crosbie to deliver an oration.

Crosbie had come to California some two years before, he had tried the lumber business at Humboldt bay, and related his lumbering experience as follows: "I bought an ax on credit, and repairing to the woods tackled an immense redwood tree, having seen how others did it. I scaffold up above the spurs, mounted the scaffold, and, full of enthusiasm, fell to work dealing giant blows. Finding after some time that I had not yet penetrated through the bark, I became desperate and putting forth more strength down came the scaffold and the mighty blow aimed at the stubborn bark fell upon my foot. The noise of my fall brought to my assistance a man who kindly bound up my wound, and told me he had been chopping on the other side of the same tree for some days, and certainly had a prior right. This caused me to reflect, and after mature thought I concluded that a man who had no more judgment than to commence chopping on a tree without first going around it and ascertaining whether or no there was a prior claimant, would not prove a success as a lumber man, and as I had not paid for the ax, and didn't possess the dust with which to perform that honorable duty I would seek other diggings. So I tenderly laid the ax at the foot of the tree, and after assuring my newly-made acquaintance, that inasmuch as he had rendered me so great a favor, I would relinquish my claim in and to the premises. I got in with a pack train, and made my way to Yreka, and finally to Humbug. Here I have tried mining but find it up-hill work, for I wasn't cut out for a miner."

So, on this morning of the Fourth, we fixed Crosbie up with a "bran new" woolen shirt, tied a big, red handkerchief around his neck, put him on an extemporized platform, and I will say that I never heard a finer effort in this line than he made on this occasion. One thing is sure, from that date commenced his success as an attorney.

As before, we miners had settled all of our difficulties by arbitration, pistol, or knife, this speech of his aroused our ambition, and we resolved to take a step in the way of *civilization*. So, a day or two afterward, we called a meeting, elected a Justice of the Peace, and proceeded to *persecute* each other in a more *civilized manner*. The result was, more trouble, more shooting, and less dust in our purses.

The justice was *affable,* and always ready to *receive* and *welcome "visitors"* rendering his decision in the most approved style, to wit: *against the miner who had the longest purse.* From this date commenced the "advance of civilization" on Old Humbug. But Crosbie was full of paying business, and he and his friends were happy. This inspired our "local bard" to perpetrate the following:

"MINER'S LAMENT.

"Air — 'Jeanette and Jeanot.'

"Oh, I'm going far away from my creditors just now,
And I have not got the dust to pay — they're kicking up a row;
Ther's no chance for speculation, and these mines ain't worth a dam,
And I'm none of those unlucky 'coves' that work for Uncle Sam.

"There's Jack Taylor swearing vengeance — oh, he says he'll give me 'fits,'
And the Sheriff, he is after me with his pockets full of writs;
And every time I turn I am sure to get a 'dun,'
So the best thing I think I can do is for to 'cut and run.'

"When I came into these mines for to help to turn the stream,
I got credit on the strength of that glorious golden dream;
But when we got it done, oh, it proved to be a sham,
And we who dammed the river by our creditors were damned.

"There's that durned unlucky fellow that wrote home about the gold,
Oh, he'd ought to be in the place the Bible says ain't cold;
For he wrote about the specimens and lumps of gold so big,
But he never said a word about how hard we had to dig.

"Now I'm going far away, and I don't know where to go;
'Twon't do for me to go home again; they'd laugh at me, I know;
For when I came away — oh! I said I'd 'make my pile,'
But if they could only see me now — should rather think they'd smile."

More about Crosbie Hereafter.

Later in the season Study and myself concluded to go to "Scott's bar," on Scott's river, on a prospecting tour, as the water had given out on our claims; so we "laid over" our claims till winter, and started.

We, with three other miners, commenced to sink a shaft on what was called "Poor Man's bar," some two miles below Scott's bar. This "Poor Man's bar" had been prospected to some extent before, but as it was very deep and full of large boulders, it was very costly work to sink a shaft there, and all who had tried it had failed, which was why it was called "Poor Man's bar." The five of us sunk a shaft sixteen feet square and about twenty feet deep, to the bed-rock, having to blast many boulders in doing so. We were about four weeks at it, and when we reached bed-rock we found that the rock pitched or sloped to the river. We got some eight or ten dollars in small specimens out of a crevice, and, as the rainy season was coming on, and Study and I had very good, paying ground, we concluded to return to Humbug, which we did, as will appear further on.

We left this bar, and, as we afterward learned, the other three men, in company with another man, sunk another shaft at the edge of the one we had sunk, and running twenty feet toward the river. Reaching bed-rock, they cleaned up about $20,000 out of a shaft 16x20 feet, and then sold their claim for a large sum of money to some capitalists, who subsequently flumed the river and took out an immense amount of money.

This "Poor Man's bar" proved to be one of the richest bars in Northern California, and furnished further evidence of the truth of the old adage, "a fool for luck," etc.

At least, I am poor, and blessed with *babies,* while the men we left went home to the States, full of wealth, and blessing the day they stuck to "Poor Man's bar" on Scott's river.

Study and I on hearing how near we had been to a. large fortune, would, while sitting in our lonely log cabin during the evenings, talk of our luck and indulge in a few remarks in regard to *luck-fools,* etc.

After a few weeks on "Scott's bar" we concluded to prospect down Scott's river, and up Klamath to the mouth of Humbug, and on home.

The distance proved farther than we had contemplated, and as we carried our "outfits," consisting of blankets, pick, pan, shovel and "grub," on our backs, our provisions got low, and we were pushing on up the Klamath river, when one evening, as we were approaching the Humbug trails, we were suddenly *surrounded by Indians,* who didn't appear to be at all friendly disposed. They "escorted" us to their camp where a rabble surrounded us and gave every sign of hostility. We had only our "navy" revolvers with us, which would have availed us but little in case of the attack we were satisfied they were meditating; at this moment a young girl came forward and taking a close look at us called to another and older one, she in turn scanned our faces closely, talking rapidly to the surrounding Indians. A painted and ugly-looking Indian came forward and taking a good look at us, asked in broken English and Chenook if we knew the two squaws. We now recognized them as being the two we had fed during the snow storm of the past winter, and they had already recognized us. The Indian said, "good," then left us for a short time, returning with his face clear of paint he said we need fear no danger, as the Indians would not molest us. He conducted us to his lodge and gave us plenty of such food as he had, (they baked their bread in the hot embers and no better or sweeter bread can be baked by any other mode.)

We stayed all night and had breakfast with this Indian, (who proved to be Chief William) and told him if he would let us across the river in his canoe, we would find our way over the mountain to Humbug. But he persisted in escorting us with eight or ten of his braves across the river and to the summit of the mountain, within five or six miles of Humbug City. He then said, "go quick," "heep bad Injun," "plenty kill 'em white man," "no stop, go!" We had been satisfied from the first that there was something wrong and that we were in eminent 'danger, but had not supposed that "William's" tribe had as yet gone on the war path. However, upon being told to go, we "stood not on

39

the order of going" but went at once after thanking him, for he refused to take pay.

Chapter Five

On our arrival at Humbug, we found the miners "up in arms," and organizing a company of volunteers to go to Jacksonville, in the Rogue River Valley, Oregon, seventy-five miles north, a courier having brought in word that the Rogue River, Shasta and Klamath Indians had "broke out," and were killing, pillaging, and burning everything before them; and it was believed that the Indians who had just escorted us had killed eight or ten men at the mouth of Humbug a few days before.

We afterward learned that William's band of Klamaths joined "Old Sam's" and "John's" band of Rogue River Indians, and fought with them throughout the "Rogue River war" of 1853.

I joined Captain Rhode's company of "Humbug boys," as also did John Scarbrough, one of my former partners; and we proceeded to Jacksonville, as did Captain Goodall's company of "Yreka boys" and seven or eight soldiers from Fort Jones, under Colonel Aldrich (if my memory don't fail me as regards the name). Reaching Jacksonville without adventure, we went into camp near Table Rock on Rogue River.

From here, twenty-one men, including Crosbie and myself, John Melvin (Greasy John), "Grizzly," and others, whose names I have forgotten, were sent out as scouts. We were each armed with a "muzzle-loading" rifle, a brace of Colt's "navy" revolvers, and a knife — except Crosbie, who had a patent gun with two cylinders, which he could fire sixteen times without reloading. We crossed the mountain to Evans Creek, twenty miles distant, where we "struck the trails" of Indians.

We followed these trails up the creek some miles, until we were satisfied that the Indians had very recently passed up into the mountains.

We knew their fighting qualities, Old John's and Sam's bands of "Rogue rivers" being said to be the bravest Indians and the most stubborn fighters in the northwest. That the reader may form some idea of their bravery, I will here re*late that when one of these renowned chiefs was being taken to the military prison at Alcatraz, near San Francisco, on an ocean steamer, he actually captured the vessel, having no other weapon than a capstan bar; and held the deck for some time before he was overpowered, then as he lay on the deck in irons, he said, grating his teeth, that if he had had one of his warriors to assist him, he would have kept the "hy-as kanim" (big canoe). Then many of the brave (?) white men on board wanted to hang him, but the captain told them that an Indian who could do what that one had was too brave a man to suffer such an ignominious death. This is told as a fact, and I have no doubt of its truthfulness.

But to my story: we returned down the creek a few miles and being hungry made a stop, to let our horses graze awhile, and to partake of such provisions as we had with us.

Some of us picketed our horses and others "hobbled" theirs on the creek bottom, which was covered with luxuriant grass. We then fell to work *in our own interest,* and after satisfying our appetites, stretched ourselves on the grass under a few pine trees that grew in the bend of the creek, to rest, while our horses fed. The bottom here was three or four hundred yards wide and the creek running through it was fringed on each side with willows and other brush. From the willows to the foot of the hills, or mountain spurs, was level prairie. The foot-hills were studded with sugar and "bull pine" trees, and were clear of underbrush. The bend in the creek where we rested was in something the shape of a horseshoe, and our shade trees stood near the centre of this bend.

While resting here, some lying down, others sitting up talking, our horses quietly grazing, none of us suspecting any danger, or that there was an Indian within miles of us, we were suddenly *saluted with a volley,* and the unearthly yells of hundreds of Indians from the bushes which almost surrounded us. Our horses stampeded, and scattered excepting one that was being held by one of the boys. This he immediately mounted, and "struck out," for our camp on Rogue river. The first glance showed us that we must retreat to the foot-hills; this we did as fast as we could, assisting our wounded along, leaving our dead as they lay.

Reaching the timber, we found that seven of our comrades had been killed and that seven more were so badly wounded that they could not stand up after we got them there.

The one on the horse we believed — and it was soon proved — had escaped and gone after the rest of the company. Our wounded had retained their arms and ammunition.

The Indians first proceeded to mutilate our dead after their most inhuman fashion, cutting, stabbing and gashing, all the while yelling in the most fiendish manner that the mind of man could conceive. Then, after securing our animals, they swung around on to the mountain above us, so as to work down on us from tree to tree. A few well-directed shots had convinced them that it would not be a healthy undertaking to follow us across the bottom. These movements on their part gave us sufficient time to select our fighting-ground. This we made on the first high ground out of gunshot of the bushes along the creek. As good fortune would have it, a log lay across the narrow ridge. Behind this log we laid our wounded, among whom was "Greasy John," severely wounded in the hip. "Grizzly" had fallen and was one of the dead; Crosbie fell by the log with the wounded, being, as I supposed at the time, more dangerously wounded than any of the others.

The Indians gave us but a short time to prepare for them. We all realized upon reaching the friendly trees that we must stop here and fight it out, or leave our wounded comrades to the tender mercies of these inhuman fiends, and even then, in all likelihood, be overtaken and killed in detail ourselves.

Our only thought was to stand by our comrades, and fight for them and ourselves to the bitter end.

Those that were able to fight could command two rifles and four revolvers each, as we could use those of our wounded as well as our own. Some of our wounded comrades could load our revolvers when emptied, as a ball that fitted one, would fit all.

Our respite was short. The Indians, armed with guns, bows and arrows, — few of them had revolvers at the time — soon came down on us, jumping from tree to tree for cover, all the time firing and making the mountains re-echo their bloodcurdling war-whoop. They seemed determined to "finish us up" there and then, at all hazards. They charged down to within a few yards of our log and trees, but here they met such a withering fire from our Colt's revolvers, that those who were able were only too anxious to retreat to a more respectful distance, and for awhile contented themselves with firing on us from trees behind which they had taken cover. On this first charge there were but five of us on our feet — Crosbie lying by the wounded as dead. "Greasy John" and one or two others would from time to time raise on their elbows or to a sitting position, and over their log fire a few well-aimed shots, then sink back faint and exhausted, soon revive, reload, struggle to a position and blaze away until their strength failed. This they repeated during the entire fight. The wounded would load our revolvers and pitch them to us as fast as we emptied them, when we were being pressed by these charges.

About this time Crosbie raised to his feet, having got over his "scare" (as he afterwards acknowledged for he had lain unhurt all the time). There he stood, his face flushed, his eyes flashing with daring and his repeating rifle firmly grasped, and as his glance took in the position of the five who were stationed around the wounded, under such cover as was most convenient, and our poor and wounded comrades, who in different positions were either engaged in reloading pistols, or helping one another dress their wounds, using pieces of torn shirts or drawers for bandages; then at the few "good Indians," that had fallen so near our log that their friends dare not attempt to remove them, all this time standing in open view amid the firing, and while friendly voices were calling to him to "take cover," his voice rang out clear as a bell and above all other sounds, as he started up the comical song, "Jordan is a hard road to travel." In all my life, I have heard but few voices that could equal his for power and sweetness, and as he leisurely walked to a tree he sang:

"I looked to the east, and I looked to the west,
  And I saw a chariot coming
  With four bay horses running their best,
  To tote you to the other side of Jordan."

Then his gun sprang to his shoulder, there was a flash, a report, and an Indian's "heel flew up."

Again his joyous voice rang out clear and sweet:

> "Haul off your jacket,
>   Roll up your sleeves,
>   For Jordan is a hard road to travel I believe;"

to the accompaniment of cracking rifles and pistols, our defiant shouts, and the hellish yells of the infuriated Indians; then flash, bang! — another Indian called for. Then, as

> "Adam and Eve in the garden of Eden,
>   Viewing the beauties of nater" —

Bang! —

> "The devil stuck his head
>   Through a gooseberry bush,
>   And I hit 'im a whack with a tater."

And again the trusty rifle would speak its warning, notifying the Indians that we had been reinforced by a giant.

To try to describe this man, as he jumped from tree to tree, firing, singing, and by turns calling to us to fire "slow and sure," that our friend would soon come back with the rest of the company, would be a difficult undertaking. "Save your bullets, boys," he would say, "till you have a dead thing, then sling 'em in."

As the Indians would at intervals attempt, in various ways, to get to us under cover, Crosbie's voice would again ring out: "Haul off your jacket," etc. This song he continued to sing, from time to time, for hours, to the strange accompaniments described. The "*chords* were *jarring*," but they beat none at all.

Some time after he had come up to the fighting point, and while resting a moment, one of the fingers of his left hand was shot clean off at the second joint. Coming to the tree that I stood behind, he pulled the handkerchief from his neck and one from his pocket, and said, as he looked at the blood spurting from the artery, "Buckeye, tie that up," and again commenced his song, "Jordan is a hard road to travel."

Suffice it to say, that for some four or five long, weary hours (long they certainly were to us six surrounded men), we struggled to save ourselves and wounded comrades from these inhuman fiends. It would require a more able pen than an old-timer's to portray the scene. At every respite we would gaze at our wounded, then across the flat at the dead, and wonder how much longer we could hold out; then, at the warning of Crosbie or some other watchful comrade, we would turn to repulse another attack. "Greasy John" would load a revolver, then grit his teeth and say: "I wouldn't care a d__n if they hadn't shot me" (where it will make riding uncomfortable).

At last we heard a cheering far above the Indians on the mountain, which assured us that the long looked for help was at hand. The ground was not to the liking of the Indians for a general fight. So they at once decamped being warned by the shouts of our advancing friends or by their own lookouts. In a few moments there came dashing among us some dozen or so old miners who had rode their horses till they fell dead or gave out in climbing the mountain, then outstripping the rest on foot, rushed over and down the mountain, the sweat streaming from every pore. In all my life I never saw a more completely given out lot of men than these, the first to reach us, were on their arrival. They cried, hugged, and patted us on the back by turns. But few words were said until the rest of the command arrived. Then after examining the ground fought over, looking at our dead and caring as best we could for the wounded, came questions from all quarters regarding the fight. All wished to know how the boy "Buckeye" stood fire. I was accorded the praise of having saved the party in the first and most desperate charge. The others saying that I stood uncovered, shooting right and left, apparently as cool as though I was shooting at pigeons. But all agreed it was Crosbie's cool fighting, cheering words, and above all his joyous song during all the other desperate charges, that saved the devoted few from despair and final destruction.

I mention these facts to show how a scare will act on different persons.

Crosbie always said, that when we retreated across the flat to the timber and fell by the log, he was *frightened to death,* and only recovered after the first charge was repulsed, while all agreed that I had fought like a lion at bay, and probably saved the outfit at first. But I myself was proudly conscious (?) that if I fought at all, it was from *instinct,* and as a scared boy — for I certainly was as badly, and probably *worse scared than Crosbie* — and had no recollection of helping "Greasy John" across the flat, as they all said I did, nor anything else during the first charge, or until Crosbie raised and commenced his song. The facts in the case are, that I was *scared into a man,* while Crosbie came out of his scare and coolly *fought and sung* into one.

We afterward learned, that our friend who got away had rode as fast as he could to Table rock and given the alarm, telling our boys that we were all killed, or soon would be, but to hurry to our assistance. This was all-sufficient to call forth their utmost energies, and as soon as a man caught a horse, he galloped away regardless of orders or command, using his own judgment, and straining every nerve to reach us first, regardless of danger; and here a struggle commenced, which lasted for twenty odd miles, each striving to be the first to the rescue.

After all of the company came in, we encamped where we were for the night, putting out our guards. Next morning we took up our march to our former camp on Rogue river, carrying with us our dead and wounded. The dead we buried upon our arrival with the honors of war, our wounded we left in the care of the hospitable citizens of Jacksonville, where nearly all the settlers of the valley had assembled for mutual protection.

We remained in camp here for several days, collecting and killing beeves, and "jerking" the meat. This latter is done by cutting beef into thin slices or strips, it is then salted a little and the strips hung on sticks over a slow fire to dry. When thoroughly dried, it was put up in convenient packages for transportation. This required several days, as we thought best to prepare for a long trail, knowing that the Indians would fight only on their chosen ground.

While collecting and preparing provisions for the expedition, we amused ourselves by running foot-races, jumping and wrestling. We had a man with us by the name of Lout Price, from Cottonwood, California, who outran every one that tested his speed, as I had all that had been pitted against me.

About this time, General Joseph Lane, accompanied by a Mr. Armstrong, a wealthy gentleman from the Willamette valley, came to the command. The former took command of the volunteers. It is hardly necessary for me to say that General Lane commanded the Indiana volunteers in the Mexican war, and the Oregon volunteers in 1850, against these same Indians (Rogue Rivers). He was then delegate to congress from Oregon territory, afterward senator, on the admission of Oregon, and, finally, a candidate for the vice-presidency on the ticket with John C. Breckinridge.

He was a brave and generous frontiers-man, self-made, full of resources, and always equal to an emergency. It is said of him that he saved his command in Mexico with his cigar. His command, being encamped, were surprised by a large force of Mexican cavalry. His cannon were ready loaded with grape-shot, but there was no fire with which to "touch them off." Lane saw that these guns must be used to hold the Mexicans in check till his men could form to repulse the charge, or the whole command would be captured. So, as fast as the guns were trained, General Lane would "touch them off" with his lighted cigar, and in this way he saved his command.

General Lane was Oregon's best friend, wielded more influence in congress than any other man in his day, and it was indeed a "cold day" for the Pacific states and territories, when they lost the strength and influence of this noble old veteran.

Our officers concluded to send scouts to Evans creek, to ascertain what route the Indians had taken after our fight. Past experience having taught us that horses were of no use in scouting these mountains, Lout Price was selected to perform this dangerous duty, as he was believed to have more mountain experience, and to be the fleetest of foot of any. (Many thought I could "hold him level" in a long race, but up to this we had never tested our speed, and I guess each of us feared to test the matter.) When I learned that Price had been selected to perform this mission, I requested the privilege of accompanying him, and he gladly seconded my request. After some opposition from older men, my request was granted, for they all knew I was endowed with great endurance.

Having received our instructions and provided ourselves with a little of the "jerked" beef, we shook hands with our most intimate acquaintances and were set across the river, when we pushed out, up and over the mountain to the scene of our former battle.

Thence slowly and cautiously we made our way up Evans creek, keeping near to or within the bushes that fringed its banks, using every precaution possible to prevent being ambushed or surprised. We could discern no "sign" indicating that Indians had been there since our fight. Toward evening we found it necessary to cross a bald ridge to another small creek that emptied into the one we had been following up.

After a short rest, we started up a long gentle slope to cross this low elevation. Arriving at the summit to our surprise we discovered the Indian lodges not more than three hundred yards distant on the other creek. As we took in this sight we were made aware that the Indians had discovered ns, about the same time we saw them!

They *"raised the yell"* and started for us. We didn't think it necessary to stop to "count noses," but whirled, and struck for Evans creek and the brush at our best pace. Now was the time to test our speed. But we did not think it wise to stop to arrange a wager — rather run for glory, Evans creek and the brush; knowing that our only hope of safety was in reaching the friendly bushes before the Indians could get within rifle shot. We dropped our pouches of "jerked" beef, and as we only carried our revolvers and knives, we were in "light running order." *Then* commenced a race to save our hair, and a more equal one of five or six hundred yards was scarcely ever made, as we strained every nerve. We ran side by side, and as I looked at Price, I thought "you are a good one for not leaving me." Price afterward said he thought the same of me — as we approached the brush Price "panted out" to me, "go up the creek, and hide in the thick underbrush, I'll go down stream. Lay low until dark, then take for the mountains and for camp."

It being nearly dark and as I didn't think we would be long separated, I acted on Price's orders, believing we could better elude our pursuers.

On getting well into the brush I crawled up the creek a short distance making as little noise as possible, and "cached" myself. I could hear Price crushing down through the brush, making as much noise as would a yoke of stampeded oxen, and at once divined his motive, it was to draw the Indians after him and give me an opportunity to escape, as he had confidence in his own ability to out-wit and elude his pursuers. I could hear the Indians yelling on his trail, the sounds growing fainter as they passed from my place of concealment.

At dark I could not hear anything of Price, or the Indians, so I worked my way slowly and cautiously across the creek and toward the mountains, creeping and stopping every few feet to listen, at every crack of a twig, or flutter of a disturbed bird. I would grasp my revolver in one hand and with the other feel if my hair was in any way loose. After what seemed to me an interminable time, I came to the edge of the brush, on the opposite side of the creek, then I had to cross a flat some two hundred yards wide to reach the timber at the foot of the mountain. This flat I crossed by crawling in the most cautious manner possible; feeling before me to see that there were no obstructions that might cause me to make sufficient noise to attract the attention of any hostile who might be prowling around, or left near on the watch.

Upon gaining the timber and mountain I felt comparatively safe, and if Price had only been with me I should have been as happy as a clam at high tide, but as he was not I must do the best I could.

I studied the lay of the mountains, and the course of the creek, being far above where I had ever crossed before. I knew I would have many spurs and gulches to cross, as I dared not venture down Evans creek for fear of running on to the Indians. So I slowly pursued my lonesome way, striving to keep parallel with the creek, till I reached the place we had before crossed at, or still better find Price, being satisfied he had eluded his pursuers as I had mine.

On I went in total darkness for hour after hour. Finally, becoming tired out (as I was continually falling over logs and brush, and getting scratched and bruised), I found a large tree and sat down at its foot to await the rising of the moon, or till daylight. It was dreary and lonely waiting, "but the longest night must come to a close," and this, like all others, at last came to an end. The moon came up toward morning, and shed sufficient light for me to discern my way across the mountains and back to camp, where I arrived about 10 o'clock in the morning, to find the camp in commotion. Price had got in the night before, and, relating our adventures, was severely censured for (as they would have it) "forsaking the boy." He assured them that I would "turn up all hunkey"; saying, "he was as 'cool as a cucumber'; and while we were running he could have left me easily, but would not. I left him in the brush near night, and he wouldn't dare cross the mountains, from where he was, it was so dark; but after daylight he will come in, you can bet your lives."

He wouldn't tell them that he had left me in order to decoy the Indians after himself, and thus secure my safety. I verily believe they would have hung this brave and generous man if I hadn't put in an appearance during the day. But, upon my appearing on the bank of the river and hailing for a canoe, there went up a glad shout, and I assure you I didn't have to wait long for a boat. Once in camp, I was fed and questioned: and, when I gave my version of our adventure and Price's generous action, all were ready to "shake," and beg his pardon for the naughty things they had said.

Afterward, at different times, many of our friends strove to have us pitted against each other in a race, but each of us preferred to let the question rest, and remained of the opinion that the other ran that day to *keep up,* and was too brave to leave a comrade in peril.

Chapter Six

The command now being well supplied with "jerked beef," and everything being in readiness, we removed across Rogue River and on to Evans Creek, where we camped that night. Next morning we followed the trails of the Indians, which led us high up into the mountains. These trails we followed for some days, when Bob Metcalf, Lout Price, and myself, who had been acting as scouts, upon gaining the summit of a high ridge, heard the barking of coyote dogs in the canyon below. This assured us that we had at last brought these wily savages to bay, and closer inspection satisfied us that they had selected their position for a struggle.

General Lane was notified, and was soon on the ridge overlooking the canyon. The command coming up, the order was given to dismount, then leaving the horses in care of a guard, General Lane ordered a charge down the mountain, himself leading, swinging his hat and hurrahing for the man who fired the first shot.

The Indians had set fire to the dead pitch pine trees and dry brush surrounding their camp, so we had literally to fight in fire and smoke. We reached them in a few moments and there ensued a hand-to-hand struggle which lasted a few minutes.

General Lane was wounded in the same arm in which he had before received a Mexican ball. His friend, Mr. Armstrong, was killed (shot through the head). My partner, John Scarbrough, while fighting by my side, was shot through the heart. He fell, then jumping to his feet said *"I'm killed, write!"* then fell dead without a struggle (he had a wife and six children in Indiana). The Colonel in command of the seven or eight "regulars" was shot through the shoulder and several others fell dead or badly wounded. I broke off my gun stock in striking an Indian, but this made it all the more handy while in close quarters.

The Indians soon learned that close quarters wouldn't do for them, so they scattered and fought from behind trees in the midst of the smoke and fire. As my gun was broken and the boys were playing on them at long range in Indian fashion, I went back a short distance and found General Lane sitting on a log with his arm undressed and bleeding. As I approached he asked why I was not down with the "boys?" I showed him my gun barrel, and as he knew how it got broken he gave me his shotgun and ammunition saying "break that in the same way if you get the chance." I took it, and our men having formed a skirmish line across the canyon below them and were working up on either side from tree to tree and slowly crowding the enemy from their cover, I advanced up the left side of the canyon till I reached a large sugar pine tree, where I found Tom Hayes (an old soldier of the Mexican War) behind it. He told me he thought we were the farthest up on the left flank so I stopped with him, and was peering into the dense smoke which hovered over the little flat that the Indians occupied. I was able to see but a short distance. Hayes would load his rifle, aim, fire, take a hasty look, and load and fire again. I couldn't see what he was shooting at, finally he remarked that he must have got the sights of his fine target gun moved, and said try my gun and see what ails it. I said that he couldn't see an Indian from where we were.

He said "yes I do! come on this side of the tree, and look over that big log in front of the big tree, pointing as he spoke. Watch close and you'll see an Indian come up after he has reloaded, he is shooting at the boys below, and hasn't discovered us." (The continuous firing by Whites and Indians, accompanied by their shouts and yells and the barking of the coyote dogs created such a din, that one could scarcely hear the other's voice, much less could you tell by the report what direction a shot was fired from.)

I gave Tom my shotgun and taking his rifle closely watched the tree he had pointed out to me. I soon saw something rising from behind the log and close to the tree Tom had pointed out, and as it continued to rise I could see through the smoke that it was an Indian, I waited till He raised his gun to shoot, then taking a quick aim at his shoulder I fired, at the crack of the gun he uttered a fierce yell and jumping high in the air (his gun going off as he went up) he fell over the log toward us alighting on his head and shoulders, some one had made a "good Indian" of that fellow sure. This was too much for Hayes, he sprang out from the tree swinging his hat and shouting at the top of his voice, but he came back faster than he went and with a different cry. The Indians had now discovered" our position and a stream of bullets poured at our tree, one of the first passing through Hayes' wrist breaking both bones. Seeing that it was getting too hot for us where we were, and that Hayes had got a "furlough" and was ready for the pension rolls of his country, we beat a hasty retreat to our comrades below. Fighting continued for some hours when the Indians called to Metcalf (who had a squaw for a wife) for quarters. After a while General Lane instructed Metcalf to tell them to come into camp on the ridge where our horses were left and he would treat with them, this they did, giving up their arms. There were two or three hundred warriors alive, but scarcely a dozen of them were without wounds of a more or less serious nature received in one or the other of our two skirmishes.

We all noted throughout the fighting above all other sounds the shoutings of old chief John, giving his orders and "medicine cries."

We encamped for the night on the ridge, the Indians bringing us water from the canyon.

The next morning we buried our dead on the battlefield, then constructed litters on which to carry our wounded out of the mountains. This we did by lashing poles to the sides of horses, one horse in front of the other, then stretching a blanket from one pole to the other between the horses, thus forming a cot or litter, upon which we laid those of our wounded who were not able to ride on horseback. All being ready we took up our line of march over the rough route we had come, much of the way we had to clear a trail of brush and trees with our hatchets to enable the horses carrying the litters to pass, we were several days in reaching Jacksonville where some of our wounded died soon after. The Indians soon came in and made a treaty of peace with General Lane. We were discharged and returned to our several homes and occupations.

General Lane afterward secured the passage through congress of a bill allowing each of the volunteers one dollar per day for the time served, and a 160-acre land-warrant. I gave my land-warrant to mother, when I next saw her. I returned to Humbug and joined my partner, Study, in mining, for some months.

About this time an incident occurred at Yreka, that I deem worthy of note.

There arrived on the "flats" two boys, aged respectively seventeen and nineteen years. They stopped in a mining-cabin about a mile from town. Before obtaining work or finding "paying diggings" they were both stricken with fever. The eldest died, and the other lay in a critical condition before the facts became known to the public.

One evening a miner came to town and related the circumstances in a gambling-saloon, when a sporting-woman named "Swan," who was *bucking* at monte at the time, sprang upon a gambling-table, grabbed a hat from the head of one of the dealers and threw into it a handful of money from her purse, saying, "Swan is sorry so much," naming the amount, which was a large sum to contribute, "Boys how much are you sorry?" It would be needless for me to tell an old-timer that the boys were *all* "sorry." Swan moved from table to table and from saloon to saloon until she was satisfied with the amount collected, then, in company with a doctor and others, she repaired to the cabin, and assisted in preparing the remains for a decent burial. She then caused the other young man to be taken to her own house where she nursed him till he was able to travel, then presenting him with a check for some two thousand dollars — purchased with the money donated — and a ticket for his return to New York, she said, "take this and go home, you have had enough of California life."

Poor woman! She sleeps in a comparatively unknown grave, where she was laid by the rough hands of warm-hearted miners. Hearing that the Modocs and Pitt River Indians at or near Klamath lake were killing emigrants who were coming in on that route, I joined a scouting party that was organized by Ben Wright, the noted Indian fighter and scout. Lout Price and "Greasy John" (now recovered from his wound) were of the party.

We had many skirmishes with these Indians, but sustained no serious loss, until one day our brave friend, "Greasy John" (Melvin), started alone on a scout along the margin of a tule lake. He not returning that night, we went in search of him the next morning, and found his body lying in a "pot-hole" or sink, riddled with bullets. But he left proof of his valor, for beside him lay his gun, pistol and knife, showing that after firing his last shot, he had broken the tubes off both the former and then broke the knife, to prevent the redskins from using them against his friends.

Noble John! He sleeps with his broken weapons beside him in an unknown grave, where he fell, but his memory is enshrined in the heart of many an old miner. We returned to Humbug soon after this, and Study and myself resumed mining.

That winter I received a letter from my uncle, Samuel Meek, informing me of the whereabouts of my father and the rest of the family, and of their good health. During the next spring my father moved to Yreka with the family.

Some time during the summer of 1854, while Allen, Study, Draper, Carwile, myself and others were coming across the Yreka flats we saw a man coming to meet us. Allen asked me, "Isn't that Bill Adams coming there?" Allen had known him in the States. I replied that I thought it was. He then asked if I thought I was able to collect my pay, for helping him drive his cattle over the Cascade trails? "I'll try it at any rate," said I. On meeting, Adams shook hands with Allen, Draper, and Carwile, but didn't seem to recognize me, as I was then "several sizes" larger than I was when he refused to pay me the five dollars. Allen inquired of him if he knew *that boy* (pointing to me). He replied that my face was familiar, but he couldn't "place me."

I then stepped up and asked him if he had such a thing as a five dollar piece in his "breeches?" If so, he would please "fork over," for I had waited long enough for it. He *recognized* me, and said he didn't think I earned it. I replied: "That makes no difference; I told you when I last saw you, that if we ever met again when I was well and able yon would pay me with interest, now we have met, and I am well, so fork over the dust." He saw that I "meant business," and said, "Well! I'll give it to you rather than have a fuss over it." So he handed me five dollars. I said, "Now the interest!" "How much?" he asked. I said I thought two-and-a-half would be about the proper thing; this he paid me without a word.

I then said, "Now I propose to 'strife' with you, and you'd better arrange yourself!" Seeing my revolver he thought I was going to shoot him, but I took off my belt and handed it to Allen, telling him to do likewise. He seeing that there was *no other doctor in the place,* "squared off" and at it we went! I soon found that I had a larger contract on my hands than I had bargained for; but I "stayed with him" till he "sung out." Allen told me I had done well; but I was not in a condition to ornament a ballroom or the dress-circle of a first-class theatre, for some days after.

Allen met him some months afterward, gave him another licking, and he fearing, I suppose, that he would eventually get one from Carwile and Draper as well, left the diggings. I never met him afterwards.

About this time I and one George L. Willey, struck "pay" in a deep bar on Humbug. For a short time we got good "pay" ($20 to $30 per day), but getting off the "pay streak," we worked some weeks without getting the "color." Willey becoming discouraged, proposed to sell out, and rather than have a stranger for a partner, I bought his interest myself.

According to our mining laws we had to "represent our claims" at least one day in each week, so leaving word with Jackson ("Whisky Jackson" for short) to hire a man for me as soon as he could, I continued in the claim alone. I soon found the "pay streak" again, and was taking out big money, when on going to work one morning I found a notice posted on a tree on one of my claims to the effect that George L. Willey (the same man I had bought it of) had "located this ground."

Miners now seemed to be "falling from grace;" that is to say, they were not the *gentlemen* they were the year before (in my opinion). For me to say that I tore down that notice and *swore* a *very little* is touching it light enough.

I returned to my cabin, got my revolver, and going back to my claims found Willey at work starting a drift, I asked him what he was doing, and he told me he had located that ground, "Didn't I pay you for this ground?" I asked. "Yes," said he, "but you have forfeited it by not representing it!" I pulled my pistol and told him that if he didn't leave in a minute he would be in a poor condition to "represent" anything. He left, and called a miners' meeting, at which I proved that I had authorized and requested Jackson to hire a man for me, and that I had been doing all in my power to conform to the miners' laws. The claim was awarded to me and Willey was warned not to molest me in my rights again; but I was not yet rid of him.

Some days later I went to Jackson's "dead fall" (all the stores were called "dead falls" by us, for they all sold whisky as well as miners' supplies; Jackson sold beef in addition). As I was passing under a shed roof I saw Willey and a miner named Hill talking. Willey had a drifting pick, with which he was amusing himself by picking at a log over his head. I spoke to Hill as I passed, and he asking some question, I stopped and turned toward him. At this instant Willey struck me on the head with the pick, and if Hill had not noticed the movement and partially arrested the blow these reminiscences would not have been written, by me at least. The blow knocked me back against a keg of ax and pick handles. In a second I had jerked out one of them and before I got on my feet, I struck and "caught" Willey on the jaw. Others interfering, we were both carried or assisted to our cabins for "repairs," he with a broken jaw and I with a broken head.

Some weeks after we had got well we met on the trail, I going down and he coming up. He being a more powerful man than I, I thought I would pass him without a word if he would allow me to do so, but when he came up to me he smiled, as much as to say, "How is your head?" That settled it; I hit him on the nose, and then came the "tug of war." I "got in" one or two more on his face, when he grabbed me up, and laying me down on the trail, was doing a first-class job in the way of polishing my upper works, when some vaqueros came along and pulled him off. I returned to my cabin for "more repairs." I had got a great deal the worst of that "racket."

Later on we had an election or" miners' meeting" at Round town, and as I was going down in company with some friends I met Willey coming out of a saloon; his eyes said to me, "Well, how do you feel since our last meeting?" My answer was a "biff" in his face and we went for each other again. I could outstrike him, and got in some good ones, but at last he "muzzled" me and again laid me down and — well, *he licked me.*

Studys Ride

My friends told me I was a fool to fight such a man with my fists, and I thought so, too, but I had been the aggressor the most of the time.

Again I met him in "shooting McGee's" saloon in Yreka. I was standing at the bar in company with many others. Study had just poured out a big glass of brandy and I was lighting a cigar when some one crowded in beside me and called for drinks; turning, I saw it was Willey. I snatched Study's glass and saying some appropriate (?) words dashed the brandy into his face. Then we "had it" again, but either the brandy had failed to help his eyesight, or I did better dodging than I had done before, for he was unable to get hold of me and I was putting a "mansard roof" on him fast when he said, "that will do!" I was glad he said it for I hadn't been at all sure of the result.

I relate the above incident only to prove, that a little brandy properly used will sometimes help a poor fellow out of a tight place.

Again I must call the attention of the reader to the fact, that I am writing wholly from memory, and without a single reference. But every circumstance herein related actually occurred, though I am liable to "jump a cog" as regards the real order and date of the happening; for a lapse of thirty-five years obliterates dates in my memory.

On one of our visits to Yreka, Study and I heard that some Mexicans had lassoed a grizzly up in Shasta valley, ten or twelve miles distant from Yreka, and were bringing him to town for the purpose of having a bear-fight. Every one who could get a horse or mule had gone to see the sport. Study and I rushed around, and finally procured a horse for myself and an old mule for Study. A venerable mule he was! Probably the one that was in the ark with Noah, that is, if that good old man carried any of these long-eared gentry to amuse Shem, Hani and Japhet on the tedious voyage. (Mules' hind legs are nice things to have among children - bad children.) All animals were represented in the ark, to perpetuate their species and qualifications. This being the case, a mule or a railroadman must have had a berth on board, for a railroadman can do more kicking to the square inch than any other animal on God's green earth — unless it be a mule. Away we went, kicking, damning and whipping (for it takes all the above-named persuasion to induce an old mule to a faster gait than a shambling trot — especially damning). Arriving at the scene of action, the grizzly and the. Spaniards were surrounded by a hundred or more men on horseback. They had stopped for awhile to arrange matters with his bearship. The Spaniards had cut a small juniper-tree, lopped the limbs, making a drag, worked the bear on to it, and with rawhide ropes or *riatas* hitched to the tree and the horns of their saddles, were slowly pulling him along. Now and then the bear would get off the boughs, and they would have to work him back again.

For some time we couldn't get a view of either Spaniards or bear, but all at once the crowd gave away on our side, and we got sight of the bear. Study's mule saw him just as he gave a "snort." This settled it. "Old Noah" (the mule) whirled and started for Yreka, and at every jump he would let off a "Yah-he!

Yah— he!" Of course every one present "raised the yell," and this only lent speed to the mule. Study "sat him" like a Trojan, and sawed his mouth, but having only a snaffle-bit, he might as well have pulled at Mount Shasta as at old "Noah's" mouth. This being a level country, we could see Study and his mule for miles, Study's coat-tails and hair flying straight out, and the mule keeping up his "music."

When I got to town that evening, I asked Study where "Noah" stopped. "In the stable," he replied.

Just compare Sheridan's ride on his black horse, from "Winchester, twenty miles away," with Study's ride on his "mool," from a grizzly, "only ten miles from town." Sheridan was eulogized — Study was "chaffed;" Sheridan was well treated — Study "stood the treats."

About this time a dozen or more miners and sports concluded to go into the mountains for a hunt. So, having provided themselves with a generous supply of provisions (not forgetting the *vinegar*-keg), they started out, and finding a convenient spot, pitched their camp, selecting their cook for the time. This "cook" was a jovial, witty fellow. Hunting commenced, grizzly was their ambition. After several days, some having brought in a grouse or two, others a deer, but none having reported a grizzly, it became the cook's turn to go out, and as he loaded his gun, he said: "You fellers don't know how to hunt grizzlys. I'm going out to-day, and you bet your boots I'll fetch one to camp." Off he started. He had got but a short distance from camp when, in passing through a "patch" of manzanita brush, he run on to a she-grizzly. Madam Grizzly "made a dive for him," he dropped his gun and "lit out" for camp. As he neared the camp (Mrs. Grizzly only a few yards behind him), he cried out, "Here we come, damn our brave souls!" It is needless to say that her majesty received a warm reception, and stayed at the camp. So did the cook. He said that was the only grizzly he ever lost, and he didn't propose to experiment with them any more.

Chapter Seven

I continued ruining on Humbug, and near Yreka, till the summer of 1855, when my father concluded to send the family back to the Willamette valley, and as he could not go with them at the time, I escorted them.

Hiring two four-mule teams, and a two-horse family carriage we started. There were in our party the two teamsters, myself and a young man, in poor health, who was going to the Willamette, my mother, three sisters and a brother who was six or seven years old. I had a saddle horse along, and my oldest sister (a young lady of sixteen years) generally rode him. All went well, after we crossed the summit of the Siskiyou mountains (the dividing line between Oregon and California.) We met some ox-teams loaded with apples going to Yreka. We bought some of their fruit, and pushed on through Rogue river valley. We had got some distance below Jacksonville, near "Coyote" Evan's ferry, when a friend of mine by the name of Green Linville, rode up to us, his horse reeking with sweat, and after speaking pleasantly to my mother he *made me know* that he wished to speak to me in private, so I told sister to get into the carriage and drive as I wished to talk with Mr. Linville awhile!

I mounted the horse and we dropped behind the wagons out of hearing. Linville asked me if I was aware that the Rogue river Indians had again gone on the war path. I told him no! he said "they have! they killed the men with the apple teams shortly after you passed them, I heard at Jacksonville that you were on the road with your family, so I came on as fast as I could to warn you."

We consulted on the situation, and concluded that as the Indians would not think we had heard of the outbreak, it would be as well for us to go on, as to turn back, and probably better, as our turning back would be proof of our having heard of the trouble; so we determined to go on at all hazards, but not to let the teamsters or family know of the danger menacing us, as long as we could help it.

I told Linville I couldn't asked him to accompany us on so hazardous an expedition. He replied, "You need not, for I shall go without asking, and won't leave you till the folks are in a place of safety."

I well knew this man's bravery and determination and was only too glad to have his company, but felt that it would be only a sacrifice on his part if we were attacked.

That evening after a hard drive we crossed the river and camped by a log corral, three or four miles below the mouth of Evans creek, a favorite camping place of the Indians.

After feeding the stock, getting supper, and seeing that everything was secure, Linville and I laid down near mother's bed (the weather being fine, we all slept out of the wagons). We had concluded to rest our stock this night and make a hard drive for the Umpqua canyon next day (some forty miles over Cow creek and Crab creek hills — a rough road).

We had also determined to go up to the mouth of Evans creek, as soon as all was quiet and we could get away, to make a reconnaissance and see if there were any Indians there, and if so, how they appeared. I lay until I thought all were asleep except Linville; I cautiously raised up and was about to crawl off so as not to awake mother, but it was "no go;" she spoke to me, so I laid down again. After awhile I tried it again, but with a worse result than before, for mother said "What is the matter with you? You usually sleep like one of the seven sleepers, but to-night you are starting up as though you *feared something.*" I replied, "Oh pshaw, mother, give us a rest; I thought I heard the horses making a noise," and down I laid again, resolved to be more careful in my next attempt.

After waiting till we were sure mother was asleep, Linville and I crawled out of camp, and as soon as we were out of hearing walked rapidly until we got within a few hundred yards of Evans creek. We were already aware of the presence of Indians at the old camping ground, for we had heard the beating of sticks and drums (these "drums" are made by stretching wet deer skins over hoops and letting them dry; they beat on them as an accompaniment to their weird singing). Cautiously creeping forward, we laid behind some brush and watched their movements; they were having a big dance and were painted up; everything went to show that this was a war dance. We lay there watching them until near morning, then quietly went back to our camp.

Before daylight we had the teamsters up, the mules and horses harnessed and hitched up, and were ready to start as soon as it was light enough to see to drive.

We had told the teamsters that we feared the Indians were about to go on the war-path and we had better go as far as Jump-off-Jo creek for breakfast. This creek received its name from an incident that occurred some years before. Some Oregonians were passing through this country, on their way to California, when one of the party called Jo being out after a lost horse, the Indians got after him. He ran for camp and friends, but on coining to this creek he found himself on top of a bluff some twenty feet high; here he hesitated, the Indians were close after him, and there being no other chance for his escape, his friends seeing his danger cried, *"Jump off, Jo; jump off, Jo."* Off Jo jumped and came down all right, and soon joined his friends, thus saving his "har." From this incident this creek took the name of Jump-off-Jo.

As soon as it was sufficiently light we were about to start, when mother declared she could not think of starting without having a cup of coffee, for she would have the sick headache all day if she went without it. Whilst I was trying to argue the case with her we saw thirty or forty Indians mounted upon ponies coming from Evans creek. Mother seeing them said as she climbed into the carriage, "George, you fear those Indians, and that is why you were so wakeful last night." I said, "You are right, mother; those Indians are on the war-path, but they think we don't know it; so keep the children quiet, and don't let the Indians see that we are afraid of them, and we may escape!" She said not a word as the Indians were close at hand, but stayed in the carriage with the children.

The Indians on coming up appeared friendly — asked where we were going? We told them to the Willamette, they then asked for tobacco, and I divided a piece with the head man. They started on and we followed, as they were going the same road that we were. They would go a short distance, then stop to consult, and we would come up and pass them. I generally stopped back with them until the teams passed (they generally stopped at small streams to drink and smoke); when the teams got a short distance ahead, I would gallop up to the wagons. When the Indians overtook and passed us again, I would ride a short distance with them and then drop back to the teams again. This proceeding was repeated several times during the day.

Finally my eldest sister becoming tired of the wagons got on to my horse for a short ride while the Indians were behind ns. But as they came up, they made such demonstrations that she became frightened and got into the carriage.

They at one time tangled up our lead mule team as it was crossing a bridge. I passed in among them and drove their ponies off the bridge laughing all the while. This was all sport (?) so far, but the villains were only awaiting an opportunity to make sure of us without alarming the few settlers who kept wayside inns or hotels along the road. As we passed them, Linville or I would manage to warn them of the danger, but to no purpose, for like rumors were current every week or two, and they paid no attention to our warnings.

When we got to Cow creek, near the Umpqua canyon, we stopped, turned out our teams, and made preparations to camp for the night. The Indians came up and asked us if we were going to stay there all night. We told them yes. In a short time they started on, saying they were going to camp a mile or so below.

As soon as they were out of sight, I told the teamsters we would hitch up and drive through the canyon during the night.

But as we had already driven some forty miles that day over a rough and rugged road, our stock was tired, and the teamsters refused to hitch up their mules, declaring there was no danger, and it was only a "scare" — they didn't believe the Indians were on the war-path.

I tried to reason with them, showing our utter inability to protect the family in case of an attack, and told them that Linville and I had planned, long before reaching Cow creek, to go into camp there, and let the Indians pass us, believing we were going to stay there all night; for, if they knew that we were going to attempt to go through the canyon that night, after traveling as far as we had that day, they would never allow us to escape; that our plans had worked well thus far, and if we remained where we were, I didn't believe there would be one of us left to tell the tale. Still they refused to move an inch.

Linville stopped the argument by picking up a shotgun and saying that if they didn't hitch up and push on through the canyon, he would save the Indians some trouble, for the teams should go, "danger or no danger." This argument proved effectual, as I had in the meantime got hold of another gun. So we hitched up, and pushed on into the canyon.

This canyon is some ten miles long, and separates what is known as the "Cow Creek country" from the south Umpqua.

In the days of which I am writing, this canyon was a terror to teamsters. It used to take three or four days to get a wagon through it. To give the reader some idea of what this canyon was at that time, I will relate a story that was current in early days.

Some packers, while passing through this canyon, found a hat lying on the ground. One of them raised it up and found a man's head under it. The head exclaimed, "Put that hat back, there is a d___d good mule under me yet!"

I don't vouch for the literal truth of the above, but it was not uncommon to see a whole packtrain mired down, the packers unloading and carrying the

Mrs. Harris defending her home and baby

cargoes to less miry ground, then helping the horses or mules out and re-packing them, only to repeat the performance many times while going through this pass.

Lieutenant Joe Hooker, later known as "Fighting Joe Hooker," afterward expended some $90,000 of government money in building a military road through this pass, and, contrary to the general rule, he did a first-class job for the money expended.

All through that long, weary night we moved on, over rocks and through mud and water. Toward daybreak we came out at what is now Canyonville — then there was only a "hotel" there. Men women and children were "give out," as were our mules and horses. Stripping off saddles and harness, we sank down on our blankets to rest, and slept till we were awakened about ten o'clock by a horseman, who came dashing through the canyon. He stopped and told us that the Indians had killed everybody between Jackson-ville and the other end of the canyon, and burned all the houses.

This report was nearly true, as there were only two or three exceptions — one, a Mrs. Neida, and another, Mrs. Harris, with her wounded child.

These two brave women, after their husbands had fallen dead, seized their guns and defended their homes. How it happened that the Indians allowed these two women to escape, after fighting them for hours, none can tell — but they did.

This was the commencement of the Rogue River Indian war of 1855-6.

We had had a "close call," and I must confess that I was scared worse and for a longer period than at any other time in my life, as during the entire trip from Evans ferry to the mouth of the canyon, I had fully realized that the least thing that would indicate to the Indians that we knew they meant mis-chief would have precipitated a fight, and as we only had one rifle, a shotgun and three revolvers among five men and one of them sick, hampered with the women and children as we were, there would have been no other alter-native than to make the best fight we could with no hope of rescue from any quarter. After resting a day and reluctantly taking leave of Linville we con-tinued on our way to the Willamette.

Linville, I afterward learned, returned to Jacksonville and took part in the war that followed. At its close he returned to Yreka and thence back East.

Generous, brave Linville, if you are still living and chance to read the poor-ly worded account of that day and night in the Cow creek hills and Umpqua canyon, you will realize that an old-timer never forgets a friend who stood by him in the hour of his greatest peril and need.

I was resolved to return as soon as my mother and sisters reached a place of safety.

We reached Corvallis without further adventure, and there heard that all the Indians in the Northwest, except the Nez Perces, had gone on the war-path.

The Governor of Oregon Territory had issued a call for volunteers to go east of the Cascade mountains, to what was then called the "Walla Walla country," embracing eastern Oregon, eastern Washington and western Idaho, and now termed the "Inland Empire" — the grandest farming country in the whole Northwest.

They were organizing companies in nearly every county in Oregon to go to the "front." I bought another horse, a fast animal, and returning home with it, my mother well knowing what was going on met me at the door and handing me my gun and pistol, said: "Go, George; if I was a man I'd go with you." So after taking an affectionate and tender leave of my mother and sisters, I, in company with some other young men of the neighborhood, went and enlisted in Captain Munson's Company I, Benton County Volunteers.

Among others who joined this company were George Elliott, David White, Lint Starr, Richard and Thomas Richardson, Wesley and Warren Hinton and Al Lloyd. I mention these names because many of them are still living.

Our company, numbering about seventy-five young men, was organized at Corvallis and immediately left for Portland, the place of rendezvous for all the volunteers, where we waited a few days till all the companies arrived, so we could be mustered into service by the Governor and furnished with supplies.

The ladies of Portland made beautiful flags for each of the companies and presented them to us through the Governor on the day we were mustered in. The Governor in presenting them made some very appropriate remarks in behalf of the ladies. It so happened that our company's flag was handed to me; I carried it awhile, as will be shown. Having been "fitted out" for the expedition, we were furnished with ponies; we called them "cayuses" (pronounced "ki-yuse," after the Indian tribe of that name, which seemed to make a specialty of that kind of stock). On these we were to pack our supplies and camp equipage; so early one morning we packed up and started eastward from Portland through the timber for Big Sandy, where a barge was in waiting to convey us to the lower cascades in tow of a steamboat. The most of the "cayuses" were wild, and the rattling of cups, kettles, pans, etc., naturally inspired them to activity; then the fun commenced; each pony went on his "own hook" through the timber, the air was full of kettles, pans and curses. Well, we got *some* of the ponies and outfit to Sandy, where we embarked horses, men and outfit on the hull of the steamer "Gazelle," which had blown up some time before at Oregon City. The hull was towed here to be used as a lighter. The steamer not having the power to breast the current, we were landed on an island just below the lower cascades; from this we waded and swam to the main land and went on up the river trails.

About this time an election was held for regimental officers, resulting in the election of J. V. Nerzneitt, Colonel; J. K. Kelley, Lieutenant-colonel; Chinn, 2nd Major; and — Armstrong 1st Major. Among the minor regimental officers elected, I remember Sergeant-major Miller. More of him hereafter.

We reached The Dalles without noteworthy incident except that two or three of the boys had carelessly let their guns go off when pointed toward themselves, which we called "accidental shooting."

We had been assured that we would be furnished with tents and blankets at The Dalles, but the promise was about all we got in that line; so we averaged two thin single blankets to three men, all through that winter campaign.

On our arrival at The Dalles I was detached as a scout by Major Armstrong, a brother of the Mr. Armstrong I mentioned as having been killed by the side of General Lane, in the Rogue river war of '53. There I had to let go of our company flag, and I turned it over to George Elliott, upon assuming the duties of scout.

My first act at the Dalles was to go to the Mission, to see Father Mesplee and John Haligan, and it was a glad meeting, especially to Haligan and myself. I remained with him over night, and told him of my father and the family, my adventures, etc. Then I went with my company which was ordered to Indian creek or Tye valley some forty miles south of the Dalles, as it was believed there were Indians all through that part of the country.

One morning I was ordered by our captain to take a few men and make a scout of a few miles in the direction of John Days river. I selected Dave White, Geo. Elliott and Dick Richardson. I wanted Lint. Starr, but he was on picket duty about a mile from camp, so I couldn't get him, though he told me to come past his post. I did, and he went with us, leaving the "post" to look after itself. We were gone some hours, and finding no sign of Indians, were returning to camp, when on nearing the picket line to leave Starr at his post, while passing through a grove of scattering trees, we saw four or five of the pickets huddled together in a knot, showing every indication that they fully believed we were Indians. I saw that here was a chance for fun. We all wore coats that were lined with red flannel. I told the boys what I believed the pickets thought, and asked them if they wanted some fun; they all said yes. Then said I, "Obey my orders and we'll have it." When I was sure we were in plain sight of the pickets I ordered a halt, and we stood as if watching the pickets for a short time, then turned into a gulch, jumped off our horses and turned our coats, this gave us the appearance of having red blankets wrapped around us. Then remounting we trotted to the top of another ridge, stopped, took a hasty look, and then, in true Indian style, dashed down the sloping hill and indicated that we were trying to cut them off from camp, dropping from side to side of our horses as we rode at full speed down hill.

This was too much for the pickets; off they started for camp, and we followed, so as to leave Starr on his post. The race became a stampede. The pickets no doubt thought they must ride for their lives; and, as they passed out of sight going into camp, we stopped at Starr's post and had our laugh out. Shortly afterward we saw mounted men coming from our camp. *This was more fun;* for we were sure the pickets had alarmed the camp, and probably nearly all of the company was out after us. This was too good to be lost; so away we went, leaving Starr, and completed a circle of the camp. When the company came near Starr, he started off in good shape, the company after him. This race lasted for a mile or so, when some of the pursuers began to fire at Starr. This warned Starr that the joke had gone far enough; so he pulled up, and bawled out, "What the Sam Patch are ye shootin' at me for?" The boys, coming up to him, asked what he was doing away from his post, and what he ran away from them for? He answered: "I wasn't runnin' from you; I saw you all comin' this way, and I thought you saw something — thought I could find it first!" They asked him if he had seen any Indians with red blankets on? He said: "No; did you?" (with a grin). Charley Hand, our second lieutenant, coming up at this time, "took a tumble to himself," and said to the men: "There have been no Indians here, so march back to camp."

Starr was *relieved* from his post, and all came to camp, where they found us eating a lunch. We asked them where they had been, but received no satisfactory answer, as all had become aware of the facts in the case by this time.

We were soon given to understand that a few such jokes would go a long ways, and if we were not prepared to lick the company, the better part of valor would be to keep our mouths shut — *for a few days, at least.* We took the hint, and looked as serious as a government mule after a hard day's drive, Next day we were furnished (?) with an *escort* (!) to headquarters (The Dalles), where we were "interviewed" by a board of examining officers — a sort of flexible court-martial — on a charge of *causing the company to run their horses down.*

Seeing that we were about to be disgraced by being dishonorably discharged, whereby we would have to relinquish all our bright hopes of fighting, freezing and starving to death in the interests of the "budding Northwest," and for the protection of women and children, at a dollar a day and furnish our own horses, guns and "rigs" (through the mighty effort of Oregon congressmen some of us did get a dollar a day for what time we served, but it was years afterward), we, of course, *felt very bad* about it, and we made the Honorable Board *aware of that fact.*

At the request of Major Armstrong, I told our side of the case, and when I had concluded, one of the officers asked me if it was true that some of the pickets had used their *ramrods for horsewhips?* I answered suavely, "Some of those pickets are present; an examination of their ramrods may answer that question." They "inspected," and found the rods badly kinked. Finally we were turned over to Major Armstrong, to be reprimanded. He told us that it was very wrong to cause the company's horses to be run down, or jaded, unnecessarily, for we had a hard and dangerous campaign before us, and much, if not all of our success, depended on our horses. He hoped we would be more careful in the future, and if we should find it necessary to drive in the pickets, we should be more careful, as we might *run against the wrong man,* and he didn't want to lose any of us from the command, for he was satisfied that if we could run the pickets in we could fight if called upon. "Now," said he, "go back to your duties, and *remember, you have a friend in Major Armstrong*" (and better one men never had). So ended the "court-martial."

Chapter Eight

Late in the fall of 1855 we started for the front. Part of the regiment crossed the Columbia into the Klickitat and Yakima country, and the rest under command of Col. J. K. Kelley and Major M. A. Chinn started up the Columbia river to the Walla Walla. Our company was with the latter division.

All went well till we arrived at the old emigrant crossing of the Umatilla river, the site of the present thriving town of Echo. Here had been an agency, and here we built a stockade and named it Fort Henrietta. Why this name was chosen I am not now able to state, but it was probably the name of the sweetheart of some young officer who had determined to "sacrifice himself" in the campaign, and took this method of leaving a memento to his "loved and lost Henrietta." Here the command remained a few days, to rest the animals and give the scouts time to look over the surrounding country. Lint. Starr, Dave White and myself crossed the rolling prairies, *a wilderness of grass.*

Excuse me for "slopping over," but as I recall the incidents of '55, and the trials, hardships, sufferings, heroism, and fortitude of the boys who volunteered to secure immunity from danger to those who chose to settle in this portion of the Northwest, and realize the changes that have since taken place, "I can't write for thinking." The Umatilla "meadows," then covered with a thick growth of wild rye grass taller than a man's head on horseback, were settled soon after the close of the war, and are now dotted with fine residences and out-buildings, orchards, tame meadows and wheat fields. The low hills over which we rode, through luxuriant bunch-grass, belly deep to our horses — at the time believing that it would never be utilized for any other purpose than grazing — are now most all fenced in, and fast yielding to the plow-share, every acre yielding, when properly tilled, from twenty to forty bushels of wheat to the acre. What we then denominated a desert is fast becoming the garden spot of the world. Thriving farms have taken the place of bunch-grass and sage-brush; the spade and hoe outdig the badger, and children outcry the ground-owl; the millions of sheep that roam the hills furnish our woolen mills with the finest texture of wool, and food for the frisky Kiota; railroads have been constructed on many of our old trails, and more are located on others; fine towns have succeeded our stockades — and developments have only commenced. *There is room for more.*

But, to my story. We three crossed over the rolling country northward and crossed the Walla Walla river about four miles above its mouth, near which was old Fort Walla Walla, afterward called Wallula. This "fort" consisted of an adobe building, constructed by the Hudson Bay Company many years before, but abandoned by them for some years, they leaving some old iron cannon, blunderbusses and some provisions in the fort. It being night when we struck the river, we worked along down to near its mouth; then, leaving our horses with White, Starr and I crept down over the sand-hills till we got near the old fort, where we could see Indian camps or "lodges." As we had gained

Culture of Pu Pu Mox Mox

all the information we came for, we returned to White as noiselessly as we went. Mounting our horses, we rode slowly for a mile or two, then as rapidly as our horses could stand it rode back to Fort Henrietta, where we reported what we had seen. A detail from each company was made to garrison the fort and look after worn-out horses, provisions and ammunition. The companies, or what was left of them — as we had left men at several points — numbering all told about two hundred and fifty men, started one afternoon for the Walla Walla valley via old Fort Wallula.

Just as day was breaking we came in sight of the old fort, and saw several canoe-loads of Indians crossing the Columbia. Some of the boys rushed down to the beach and fired at them. They returned the fire, but the only result was wasted ammunition, as neither the whites nor Indians had guns that would carry across the river at that point. We took a good look at the fort, took some pickled pork and one of the iron cannons, then went up the Walla Walla river, going into camp at the mouth of the Touchet (pronounced Too-shy) river.

The next morning, leaving a guard with the ammunition and provision train, the command moved up the Touchet. After going some distance up the stream the advance scouts (six or eight in number, and of which I was one), in crossing the spur of a hill over which the trail led, suddenly met six Indians. We instantly "covered" them with our guns, and, being so close to them, they dared not attempt to retreat, so they raised a flag of truce, and we came up to them. Many of us could talk the *Chenook* or jargon (a simple language constructed by the Hudson Bay men, pronounceable by Indians, and used as a medium of conversation between the different tribes, as well as between whites and Indians, in the Northwest).

We soon learned that one of them was no less a person than Pu-pu-mox-mox (Little Yellow Serpent, or, as history has it, Yellow Bird), the leading war chief of all the hostile tribes east of the Cascades. The others were members of his own tribe, with the exception of one Nez Perces (friendly to the whites).

Mox-mox said his people didn't want to fight the "Bostons" (Chenook for white men), but if we would go up the stream a-ways, to his camp, the Indians would make a treaty of peace.

We *conducted* (?) him and his fellows back till we met the command and Colonel Kelley, who put them under guard, and told Mox-mox he would go on up to his camp and *treat or fight,* as occasion required.

It was about night-fall as we scouts neared the mouth of the Touchet canyon, which was about half a mile long, and so narrow at. each end that not more than three men could enter it abreast, though the bottom widened out till there was a hundred to two hundred yards of prairie between the brush and perpendicular walls.

Nathan Olney (who had married an Indian woman, of whose virtues many things could be said) was the Indian Agent at The Dalles, and accompanied our command. He knew the country and the Indians well. Hearing of what had happened and been suggested, he came galloping up, and said: "Boys, don't you go into that canyon to-night! That old scoundrel, Mox-mox, has laid a trap for you, and if you go in there, there won't be a man left in the morning, and I propose to start for The Dalles while I have a chance. We told him he had better report his belief to Colonel Kelley, and he probably did, for we soon received orders to go back down the stream a short distance to a nice little bottom, which afforded a good position for a fight, and camp there. While marching down there, Moxmox and some of his Indians attempted to escape by running; but our boys could outfoot them, and caught and brought them back to camp, where they were closely guarded till morning, when we scouts were again sent forward to see if the command could pass through the canyon. On gaining the top of a bluff, we could see that there were no Indians in the canyon; so we proceeded to closely examine. It was evident that Olney was correct in his surmises, for everything indicated that a large body of Indians had been there in waiting for us during the night.

The command moved up, and after passing through the canyon we came to the recent camp of the Indians. There were hundreds of lodge poles standing from which the rush matting, skins and other articles then used by the Indians to enclose their wick-i-ups had just been hastily stripped, their fires were still burning and there were hundreds of the warriors to be seen scattered around on the adjacent hills. Here we stopped for some time, as the Indians made us know that they wanted to speak with us and their chief Mox-mox. They came up a few at a time under flags of truce, talking with Olney, Kelley, and their chief, and finally told us that if we would go back to the mouth of Touchet, and thence up the Walla Walla to Whitman station, they would come in and make a treaty, for *they didn't want to fight us.*

So we returned to the supply-train, many of the boys regretting that they had to forego the pleasures (?) of an Indian fight. But those of us who had participated in other Indian "troubles" were not sorry, but believed we would yet have all the fun (?) we could relish, *and we did.*

The next morning as we moved up the river toward Whitman station, our company (Company "I"), in ascending a bank of the stream, were greeted (?) by two or three hundred Indians mounted on fleet ponies. They formed a circle, were riding at their utmost speed yelling and shooting at us as they approached, careening over on the sides of their horses for shelter from our squirrel guns, yagers, "old hammered barrels," revised flint locks and shotguns. This "opened the ball," the Indians maintaining their *circulation* with the usual accompaniments to these *friendly receptions,* and we had a running fight from the mouth of Touchet to what is now called Frenchtown, some twelve miles below what is now Walla Walla City, and about five miles below the mouth of Mill creek.

Whitman station (the Indian naine is *Wa-eel-at-pu*) — the scene of the Whitman Massacre, which occurred in 1847, I believe — is just above the mouth of Mill creek.

But before proceeding to describe the battle at Frenchtown, I must digress some.

Dr. Marcus Whitman came to the Walla Walla valley years before as a missionary. He was accompanied by his family, Rev. Eels and family and Rev. Spaulding. Dr. Whitman located here, Rev. Spaulding on the Lapwai among the Nez Perces, and Rev. Eels among the Spokanes. I think I am not clear as to the location of Father Eels, but I know that to *his* energy and devotion belongs the honor and credit of founding and erecting the Whitman College, at Walla Walla, in memory of the man who with many others was foully murdered.

To Dr. Whitman, it is believed, belongs the praise and credit for saving the State of Oregon and the Territory of Washington to the United States by his timely appearance at the capital, and showing the worth of this part of the Pacific Coast to the Government. Sure it is that he was a great and good man, and that he lies in an untimely grave. A monument to his memory (with a cut of which I hope to embellish this book) will soon stand out in bold relief as a reminder of the trials, hardships and vicissitudes that old timers and pioneers had to pass through and suffer before less venturesome but more wealthy men could be induced to come forward and assist in making two of the finest States in the Union.

Of the massacre at Whitman station, which has been thoroughly written up 037many able writers, who had statistics to assist them in compiling their works, I shall make short mention, as I am writing mostly of myself, and of men and incidents that came within my own knowledge. But I shall venture, from time to time, to give my opinion on matters that I am forced to speak of, in trying to portray to the reader the incidents that occurred prior to my arrival in this country, and of circumstances as I remember of having heard them related by eye-witnesses a few years after their occurrence.

From the many conversations I have had with different survivors of the Whitman family (those who were living at the station at the time of the massacre)— prominent among whom were the Kimball family of four: Mrs. Munson, *nee* Miss Sophia Kimball, Mrs. Wert, *nee* Miss Kimball, and Nathan and Byron Kimball, all of whom were my neighbors for some years at Shoalwater bay, and each of whom are, I believe, now living at Astoria, Oregon — and from my own knowledge of the Indians and their superstitions, especially in regard to *doctors* and *being doctored,* I am led to give some opinions, and my reasons for having formed them.

It appears that some emigrants, who wintered with Doctor Whitman, had the measles; that the Indians contracted the disease; that Doctor Whitman attended many of them; that they would take his prescriptions and then revert to their own mode of treatment, which consisted of coming out of their sweat-houses reeking with sweat, and plunging into cold water, *and* — well! "another good Injin," and, as is usually the case, *mischief-makers saw their opportunity*, and at once commenced to inflame the minds of the ignorant savages. Some of these mischief-makers had been fostered by Doctor Whitman. Although they were half-breeds, they persisted in their misrepresentations and inflaming the superstitions of the Indians until the latter were worked to a pitch of excitement which culminated in the fiendish, brutal and hellish atrocities that took place at the Whitman mission.

As Judas had done with his Master, so did Whitman's half-breed friends with him, with the exception that the one acted from pecuniary motives, while the others were prompted by prejudice and superstition to commit their fiendish crime.

I do not believe that the representatives of any Christian Church would lend aid to or countenance so damnable an outrage, nor do I believe there is a particle of evidence that would lead a reasonably intelligent and unbiased mind to think they did.

I will say that it is well known among old pioneers, who have had any considerable acquaintance with the Indian modes and habits of doctoring among themselves, that when a "medicine man" loses a considerable number of patients he is held responsible, and not unfrequently his life atones for the *offense* of having failed to cure.

And the fact of Whitman having prescribed for what to them was a new and strange disease, and the fatal results following because of their own ignorance, led to the dreadful scenes at Whitman station on that fatal day.

But I must return to the fight.

Chapter Nine

When we were first attacked, at the mouth, of the Touchet, I was riding a pony that couldn't have outrun a cow; and, not wishing to be the *hindmost man* in case of a *possible retreat,* I stopped to change the pony for my fast mare, which I rode only when I thought a hard or fast ride might be necessary. Lint. Starr and Dave White stopped with me, though they were "eager for the fray," as a charge had been ordered. It took me but a minute or two to change my "rig" to the mare; then forward we dashed, and overtook the foremost of the command, which position we maintained.

Just before we came to the mouth of Dry Creek, we noticed one of our boys (Addington by name) dashing ahead, and almost among the Indians. We were satisfied that Addington had lost control of the high-spirited horse he was riding, and that if some one didn't get to him quick, he would lose his hair; so we gave rein. My mare was the fleetest, and I thought I never knew her to do better work than she did then, as she bounded over the sage-brush and badger-holes to the rescue of Addington. Just as I reached him an Indian either knocked or punched him off his horse. The Indians gained a horse, but lost a brave. Addington was not lost, for the rest of the command came galloping up as fast as they could.

First charge at the Battle of Walla Walla, 1855

At the mouth of Dry Creek the Indians made a stand on a high knoll, and were setting the grass on fire, when some of the boys dashed through the bushes and into their midst, while others had gone around the knoll, thus forcing them to a still further retreat, which they continued on to French-town, as before stated. Here they had arranged for the final struggle. Ten or twelve hundred Indians were posted in the timber along the river and across the valley to the foothills. Coming up, we saw at once that the retreat had ended, and the fight must begin in earnest. A point of brush that extended out into the flat some distance, and a fence that a Frenchman had built around a cabin and piece of bottom land, afforded the only shelter for our men; and behind these they took position as fast as they came up, dismount-ed and secured their horses. At the mouth of Dry Creek I came up to Elliott, who was carrying our company flag. He said:

"Take this flag and carry it to the front, my horse is played out." No sooner said than done. I caught the flag and in company with Starr and White came up to the point of brush where sixty or seventy of the boys had already ar-rived and taken their stands, and were sustaining a heavy fire.

I found a short chunk or piece that had been cut off an alder log, this I picked up and carried out a few steps from the point where I threw it down, and having driven the spear of the flagstaff into the ground by it so the rest of the company could see where our men were as they came up, I lay down be-hind the chunk and kept my head close to the ground, for the bullets were whizzing uncomfortably near me.

I had lain there but a few moments when our captain (Munson) dashed up on a fine black horse that he had succeeded in "drawing" from the govern-ment, and dismounting, he let go of the horse, jerked up the flag, and without looking to see whether there was one or fifty of his men around him, or whether there was a hundred or ten thousand Indians in front, rushed wildly forward waving the flag over his head and shouting *"Company I, charge!"* Forward he went on foot, his horse having already gone to the Indians.

Not more than seven or eight of his company had yet come up, but those present were not to be outdone by their captain, so they charged with him. I having, as is related in a previous chapter, been caught out in open ground by Indians, didn't relish the movement, and for a moment I *played that I hadn't got there yet.* But as Starr, White and some of the other boys charged with the captain, I saw that I must "face the music," so *I charged rather slowly, I admit.* When we got thirty or forty yards from the bushes the Indians raised from behind the sage-brush and other objects that up to this time had concealed them, and opened fire full upon us. About this time Sergeant-Major Miller came up and ordered a retreat. This left our little band in a tight place, but, as luck would have it, at that moment Captain Munson got shot in the arm, which caused him to drop the flag and retreat (he had probably gained glory enough for one day). When we turned to run I was, of course, in the lead, but turning around to see who had the flag, I realized that it was being left, and before I had taken the second thought I had run back, picked up the flag, and then I guess I did some of the finest running that a scared man ever did in Walla Walla valley. Owing to bad marksmanship or something else I reached the fence, when a rifle-ball grazed my temple, barely drawing blood, and scaring me so bad that I fell down, got up, fell down again, and finally found myself in the hands of Starr and White, who were trying to get my hands from my head and asking if I was badly hurt. I told them *I was killed too dead to skin,* and from the sight of a few drops of blood and the feeling of my temple I thought I was.

The boys got my hands down, and seeing I was only scratched, and not hurt a bit, *they made me know I was alive.*

Our men seeing the danger in leaving the point of brush, came back and met the Indians hand-to-hand, with knives, pistols and guns, and taught them to keep at a more respectful distance.

As soon as I saw that our men had driven the Indians out of the brush, I "came to," and helped care for our wounded and dead. There were five or six killed (*besides me*), and twelve or fifteen wounded. Among the killed was my young friend, Lieutenant Burrows, who fell by my side. I believe he was from Linn county.

A more determined struggle than this, at the point of timber, was scarcely ever made in the Northwest. The Indians seemed determined to hold the point of brush after they had gained it, and convert the short retreat into a stampede, but they had to deal with men of equal determination, who saw the value of taking and holding the point of advantage. Many were the incidents of bravery exhibited by volunteers and Indians on this the first day of the battle of Walla Walla, or Frenchtown.

About this time the rest of the command came up with the supply-train and the Indian prisoners, and encamped at the cabin before mentioned — the cabin we used for a hospital.

We were all convinced that Chief Mox-Mox had all the time been planning our destruction, and demonstrations plainly showed that he had ordered this fight and wanted to escape from us. So, while the guards were forming camp, they concluded to tie the prisoners. The Nez Perces proved to be friendly, and requested to be tied; but one of the others, "Wolf-skin" by name, jerked out a knife he had concealed, and stabbed Sergeant-Major Miller in the arm, when the others attempted to escape. This settled it, and all but the Nez Perces were killed.

There have been several versions of this so-called "butchery of prisoners," but I am satisfied that the above is correct; that the boys were justified under the circumstances; and that, if the same principle had actuated our regular soldiers that did our command at that time, and Wright's command at Spokane, later, there never would have occurred the Nez Perce war of '77, or the Bannack war of '78.

Ambuscade, treachery, torture and sneak are the components of the Indian, and fear is the only civilizing element that will bear heavily on him.

It is related that when Governor I. I. Stevens and some other representative men from this country were trying to obtain some remuneration from the government for the services of the volunteers during the Indian war of 1855-56, a representative from some one of the Eastern States opposed the bill, and during the course of his remarks said that the volunteers under Colonels Cornelius and Kelley had "murdered a friendly chief, who had come and delivered himself up." This "fine-haired man of the East" had probably never seen an Indian, and knew nothing of the hellish work they did when on the war-path. He said, "It would not have appeared so bad if the volunteers had served the 'Yellow Serpent' (or "Yellow Bird"), the head chief of the hostiles, as they did Pu-Pu-Mox-Mox" — not knowing that "Yellow Serpent" and Pu-Pu-Mox-Mox were one and the same person, and that person a combined snake and viper.

As has been the case in nearly all the frontier Indian wars, the volunteers, who bared their breasts to the bullets and other missiles of hostile Indians, were traduced, and their remuneration retarded, by such ignoramuses and *Cooper* Indian lovers.

The man who wrote:

"Lo! the poor Indian,
  Whose untutored mind
  Sees God in clouds
  And hears him in the wind;"

Should have rendered it:

"Low! the poor Indian,
  With his untutored mind,
  Clothes him up before,
  And leaves him bare behind."

While I do not fall out with other writers, I will say that almost a lifetime spent among the Northwestern Indians, and noting the progress of their civilization under the Governmental system of reservations, red blankets and dishonest agents, has led me to the conclusion that churches and preachers have caused more destruction of property, misery, torture and loss of life than all other acts combined instead of agencies and agents, forts, soldiers and school-houses, interspersed with gunpowder, Miles and Crooks (and of the latter plenty). For it is a well-known fact among pioneers, that firmness with a display of power has been *the only civilizer* that has proved effective among our western tribes.

I don't believe there is a single instance of a tribe of these Indians having been civilized to any extent until they were first thoroughly subdued, either by soldiers or volunteers.

But to "resume the fight." Col. Kelley soon came on to the grounds, and as it was plain that we had a large contract on hand, he posted our men, and had rifle pits dug across the flat and to the foot of the hill. During the rest of the first day we fought from our rifle pits and behind trees and bushes. About half a mile above our hospital cabin and camp was another cabin which the Indians occupied. Along toward evening the captain of one of the companies brought up the cannon we had taken from Port Wallula, and trained it on this cabin, but after two or three shots were fired the gun burst, killing or wounding two or three. I believe the captain was one of the number.

Late that evening, while I was assisting in bringing a wounded man in from our extreme right in the timber, I overheard Starr telling White that he would be "continentally gougered" (his only cuss-word) if he didn't find George, if it took him all night. Upon my calling to them, Starr came forward, and I asked, "What's the rumpus, that you're so anxious to find me!" He said that one of Company H's men had told him he had seen the scout Hunter fall, and he thought he was killed. He had probably seen me at the fence with the nag, when *scared to death*. I will here state that the next morning I *tenderly* put that flag in its cover, and *hid* it in a pile of rails where it remained till after the battle. It having been perforated with bullets, we sent it home for repairs, being convinced that flags and Indian fighting didn't run in the same channel.

An anecdote was told of Col. Kelley on this first day of the fight. He being very near-sighted, came on to the field, and looking over the sage brush, asked agent Olney if those were Indians over there! Before Olney could reply, a bullet passed close to the Colonel's ear. This seemed to be a satisfactory answer, and he and Olney withdrew, thinking, no doubt, that the rear was the most healthy place.

Colonel Kelley was regarded by all of us as a brave and efficient officer, and a good, kind-hearted man. Major Chinn was not so well liked.

The whites and Indians camped about half a mile apart during the battle. The night of the first day the Indians fired into our camp, causing us to extinguish our fires. Some of us returned their salute the next night by throwing some lead into their camps.

The morning of the second day, after we had breakfasted, we found that the Indians had already got into some of our rifle pits, and seemed disposed to remain there, but they changed their minds and took a back seat when our boys came up on double-quick. Then guns and revolvers were soon emptied, and so were the rifle pits. Then the scenes and routine of the day before were reenacted with slight diversification. We could drive them but a short distance, when they would flank us, and we would have to fall back to our rifle pits and point of brush to protect our camp. We kept twenty or thirty mounted skirmishers on our extreme left to prevent their flanking us, our right being protected by the river and timber. They also kept skirmishers on their right, as their left was on the river.

In the afternoon of the second day I was in the timber with several others of our company. The command was scattered out, ten or twelve in a place clear across the flat, and when the Indians would advance on any one point the others would rally to their help. Whilst in the timber we were under a heavy fire, but could only see the smoke from their guns, and they were shooting close. There being a large alder tree near me, I climbed some twenty feet up it to its fork, which enabled me to overlook the ground occupied by the hostiles. I soon discovered that the Indians had grass on their heads and backs.

I told the men that the Indians had grass caps on their heads, and when they saw the grass raise they should aim just under it.

It was but a short time until the grass caps commenced flying; then the Indians made a rush for the point I was at, and our men, in accordance with orders, started to fall back to the next squad, when some one called out, "Stop boys! Hunter is in the tree yet." But I was not there long, I can assure you, for I tumbled down regardless of limbs or clothing. Suffice it to say they didn't get me, and I had enough of the tree game.

On the third day, I was out near the foot-hills, in company with some Wasco boys. We would leave our pits and crawl to the top of a ridge and lie in wait. The Indians were doing the same thing on another ridge a hundred yards or so in front of us. We would exchange shots and then fall back out of sight to reload. One of the Wasco boys wore a heavy elk-skin coat, and on one occasion as he was crawling to the top of the ridge, keeping his head lower than his back, a ball struck him on the back and glanced along the coat, making a crease that looked as though a hot iron had been drawn along on it — a close call, but the Elk skin saved a good man. On the fourth and last day, I was on horse back with some twenty of our company, under command of Lieut. Hand, the most of the time. The Indians in front of us would ride up to within one or two hundred yards, and fire, then circle away. It appears that two of the boys that we had left at Henrietta had gone out to look after the horses, when the Indians came upon them, and killed and scalped them. And one of these scalps was being shaken at us by the Indians in front of us. Seeing this, I told the boys that if I could get near enough to an Indian I would take a scalp to get even.

During the day an Indian, a medicine man, would ride close to us, turning, twisting and shaking a feathered stick or baton, urging the other Indians on to fight. But he came around once too often, for, I with some others, had dismounted, and as he made his last round the horse and rider both went to grass at the crack of our guns. With drawn knife I rushed for him, as did all the others, both afoot and on horse, but as I stooped to grasp his hair he gave me his dying look. That look settled it with me! I gave the knife to "Nick" Belcher, who made short work of "lifting his hair." This was the first and last Indian that I ever attempted to scalp.

Along in the afternoon of that fourth day word was passed along the lines to hold our fire, as our ammunition was running short. But about four o'clock an escort arrived with plenty of ammunition.

That night the Indians gave it up and left the field in our possession.

A day or two after the battle at Frenchtown, Governor I. I. Stevens, with about twenty other white men, escorted by about a hundred of the friendly Nez Perces (pronounced "Na-percy"), came into our camp.

The governor, with his party, had been out among the Flathead and Blackfoot Indians, making treaties, I believe.

He said he thought our fight had saved his party. This assertion he repeated many times in the halls of Congress, while trying to secure remuneration for us.

Chapter Ten

After the battle, I, in company with four or five others — one of whom was Nathan Olney — started to The Dalles with dispatches. The snow was about six inches deep, and it was still falling. Our outfit of provisions for this two-hundred-mile journey in the snow consisted of about ten pounds of parched corn. The command had been short of provisions for some time, depending mostly upon the cattle we found among the hills and along the creeks. We had found some Indian caches (deposits) near the battle-ground, in which were some corn and potatoes, which we relished greatly.

We went that day to McKay Creek, and camped near McKay's house. We found a shoat in the bushes near-by, and that pig was soon dead, skinned, and in our camp-kettles, with some dried peas we had found cached; so we had a fine supper and breakfast of pork and peas. We reached The Dalles all right. I remained there but a day or two, when I got a change of horses, and, in company with Starr, returned to the command on the Walla Walla.

We found that the Indians were making for Snake River, to cross at the mouth of Tukanon.

One morning, when the command was at or near the present site of Walla Walla City, Lint. Starr, Dave White, Elliott, and one or two others proposed that we should go out toward the Touchet and Tukanon, and see if we could find any Indians, or, more particularly, Indian horses for a change, as ours were pretty well jaded. Having obtained permission, away we went, nothing occurring till we had traveled twelve or fifteen miles, when we saw quite a band of Indian ponies in a gulch about a mile from us. They seemed to be feeding near a small patch of willows and small trees. "There they are," said some of the boys; "let's go for 'em!" "Hold on," said I. "I don't like the idea of those horses being so near the brush; they seem to have been driven or ridden there lately." They all laughed at my notion; and Starr asked when I had learned so much caution? "Well," said I, "I believe there are Indians with concealed horses in those bushes, and that those horses are left out there for a bait for us; but if you will listen to me we will try for them." This was agreed to. I told them if there proved to be Indians in there they should jump their horses into a deep ravine, near which the Indian horses were grazing, and follow that till out of gunshot of the bushes before starting for the hills again.

So, after the horses we went. When we got within a few hundred yards of them we started at full speed, yelling at the same time to stampede the herd. Just then guns commenced cracking in the brush, and out came about twenty mounted Indians. It was just as I had surmised.

They had set a trap for us and were springing it, but they were a little premature, for they fired before we were close enough for them to make sure work on us.

The gulch was but a few rods from us, and into that we went, out of sight of the red devils, and then commenced a race. We ran down the gully a few hundred yards, and across a flat or bottom for a mile or so. When we struck this flat we were four or five hundred yards ahead of the Indians, and our horses could outrun their ponies, but as we neared the foot-hills I looked back — being one of the head men in the race — and to my horror saw that Lint.'s horse had "thrown up," or was weakening, and Lint, was spurring for all that was out. I saw at a glance that if something wasn't done mighty quick Lint, was a "gone sucker." So I told the rest of the boys to ride over the top of the ridge, out of sight, and jump off, take the ends of their riatas in their hands and crawl back nearly to the top and wait till Lint, and I passed, then to bang away at the redskins and check them, so as to give Starr a chance to get ahead. All the rest of us were well mounted, and could easily outrun the Indians. I then held my mare back to give her the appearance of having given out, and let Starr overtake me. I had a heavy, bone-handled, Indian riding-whip (these are made by boring into the end of a handle, and fastening in two or more rawhide-thongs; they are a formidable weapon against horse or man). As Lint, came alongside of me he asked, "Has your mare thrown up the sponge, too?" "No," I replied, and leaning over, I brought the whip down over the loins and into the flanks of his horse. A few doses of this medicine infused new life into the animal for awhile, but I knew it couldn't last long.

As we rode up the sloping hill I hurriedly told him the plan I laid to give his tired horse the start. He insisted on stopping with the boys, but I soon made him know that would endanger the whole of us. So he "gave in," and as we passed over the ridge, out of sight of the Indians, I jumped off my mare, and was with the other boys in a moment, while Lint, went on. I had barely time to get laid down with the boys at the crest of the ridge, when the Indians came galloping up hill full upon us. Five or six rifles rang out, followed by a fusillade from navy revolvers. As this was not down in the Indian guide-books, they went down the hill faster than they had come up, some being dragged by the heels (they were tied on their horses), others reeling in their saddles and giving every evidence that the pills we had administered were operating. Three or four of their ponies fell before going far, and their riders scampered off on foot.

We didn't stop long to enjoy their movements, although they were pleasing to us, but we jumped on to our horses, and away we went after Starr, soon overtook him, and told him the result of our tactics. After awhile we saw some of the Indians come over the ridge half a mile from where we had crossed it, but they didn't attempt to follow us, and we had had all the horse-hunt we wanted for that day.

Soon after this, Starr, White and myself went to The Dalles with more dispatches. On this trip my horse fell over a bluff with me, bruising my hip so badly that when I arrived at The Dalles Major Armstrong granted me a furlough and allowed Starr and White to accompany me home, as we were told that there were now regular troops in the field sufficient to cope with the Indians, and that the volunteers would be discharged and sent back to the Willamette valley as fast as they came into The Dalles; and they were.

I returned home to Corvallis, accompanied by Starr and White, for I knew I wouldn't be able to ride for a month.

In the spring of '66 the government troops under command of Colonel Steptoe and Major Luginbeale took the field, followed the Indians across Snake river, and met with a disastrous defeat near the two buttes afterward known as Steptoe and Kamiacken (the latter for the chief who licked Steptoe). They retreated and crossed Snake river at the mouth of Turkanon, where they built a stone corral or fort that they named Fort Taylor, the site of what was afterwards Grange City, mention of which will be made hereafter.

Soon after this defeat Colonel Wright took command and moved into Spokane prairie in pursuit of the hostiles. Here Colonel Wright distinguished himself as a practical Indian fighter, and established the famous boneyard by gathering up all the Indian ponies he could and shooting many hundreds of them, thus breaking the hearts of the redskins and ending the war, as "poor Lo" don't fancy traveling on foot.

The close of this war resulted in locating the most of the tribes and bands of Indians on reservations. And many stock-men soon came into the Walla Walla valley or basin, as the country embracing the John Day, Umatilla, Walla Walla, Touchet, Snake river, Palouse, Hangman, Crab creek, Spokane and Colville sections — in short, that portion of the country lying east of the Cascade mountains, south and east of the Columbia river and west of the Blue, Coeur D'Alene and Pend O'Rille mountains — was called, while that portion of Washington lying east of the Cascades and north and west of the Columbia was known as the Klickitat and Yakima country. All of which was thought to be the finest grazing land in the United States, but from its high, rolling nature, dry summers and alkaline soil it was supposed to be unavailable for agricultural purposes, except along the narrow valleys or bottoms of the small streams.

That portion known as the Walla Walla country is about 300 miles long by 75 in width, while the Yakima and Klickitat country is perhaps 200 miles in length and averages 70 miles in width.

These two great sections of country were used by the few white settlers for pastoral purposes only, up to 1860, when mines were being discovered in the surrounding mountains, and thousands of gold seekers and ranchers flocked in from every quarter, and the Walla Walla country became the base of supplies, as the Oregon Steam Navigation Company put boats on to the Upper Columbia and Snake rivers, and constructed portages around the impassable falls and rapids, and transported to the towns and landings along the river such necessary supplies as were not produced in this valley. From these points along the river the supplies were loaded on to wagons and pack animals and forwarded to their destination.

Finally the new-comers began experimenting with the different grains, vegetables, fruits, etc., and met with flattering success on all soils tested. They soon demonstrated that what had been thought a desert was a fertile field unequaled in the United States, and probably not in the world.

But the lack of cheap transportation retarded its development. The early settlers had to pay from $60 to $150 per ton up-river freights (less than 300 miles), and the first surplus for export cost twelve to sixteen dollars per ton. Yet the pioneer farmers lived and thrived slowly, which would have proven very difficult in any other country under like circumstances.

Our uniformly mild climate enabled the early stock-raisers to conduct their business at a comparatively light expense, as not one winter in ten did stock require any feeding.

True, an occasional winter was denominated a "cow-killer," and very many of the cattle died, yet on the average the losses of stock would not have offset the annual expense of providing feed.

The foregoing is about as brief a history as I can write of the early settlement of the great Walla Walla basin, upon which the eyes of the United States and Europe are fixed with wonder and admiration.

Chapter Eleven

Soon after my return home to Corvallis I was again able to ride. I mounted my horse and went to Yreka and Humbug; sold my mining ground to my partner (Study); then returned to the Willamette valley for medical treatment and a mother's care.

Before we bid adieu to the California mines I must give some verses that were composed by a miner, and proved very popular in those days, on account of their appropriateness to the men mentioned and their mode of living. I, especially, enjoyed it, because I was acquainted with some of those whose names are mentioned:

"THE DAYS OF 'FORTY-NINE

"You are gazing now at Old Tom Moore — a relic of bygone days;
A bummer now they call me sure, but I'm not fond of praise:
My heart is light, I make it so, yet oft I do repine
For the days of old, the days of gold, the days of 'Forty-nine.

"I then had friends that loved me well — a jovial and hearty crew;
There were some hard cases, I must confess, yet they were brave and true;
They stood the pinch; they'd never flinch; they'd never fret nor whine;
Like good old bricks, they stood the kicks in the days of 'Forty-nine.

"There was New York Jake, the 'Butcher Boy,' so fond of getting tight;
And whenever Jake got on a spree, he was spoiling for a fight.
One night Jake ran against a knife in the hands of old Bob Cline,
And over Jake we held a wake in the days of 'Forty-nine.

"There was Monte Pete — I remember well the luck he always had;
He'd deal for you, both night and day, and as long as you had a red.
One day a bullet laid Pete out; 'twas his last lay-out, in fine;
For it caught Pete, sure, dead in the door, in the days of 'Forty-nine.

"There was Buffalo Bill, who could outroar a Buffalo bull, you bet;
He'd roar all day, and he'd roar all night, and I guess he's roaring yet.
One night Bill fell in a prospect hole; 'twas a roaring bad design,
For in that hole Bill roared up his soul, in the days of 'Forty-nine.

"There was Poker Bob; I knew him well — so fond of a little game,
And if he lost, or if he won, to Bob 'twas all the same;
He'd rush the buck and ante a slug, and go a hatfull blind,
But in a game with death Bob lost his breath, in the days of 'Forty-nine.

"There was old lame Jess, a hard old case; he never would repent.
He never was known to miss a meal, nor never to pay a cent.
But poor old Jess, like all the rest, to death he did resign,
And in his bloom went up the flume in the days of 'Forty-nine.

"Of all the friends that I had then, there is none now left to toast,
They have left me here to wander alone like some poor wandering ghost.
And as I wander from place to place, they call me a wandering sign,
Saying, 'There's old Moore, a bummer, sure, of the days of 'Forty-nine.'"

They were all good boys, but, like Jo Bowers' money, "all went."

After doctoring for some months I got tired of being a walking apothecary shop, and in company with a friend started for the Sandwich Islands, but on arrival at Portland we fell in with an old friend who had served with me in the last Indian war, a marble cutter named A. B. Robberts. He gave us such a glowing account of Shoalwater or Oyster bay that we determined to visit that place for awhile. The bay is about thirty-seven miles north of the mouth of Columbia river, and is a beautiful sheet of water as it nestles back inland, and is almost surrounded by high mountains covered with heavy timber, excepting the south side, which forms a peninsula of flat and low lands covered with timber, interspersed with small fresh water lakes and cranberry marshes. This peninsula, or that portion of it that fronts the ocean, is called the weather beach. When the tide is out this beach is probably the finest drive in the world for a distance of twenty-five or thirty miles. The beach is fringed or bordered with rolling prairie from a few hundred yards to a mile wide back to the timber or marshes.

At Astoria we met Colonel H. K. Stevens, Major Espey, Edward Loomis and I. A. Clark, of Oysterville, on Shoal water bay. In company with these gentlemen we went to Oysterville, where I remained some years. As I soon regained my health, I was joined by my brother and we engaged in the oyster business, which was then proving lucrative.

While here I joined the Masonic fraternity at Astoria (Temple Lodge No. 7, of Oregon), the nearest lodge to the bay at that time.

Game was plenty near the bay, and being passionately fond of hunting, I frequently went in quest of deer, elk and bear, sometimes alone sometimes with some white friends, sometimes with Indians of whom I had made friends.

One night while a party of us were working on the oyster beds one Wilson remarked that there were plenty of bear coming out of the mountains and along the Palix river, near the mouth of which we were oystering, and that he was going out next morning to kill one. I proposed that I would go on one side of the stream and he on the other, early next morning, and the one who killed a bear should give the other a hind quarter. This was agreed to, and on meeting at the oyster ground the next night by agreement each had a fat quarter of bear meat for the other. Here was a stand-off! We gave our surplus "bar" meat to friends,, had a hearty laugh about the coincidence, and resumed our occupation.

At another time I was engaged with my brother and others in planting, taking small oysters from the natural beds, culling and bedding them on beds prepared for their cultivation further up the bay. We owned a fine sloop of fifteen tons, which we used for this purpose. We had sailed up the bay some fifteen miles, and came to anchor at or near high tide to await low water, so we could work. I told my brother that if he and some of the men would put me ashore I would take a hunt, as we had a gun on board. Knowing the gun was loaded, I didn't stop to examine it, but "struck out" on my hunt as soon as they landed me. Before I had gone many yards I saw a big black bear quietly feeding on a crab that had been washed ashore by the tide. Taking a hasty survey, I saw a large tree which had been blown down leaving its torn up roots spreading out wide, and as it didn't seem to be far from the bear, I crawled out from the bay toward the timber till this root was well in line between me and Bruin. Then, snake-like, I crawled forward, never raising my head till I reached the root, when to my surprise I found myself within forty feet of his bearship. Carefully thrusting my gun through the tangled roots, I took deliberate aim at his heart and pulled the trigger; the result was a spat and a fizz. The gun had become wet with bilge-water. To pick powder into the tube, re-cap, and aim at his head, was the work of a moment; this time it was "snap, fizz-z-z."

My first snap had aroused the bear, and he had reared on his haunches and was looking for the cause of the noise. At the second snap I jumped up and was about to smash the gun over the log, when the bear, not having seen me, started toward me. I threw the gun and started for the timber, some hundred yards or so distant. It had been thought that the lumbering business would soon pay there, and I had a mind to examine some of the trees. Being in something of a hurry, I didn't look back till I got to them, and then only to see Bruin entering the timber several hundred yards below me. It appears that when he saw me he made off in another direction as fast as I was going in mine.

And this would have been all right (as I was not scared) if the boys on the sloop had not discovered the bear about the same time that I did, and witnessed the whole performance. Disgusted, I returned to the sloop and received a most unmerciful chaffing from my brother and the others.

At another time, some white men and myself concluded to go on a hunting and exploring tour up the river Nacell, which has its source far up in the mountains. We engaged some Indians to go with us as guides, and, taking them in their canoes in tow, we sailed up the stream as far as we could go with the sloop, then took the canoes and proceeded some miles further, finally landed, and proceeded on foot through the timber and tangled salal bushes, following elk-trails the most of the time. After traveling some hours we came to a cranberry-marsh, and discovered a band of elk quietly feeding. Getting near enough, we fired on them, and succeeded in killing four before they got out of our range. We dressed them, and as night was coming on, we camped where we were, all in the best of humor.

One of the elks killed was a small yearling; from this we cut portions and cooked it on sticks before the fire for our suppers. Soon the whites and Indians were eating and joking, as we all understood the Indian dialect sufficiently for the purpose.

Soon the whites had appeased their hunger. Not so the Indians, for they cooked, ate and jabbered — jabbered, ate and cooked, all night. Toward morning we found them roasting the bones, then breaking them and sucking the marrow. One of them, an old chief, "Toman-amus," said to me, "Injin heap eat meat! heap eat glease! no sick! Cum-tux?" (understand?). In fact, these Indians had eaten nearly all of that year-old elk during the night.

Morning coming, the Indians loaded themselves with the meat, and we started for the canoes, with a fellow named Stout leading, myself next, and the others following. We were following an elk-trail winding around through the brush when, at a sharp curve in the trail, I saw a large gray mountain-wolf just in the act of springing upon Stout. To see was to act, and at the crack of my rifle Stout staggered into the brush, exclaiming, "My God, you came near shooting me!" He thought my gun had been accidentally discharged, as I had shot right past his head. I pointed to the wolf, lying not ten feet from him, with a bullet through its brain. It was the largest wolf I ever saw, equal in size to the largest Newfoundland dog, and when we examined his immense claws and terrible teeth, we were assured that he would have made fearful havoc with the victim he attacked. But Stout said he didn't know which would be the worse — to be eaten by a wolf, or be scared to death by my shooting. This ended our hunt, and we returned to Oysterville.

About this time Pacific county, in the southwest corner of Washington territory, was reorganized. I was appointed sheriff, and at the following election was elected to the same office.

Elder Ezra Stout, the head of the Baptist Church in Oregon, came to Oysterville with his family. I met his youngest daughter, and soon afterward married her. My father-in-law soon returned to Oregon, where he owned a considerable tract of land near Oregon City.

A Frenchman, named Dupuy, killed a man at or near the mouth of the Walihut — a stream that flows into Baker's bay, near Astoria. I was armed with a warrant, and sent to arrest the murderer. He was a desperate man, and had said that no man could arrest him. My friends cautioned me, for they believed he would shoot any one who attempted to capture him. I had never seen him; so, on arriving at the mouth of the stream, I prevailed on two men to go with me to his cabin and point him out to me. They were not anxious to go, for they said he would "shoot, sure!" But I told them all they had to do was to show me the man, and I would take the chances.

We went till we came to his house, which was inclosed by a picket-fence, which was overgrown with salal bushes. On nearing this fence, some one called to me to stop, which I did, and my man said: "That's your man." I looked around, but seeing no one, I started on again; when again a voice said: "Stop, or I'll shoot you!" and again I stopped, and discovered through an opening in the bushes a man with a gun leveled across the fence at me. After we had taken a look at each other, he asked: "Is your name Hunter?" "Yes," said I. "You are the Sheriff of this county?" "Yes." "And you have a warrant forme, but you can't arrest me." I said: "If your name is Dupuy, I have a warrant for your arrest, and if I live I will perform my duty." I said: "Dupuy, you are represented to me as being a brave man. You certainly have no ill-feeling toward me for performing my duty; and if you do shoot me, there will be many to take my place; so make a good shot," and I commenced walking up to him, watching his eye. I didn't make a move toward drawing my pistol, for I fully believed he would shoot me if I did; but I was determined that if I saw his eyes drop to his gun, I would drop to the ground, and if he didn't make a sure shot, I would get up and return the compliment. He continued holding his gun on me till I was within a few feet of him (and I think that gun had the largest bore that I ever saw); then, pitching the gun over his head, he said: "I will not kill you. A man that can walk up to a gun as you have done, ought not to be killed for performing his duty." He then asked me to see my warrant, which I gave to him. He read it. He then asked me to allow him to go to his house and change his clothes. I told him, "Yes, of course," and we went to the house. He then asked me to allow him to go into the next room to shave and dress, and I granted him the privilege, after being assured by him that he would not try to get away.

He brought out a flask of wine and poured out and drank a glass of it, then handed it to me saying, "Mr. Sheriff there's some very good wine; you needn't be afraid, it twon't hurt you." It is needless to say that I sampled it, as my nerves were somewhat shaken. But the other two men would not touch it, and whispered to me when he stepped into the other room, that it might be poisoned, and wanted me to secure a shotgun that stood in a corner, fearing he would take it and make trouble. But I told them if he had wanted to try to kill me he could have done so long before, at the fence.

In a short time he re-appeared, a perfectly dressed, fussy Frenchman, and a more gentlemanly man I never met. He had killed an Englishman for tampering with his squaw-wife. He took another glass of the wine and drank it to my health, and upon seeing the "wristlets" lying on the table, he said, "Mr. Sheriff, you won't put those on my hand." I said, "Not if you will give me your word that you won't try to get away from me." He then asked if I would protect him from a mob, and I told him that while he was in my custody he shouldn't be hurt by any one. He then seemed satisfied, and promised he wouldn't try to escape. All went well.

Arriving at Astoria, I deputized Capt. Hoyt, of the river boat that then plied between Portland, Vancouver and Astoria, to take Dupuy to Vancouver to our judicial district jail. Capt. Hoyt insisted that I should iron the prisoner before he started with him, and I did so.

On taking leave of Dupuy he shook my hand, and said, "Good bye, Mr. Sheriff? I'll see you no more!" Thinking he had "weakened," I said "Yes, you will! I'll be at Vancouver during court." "No!" said he, "you'll see me no more!" Neither did I, for as the steamer was passing Oak Point, and he was walking the upper deck with the captain, he suddenly *sprang overboard,* just forward of the wheelhouse. The boat was stopped, but to no purpose. The body washed ashore some time afterward, and I got back my "wristlets."

After my term as sheriff expired I was appointed light-keeper of Toke Point light, and assisted in relighting and straightening it up, for it had been extinguished for some time.

During the winter of 1861 our oyster beds were frozen out, and my brother and I were "broke up," as were many others, and I am informed that the Shoalwater bay oyster beds have never recovered.

Chapter Twelve

Receiving a letter from my wife's father informing us of the dangerous illness of mother Stout, and requesting us to come up and stop with them, I went with my wife and daughter, who was then about two years of age, to

Oregon city. We found mother Stout's health much improved, so I bought a farm and concluded to remain near the old folks.

The War of the Rebellion had broken out, and father Stout and myself having been "Douglass Democrats," became strong Union men when Fort Sumter was fired upon.

He was living near a strong secession neighborhood, and as he was a small man and a preacher, he was frequently subjected to insults from them. A day or two previous to my arrival he had been down on Mill creek to a little store, where a big bully by the name of Beasley had been induced to bully and annoy the old Elder. This Beasley weighed not less than two hundred pounds, was young, and not being the strongest minded man in the world was easily led, and was looked upon as a "bad man to run against."

Father Stout told me of the treatment he had received at Cutting's store, and as they were having some kind of an election down there a few days after my arrival, I concluded to go down as I would probably meet some of my wife's relatives that I had not met before.

Of course, the word had gone the rounds of the neighborhood that Elder Stout's son-in-law had come up on a visit, and that I was a "Union man."

So, father Stout tried to prevent me from going down that day, saying, "You will be insulted; you'll resent it, and get into trouble."

I replied, "All right, father; if I do, there will be others full of trouble." So, go I did.

When I got to the store I got a cigar and took a seat on the porch to smoke it, seeing no one there that I remembered of having met before.

I soon noticed a knot of men assembled in the road a short distance from where I sat, talking and glancing toward me from time to time. Among them I noticed a large man, and from his looks and father Stout's description I was satisfied this was Beasley, and that they were talking of me.

Suddenly the large man left the bunch, and walking up to me, slapped me on the shoulder, and looking me fiercely in the face, said, "Do you know what I'll do if I get to see Abe Lincoln?"

I replied that I certainly did not; that he might do many smart things, but — I had much sooner believe — foolish ones.

He said, "By G___, I'll kill him, I'll kill him!" grinding his teeth the while, and, after looking at me for a moment, he turned to step off the porch.

I saw winks and grins passing from one to the other of the mob, and this was too much. I gave one spring, and struck him a blow in the back, which landed him in the middle of the road, and as he turned I said: "Do you know what I shall do when I see Jeff Davis? I'll kill him, by G___, I'll kill him? But as neither of us will probably ever have the pleasure of seeing our men, let us represent good men for once in our lives — you are Jeff Davis to me, and I am Lincoln to you."

But at this moment others interfered, and I failed to represent my man. It was probably as well for me, for he had the brute force over me.

Many who had seen this ludicrous affair came up, and we had a jolly laugh. I found many good, warm-hearted men among them, whose kindness to me in my troubles a short time later will ever be remembered.

Shortly after this my good wife was confined, and I lost both her and my infant son. With my little girl I started for the Rogue River valley, to which my father had removed a year or so before.

Arriving at "Starr's Point," as they used to call it (now Monroe), I stopped over to rest my little girl and visit among relatives and old friends.

One day there had assembled at this place (or more properly at a store where the double distilled extract of corn was dispensed) a considerable crowd of men, the most of whom were violent secessionists; and as "good Democrats" were supposed to do, they "filled up" with the "exhilarating beverage." From some cause or other the grand old Stars and Stripes had on this day been raised on a pole or staff near by, and pretty soon these half-tipsy fellows took offense at the defiant colors, and swore they would tear it down. Two or more of them started to execute the threat. Some of the crowd remonstrated, but to no avail. I being a stranger and a Democrat, I supposed that the Republicans present would protect the flag, but seeing no movement in that direction, and that if the flag was kept floating something must be done, and done quickly, I grabbed an old musket that chanced to be standing in a corner of the store, and at my best speed I made for that flag-staff. Remember, I had already served two terms under the "old flag!" My great-grandfathers had served with Washington, at Brandywine and Valley Forge, my, grandfather with Jackson at New Orleans, and I couldn't stand by and see the old emblem disgracefully lowered by a drunken rabble.

As I ran swiftly forward I called frequently to their leader to stop, but he paid no attention to me. Knowing that nearly all men carried pistols those days, and that these men were made desperate by drink, I determined to have the first shot.

I took a quick aim, and drew the trigger, the cap burst clear, but no report followed. Then there was a race between me and their leader for the flag-staff (all the rest had stopped when the cap bursted). We met at the flag-staff, and just as he was about to cut the halliards to lower the flag my gun went off (it didn't snap that time); the barrel brought down on his head proved more effective than the bullet which refused to leave the barrel! Well, he laid down, and as I now had time to draw my revolver, I sat down and informed the mob that I would shoot the first man who attempted to haul down that flag before sundown, at which time I would lower it myself if I lived so long.

This settled it. Friends removed my man to the store, and many Union men gathered to my assistance, which had the effect of stopping further demonstrations in that direction. At the going down of the sun, we lowered the flag — cheering as we did so — and laid it away with the honor we conceived to be due to the "emblem of the free."

Soon after this I went to my father's home in Rogue River valley, where I remained a short time with my parents. Then, leaving my daughter with them, I returned to Oregon City, sold my property, kept one hundred dollars and two horses out of the proceeds — sending the balance to mother for the benefit of my child — and started for The Dalles and the newly discovered mines.

Upon reaching The Dalles I again visited John Haligan and Father Mesplie. This was the last time I ever saw Haligan, but I afterward learned that he had been ordained a priest, and died at The Dalles. Father Mesplie I met some years afterward in Walla Walla, and I think he is still living in this the year 1887.

I staid a short time at The Dalles, and then went to Canyon City, on a branch of the south fork of John Day's river. On reaching Canyon City I found the camp in excitement, and raising a company of volunteers to go out and suppress the Malheur and Crooked River Indians, that had been attacking pack-trains and had killed several mining or prospecting parties. This company numbered only fifteen, and they were hired by the miners for this special work.

On my coming into the camp an old comrade, who had served with me in the Rogue River war, recognized me and said to the gentleman presiding over the meeting, "We want this man Hunter with us, if he will go." I was asked if I would go with them, and answered, "Yes, and glad to get the chance." So, I was admitted to their small company in the capacity of scout.

The miners had chosen a captain to command the outfit in the person of one Hill, from Minnesota. This man Hill had told of his exploits in the Minnesota Indian wars, and was thought to be well qualified to command the party. The name of the old comrade above mentioned was White, "Bill" White, as we called him. Bill was as brave as a lion, and generous to a fault, and in my opinion should have been the one to have commanded our party, as he virtually did, shortly after reaching the Indians' whereabouts.

After making the necessary preparations, and packing on animals sufficient provisions and ammunition to last us some weeks, we started out on the trails leading down the stream. We traveled some forty miles to the junction of the stream with the south fork of the John Day.

This was the vicinity of most of the depredations, and several small mining parties had been waylaid and killed at or near this point, while out prospecting, and several pack-trains had been attacked near here. So, on reaching the south fork, we moved away from the trails about two miles, into the hills, and finding a small spring-branch surrounded by hills that were covered with heavy timber, and plenty of good grass on this creek or spring-branch for our horses, we struck camp, and concluded to lay there for some days, at least, and watch the trails, and if we should discover a small body of Indians, attack them; but in case there were more than we thought we could handle, we would watch them and send back to Canyon City for aid.

The next day we posted a man on a high point, where he could conceal himself and overlook the trails and a large part of the surrounding country. He would be relieved every few hours. We all believed that the Indians had one or more white men with them.

We would send out one or two parties on foot each day to scout around the country, and see if there were any Indians encamped anywhere near us. White or myself generally went with these small parties, as it was known that we were the only ones that had had any experience in Indian fighting — unless it was our captain, and nearly everybody in a few days doubted if he had ever been in an Indian campaign.

These watches and short scouts were kept up for several days without any result, when early one morning I determined to make a scout up the south fork further than we had been as yet. As White had been out all the day before, I took an Irishman with me. He was a butcher by trade, a good walker, stout and hearty, and daring to the extreme. He wanted to go with me on this scout, as he had not yet been out.

I told Dennis we would have to "run for it" if the Indians discovered us, and if he couldn't outrun them there would be one Irishman less in camp. Dennis said, "Will, George, if thim haythens are after gittin' meself, I'm after thinkin' the divel'll have the pair uv us, fur its meself that's goin' to stay wid ye's?" I was not sorry to have Dennis with me, as I knew him to be young, stout and active, and believed him to be cool and brave, and last, but not least by any means, he was the best company to be found in camp, for with his wit and droll, rollicking Irish brogue he kept all of us in a good humor.

After telling the boys not to look for us till they saw us, we stowed some jerked meat in our pouches with a little salt and some crackers, and started out. I asked White to go a short distance with us, which he did. After getting out of hearing of the camp I told White I was sure we were going to have trouble with Capt. Hill soon, as I could plainly see that the boys had become convinced that he was totally unfit to lead the party.

I told White to watch and keep down all feeling that he could, and he said he would, as he was fully aware that to change commanders would prove disastrous to the expedition, and disgraceful to us, as our friends at Canyon City expected protection, and were paying us for it out of their own hard earnings.

Feeling easy on this point, I told White I should go far up the south fork and might not get back for a day or two, but to keep the boys well together, and not fear for us, for we would come back all right. He said, "I know you will, and wish I could go with you on this trip, but it won't do for both of us to go away from camp just now." Shaking my hand, he said: "George, I know you are cautious when it is required. I believe you are going on dangerous ground, and that when you come back you will have some kind of news for us. Don't go too far."

And he turned back to camp. Dennis and I pushed on up the south fork, keeping well in the bushes, avoiding trails so as to leave no evidence of our presence.

While going along I gave Dennis some signals and signs of warning that I had used years before to good effect. On we went, I leading, Dennis close behind, keeping a close watch all around us: We traveled very slow, so as not to run into danger unawares. At noon we sat down in the brush and ate a lunch off our beef and crackers. Whilst eating, Dennis said that we were near the place where the Indians had killed four miners who had been out prospecting. They had camped under a bluff which he pointed to. The Indians had crawled up on top of the bluff and fired on them just as they were getting out of their blankets. Two were killed, and two wounded who were followed up and brutally butchered in a gulch a short distance away. One or more made their escape and worked their way to Canyon City, where a party fitted out and came and buried the dead.

The story and dinner being finished, we proceeded on our way.

About two o'clock in the afternoon, as we were crossing an elevation near the trails, we got a good look ahead on the trails, and I just caught a glimpse of a man or an animal coming about a mile ahead.

I raised my hand and Dennis sank to the ground in silence; as I did I said to Dennis, "Keep still;" something's coming on the trails; whatever it is it will soon come in sight again. A minute afterward it appeared in plain view, and we could see that it was a man of some kind. He soon passed out of sight, as he went down into another gulch. I took a hasty look around, and seeing a thick bunch of greasewood just above the trails that would conceal us from view, I told Dennis to step carefully so as to leave no tracks, and follow me. I sprang over and into these bushes, Dennis after me. Selecting a suitable place, we lay down to await results.

I told Dennis that if there were only a few of them we would give them a fight, but if too many we would watch them, and when it was dark get back to the boys and come down upon them. We soon saw that there was only one, and that was a white man. But I believed him to be a renegade, and worse than an Indian, as I supposed he was looking for prey for the Indians to capture, as I couldn't think what would bring this one lone white man away out there in that dangerous locality. So I told Dennis to keep his gun on him, and at the proper time I would jump into the trail with my revolver and either capture or kill him, but for him to be sure and not miss him if he saw him make a movement to draw a weapon. Dennis said, "Divil a miss; sure I can dhrap 'im too aisy." I saw that Dennis was cool and determined, so I cautioned him not to be too quick to shoot, for it might be an innocent party.

In a few minutes he came along, walking as fast as he could. Just before he got opposite us I jumped into the trail in front of him. Seeing that his first impulse was to run, I said to him, "Don't run, or you are a dead man!" He said, "Thank God," and started toward me. But I said: "Stop; don't come a step nearer; look at that bush and you will see a man covering you with a gun, so if I miss you (and I ain't in the habit of missing) that man will kill you. Throw up your hands!" All this I said while I still covered him with my revolver. Up went his hands. I asked him if he had a pistol; he answered, "Yes." Then I said, "Unbuckle your belt and let it drop, and be careful you don't touch your pistol, for one false move, and you'll pass in your checks." He dropped his belt. I said to Dennis, "Come and get his pistol; I'll 'copper' him." And Dennis came and got it. I was satisfied that was all the weapon he had, so I told him to go in front of us to the brush on the stream and we would have a quiet talk, pointing the way. I left Dennis on a little raise to keep a close watch and see if any others were coming.

After getting away from the trails I asked, "Who are you, anyway?" He told me his name, and said he was coming to the John Days mining camp with a family by the name of Rexford and others, with about 300 head of beef cattle from near Yreka; that there were three families together — eight men all told, besides the women and children; that they had come via Goose lake and Crooked river, and that two days before, the Indians had attacked them one morning while in camp on a tributary of the John Day, stolen all their horses, killed all their work oxen, and surrounded them near the stream where these families had fortified themselves the best they could, and that the Indians were taking their time to kill them, as they had plenty of good beef to eat; that he had made his escape the night before by crawling through the brush for some miles, and was trying to make his way to Canyon City for help. He asked how far it was to Canyon City, and when I told him he said, "My God, they will all be murdered before I can get help."

I said, "I don't know about that." For by this time I was satisfied that he was telling the truth, as there was a young man with us by the name of Rexford, who had told me he expected an uncle out from California with cattle, and he feared he would have trouble with the Indians. So I told him that I had some scouts twelve or fifteen miles below, and if he would make good time I would soon have help to the families. But I warned him that if he was lying he had better pray every jump he made, for his stay would be short and he would get a "free pass over the road."

He said, "Let's be going; I am ready." We gave him some jerked beef and crackers (which he stood in need of). He ate as he walked swiftly in the lead, Dennis and I after him. I told him to set the gait, that Dennis and I could keep up, and the sooner we reached my camp the quicker relief could be afforded the imperiled families. And as we now took the trails, we could make good time, and good time we did make.

Getting into camp about four o'clock, we found all in an uproar. As I had foreseen, Capt. Hill had come in conflict with the boys, who said they wouldn't stay a day longer, or go a foot further with him as captain, and were determined to elect either White or myself captain. They were satisfied with either of us. They said Hill was an old ass, and didn't know any more about Indians or mountains than a "hog did about a holiday."

Here was a go. I had a short talk with White, and he agreeing with me, I got the boys together and told them that they were probably correct to some extent m their opinions of our captain. But now we had assurance of the whereabouts of the Indians, and the lives of innocent women and children depended on the promptness of our action, without a doubt; and if we made any change in regard to the commander of our company and then failed to rescue the families, the blame would be laid at our doors. And further, that the parties who hired us to come out would feel under no obligations to pay us for our time if we took the responsibility of reorganizing without their sanction. Then White and I took Capt. Hill to one side, and told him that, as he certainly was not conversant with those mountains, he had better make some concessions, and still remain in command; assuring him at the same time that we would do all we could to help him out. He said he was perfectly willing to be advised by White and myself, if this would be satisfactory to the rest of the boys, and so stated to them. This settled the matter, and I will say that Capt. Hill kept his word and proved to be a good man. I told them all I knew about our prisoner (for as such he had been regarded up to this time).

I had young Rexford stand by, while I questioned our "coppered" man, as Rexford could soon see whether or not he was an impostor, and if he was not we would soon be on the trail to the relief of his uncle and the families. But if we found him to be a renegade we would make short work of him.

Warning him that we had our own way of knowing when he lied, and if we found that he was deceiving us his life wasn't worth a cent, and he had better say his prayers, for his time was short, we proceeded to question him very closely. He related the same story he had told me when I stopped him on the trails. He told the given names of Mr. and Mrs. Rexford, and the names of each of the children, and the names of others of the party, and otherwise recited until young Rexford said, "That's enough; my uncle's family is surrounded, as this man says, and they are probably murdered by this time."

Chapter Thirteen

This satisfied all of us, and we immediately set to work preparing for the rescue, and to get to the Rexford camp as soon as possible. The man had told us that there were 100 or 150 Indians surrounding the people, so we gave him a pack-animal, and told him to ride as fast as he could to Canyon City, report the situation, and have all the men they could muster sent out to help us, as we proposed to reach the families as soon as we could, and would hold the Indians in check till they came to our assistance.

After consultation we concluded to divide our little company into two parties, leaving Captain Hill and seven men with the pack-animals, provisions and ammunition, to come on, following our trail as fast as he could. White and myself, with six men, were to push on and try to get to the beleaguered people that night, if possible; for the man who had escaped had given us the location of the wagons as near as he could.

So, after dark, we started on our dangerous mission, leaving Captain Hill to pack up and follow us as fast as he could. It was not so dark, but we could see to travel at a good round pace on through the night. We rode, White in the lead, he being the best posted as to the lay of the mountains and streams, I bringing up the rear. We traveled swiftly along the foot of high hills, flitted across small bottoms, and up and over spurs of the elevated lands like so many spectres, for hour after hour. Not a sound could be heard but the clattering of our horses' hoofs as they flew over the rocks and through the brush and timber; not a word was spoken, but in Indian file we all followed our brave leader, with guns and revolvers ready.

Thus we traveled all through the night, and till about four o'clock in the morning, when I made a signal for a halt.

For an hour or so I had been thinking we had gone too far, and when White halted at the given signal, and I rode up to him, he asked, "What is it, Hunter?" I said: "Bill, don't you think we are on the wrong trail? That man couldn't possibly have traveled as far as we have rode in the time he said he was on the trail; and he told us that the wagons were on a creek, and there is no appearance of anything like a creek ahead, as far as I can judge by these high, rocky hills."

He thought awhile, then said: "You are right, Hunter; they are not in this direction, but where are they?"

I said: "I have been thinking for some time that fellow was mistaken about that camp being on a tributary of the south fork, as the main branch is small up here in the mountains; and, as the trail leads over spurs of the mountains, when he came to the stream, it being so much larger than it was above, he has made a mistake. I believe the camp is on the main south fork, and that we have passed it some miles to our right."

"You are undoubtedly right," said White; "there is no other stream in this direction, that I can think of, that he could have walked from in the time he says he was walking; so, what shall we do?"

Says I, "Stop and let the horses rest till it is light enough for us to see around, and then be governed by the lay of the land."

This motion was acquiesced in by all, and soon our horses were relieved of their saddles, and picketed out on grass; and each of us, wrapped in a blanket, sat down by a tree, or laid down, to get what rest we could.

As soon as it was light enough to see we sent two of our men back on the trail to intercept Captain Hill and his party, and prevent their following our roundabout course with the pack-animals, and tell him how to cut across the country to the south fork.

This left only six in our party, but after taking a good view of the surrounding country we struck for the south fork. None but those who have traveled over that portion of the country can have an idea of that day's journey. It was a continuous stretch of lava rocks, over ridges and canyons without a trail. The most of the day we were compelled to walk, and lead our horses over the rocks, spurs, and deep canyons.

About four o'clock in the afternoon we heard the distant report of a gun, ahead and to the right of us, which assured us that we were correct in our last conjectures, and that we were yet in time to assist some, if not all the imperiled.

So, with swelling hearts and increased energy, we pushed on toward the sound as fast as possible. As we neared the stream the hills were less rocky, and when we reached the hill from which we could overlook the stream there were but few, if any, rocks. Gaining the summit of the last hill, we stopped there and had a fine view of everything in the narrow bottom along the stream below us.

We saw the wagons in a sink on the bottom near the stream, close to a small patch of willow brush. We also saw that the men had fortified to some extent, with brush and dirt, to protect themselves and families, in which, it will appear, they had been successful.

It appears that up to this time the Indians had no idea that any of the whites had escaped to give the alarm. And well knowing that there was no place nearer than Canyon City that they could get help from — and that there was little or no travel on these trails — they felt secure, and sure of soon having the whites in their power, without jeopardizing the life of one of their own people. And as they had plenty of beef, they were taking their own time cooking, eating, and keeping a close guard over the whites, occasionally firing a few shots at them from a distance — in short, they were having a picnic.

After taking a good look at all below us, and studying the lay of the land to be ridden over, we saw that there were forty or fifty Indians scattered around on horseback just out of gunshot of the camp, riding around and occasionally shooting at the besieged, while others were cooking and eating beef in the edge of the brush six or eight hundred yards above the camp. We could see that if the Indians were at all on the fight we had a desperate feat to accomplish if we got to the surrounded wagons; for we would have to ride boldly down a sloping hill in plain sight of both whites and Indians for fully three-quarters of a mile, and then charge through the Indians to the wagons as best we could.

It was yet light, and would be for some time.   Their actions showed that the Indians were aware of our presence and would give us a warm reception.

White turned and asked me, "Shall we go down there?" I said, "Yes! What did we come for?" He said, "You are right, Hunter, but some if not all of us are going to pass in our checks!" His cheeks were as pale as they afterwards were when we laid him in his coffin, but his eyes showed a steady determined gleam, that spoke of a fierce, determined soul within, and that he had harbored no other thought but of going to the help of those poor surrounded

Preparing to rescue a besieged camp

women and children, even though it be sure death to him and those who were with him.

He continued saying, "You are the best mounted; take the lead and command; I will be close after you." "All right," said I. Then turning to the other boys, I said: "Follow White, and keep a few yards behind each other; swing your guns, and take out your revolvers, and when we get within gunshot, fire as fast as yow. can, and give back yell for yell. But above all ride as though the devil himself was after you. If any of us fall, don't stop, but let some of us get to the camp at all hazards. Every man for himself on this ride." Then I turned and shook White's hand, as I had done the others, and we started down the hill on a slow trot.

Turning in my saddle, I saw first one, then another of the boys tighten their belts, but not a twitch of a muscle, or a quailing eye could I detect among that little band — every one sat his horse as firm as a rock, each face reflected the determination that dwelt within each brave breast. There was not an indication of fear or wavering on the part of any one. All seemed inspired by the one sole motive, to reach the surrounded wagons, or lose their lives in the attempt.

Slowly and silently we moved down the sloping hill; not a word was spoken, keeping in the order in which we started; each grasping a revolver in one hand while with the other he guided and restrained his horse.

On down we went till within a short distance of the bottom. The Indians were circling in front of us, or laying in the bushes above the wagons. I raised in my stirrups, took a hasty look and cried at the top of my voice, "Now, boys!" and away we sprang, my horse at his utmost speed, the others after me. A few seconds and we were among the circling rabble, rifles and revolvers cracking, whites and Indians yelling at the top of their voices.

It was done as quick as I can tell it, and through the yelling horde we burst like a thunderbolt; a moment more and we were safe under the bank near the wagons. The men at the wagons were about to fire on us as we approached, when a woman cried "*Don't shoot!* it is white men coming."

This was well said, and in time, for they had a straight line on us, and would in all likelihood have killed or wounded some of us if they had shot.

As it was, it seemed we had all miraculously escaped unhurt. Fifteen or twenty Indians circled very close to me, near the foot of the hill, but White dashed to my side while a stream of bullets poured into the circle from his revolver (my own was not idle by any means nor were those of the rest of the party). But as I said before, we gained cover and the wagons, where we jumped from our trembling horses to be clasped by the hands, arms and knees, by men, women and children. To describe that scene would require a better pen than mine — it beggared description.

Let the reader picture in his mind these families surrounded for days by the fiendish redskins, their horses stolen, their oxen killed, far from help, not expecting any — for they were fully of the opinion, that the brave young man

95

who attempted to escape and go for help, had been killed, or got lost - all hope having left them. Then imagine their feelings as we came dashing through the ranks of the painted devils, to their sides! They would cry, shake our hands, and bless us by turns. They told us they saw several Indians taken away by the others, and there were two or three dead horses left on the bottom.

It was quite awhile before we could make them understand that they were endangering themselves as well as us; for we now fully expected that the Indians would make a determined attack upon us, and try to "clean us out." At last we succeeded in making them understand the situation, and something like order and quiet prevailed.

We soon had good lookouts posted, and the women prepared us something to eat, while the men unsaddled our horses; and secured them where they could get a little grass.

As soon as we had eaten our lunch, White and I concluded to make a scout and find out, if we could, what the Indians were doing. As it was now after dark, and all had been quiet since we reached the camp, we feared the Indians were up to some devilment. The women objected, said we shouldn't go, they were sure we would be killed if we went, and then all of them would be killed. But we soon convinced them that it was necessary for us to know what the Indians were doing, to be able to offset them in their movements.

After arranging our signals, White started down the stream, and I up, with the understanding that neither of us should go over a mile from camp, and we should both return under the shadow of the hills and meet and compare notes. If either of us "saw any Indians, we were to gather all the information we could, and return as before stated.

So, I stole slowly out of camp, and cautiously worked my way up the stream, finding some of the cattle here and there, quietly lying down or feeding. I stopped every few steps to listen. Everything told me there were no Indians near me — for if there were, the cattle wouldn't be so quiet — but still with great caution I moved on up the stream for a mile or more. Not seeing or hearing anything but the beef-cattle, I had long ere this come to the conclusion that the Indians had left, probably thinking all of the Canyon City miners were near, and not thinking that six men would have the hardihood to rush through their midst, without there were more close at hand.

Having gone as far as I agreed to, I cautiously crept across the flat to the foot of the hills, and worked my way back along them, frequently stopping to listen. After slowly moving along for some time, I heard the bark of a coyote (wolf) a short distance ahead of me, and as this was to be White's signal as agreed, I knew he was near, and coming toward me. The low twittering of a bird told him where I was. We soon met, and when I told him of my lookout, he said it was about the same as his. He had seen nothing that indicated the presence of Indians. We were both of the opinion that the Indians had withdrawn to reconnoitre and see if there were more whites coming, or more likely had retreated back to their strongholds on the Malheur and Crooked rivers.

White imitated the low whinny of a horse, which notified our friends of our coming back, and that all was well.

We were soon in camp again and surrounded by the whole party, who eagerly asked all manner of questions at the same time, which we answered as best we could.

After posting guards and making the necessary arrangements for reliefs, we laid down to sleep some, White and I to be awakened a short time before daylight.

Being called near morning, we started out together up the stream before the families were up. We moved slowly up through the brush and found the cattle quietly feeding, which satisfied us that the Indians were not near. So we moved quietly but more swiftly. Getting something more than a mile from camp we stopped and waited till it was broad daylight. Then we made a close examination and shortly found the trail of the Indians, leading up out of the bottom and over the high hills, in the direction of Crooked river. As they had with them all the horses that belonged to the emigrants, they left a broad trail which we followed two or three miles, and until we were sure that they had left for good. We then returned to camp, got our breakfasts, and sent some of the boys out on horseback to make a more thorough scout. On their return they reported that they had followed the trail some miles and were convinced that the Indians had left. We then stationed one or two to keep watch and the rest of us drove up some of the beef cattle; and, selecting some steers, lassoed them, yoked them up and hitched them to the wagons. Then having packed the provisions and other effects to the top of the hill, we led, herded, and drove the teams up. That day was fully occupied in getting the steers to work, and the wagons to the summit of the hill.

The next day we were moving slowly along when, toward noon, we saw coming toward us our other ten men with the packs. We soon met and exchanged experiences.

In trying to make a cut-off they had run on to canyons that they couldn't cross, and would have to head, and probably traveled further than we did, then being encumbered with the pack-animals they had necessarily moved slowly. They told us of a gulch a short distance ahead, to which we proceeded and camped for the night.

Securing the teams, and leaving a few as guards, the rest of us returned to the creek, collected all the beef-cattle we could find and joined the camp that night. The next day we moved on slowly, and had just passed the head of a canyon, when we saw some miles ahead and coming over a high point toward us what seemed to be a large body of mounted men, and as we didn't think our "coppered" friend had time to get to Canyon City, raise so large a force and return so far, we feared that these were Indians returning to attack us. So we turned the teams and cattle back telling the emigrants to go back to the canyon and fortify the best they could, that we, the sixteen, would go forward and if those coming proved to be Indians, hold them in check till the teamsters could arrange the camp for the protection of the women and children. But we had not proceeded far, before we were convinced that the advancing party were white men, and there were about a hundred of them. So we signaled the teams to come on, and rode forward to meet them.

Coming together we found them to be a party of miners, who on hearing of the surrounded emigrants, and that Captain Hill's company had gone to their assistance, collected such animals and arms as they could find, then "come a-running." Mounted on fat and poor horses and sore-backed mules, some with saddles, some with pack saddles, some with only a blanket to ride on, and some riding bareback. They were armed with every conceivable weapon, from a butcher knife to a rifle.

They were the hardest looking "company of soldiers" I ever saw. Yet I would have guaranteed a most gallant fight if they had met the marauding Indians.

After shaking hands with our reinforcing friends, we pushed on to the mouth of the Canyon City branch of the south fork of the John Days river, where we camped for the night, and each told of his adventures. The women's stories were listened to with great sympathy and feeling, while they rejoiced at their escape from the ravishing fiends.

While talking that night we were told of a murder that had been committed on the trails between The Dalles and the John Days mines, by one Berry Way. It appears that he, with his partner, were coming up from The Dalles with a few animals packed.

Way killed his partner one night, and brought the train in to Canyon City, and the bloody blankets that the murdered man had slept in gave him away; search being made, the body of the murdered man was found. Way was arrested, tried, and hung. This was the first man that "stretched hemp" in the mining regions of Oregon, Washington, or Idaho. This resulted in an ill feeling between roughs and officials that terminated in a shooting scrape.

The next morning the miners escorted Rexford and the families with the beef-cattle on to Canyon City, where they arrived without further peril or adventure.

Capt. Hill, with our party, returned to the place where the Indians had crossed the high hills, or mountains, and followed their trail, as we had no idea of letting them off so easy. We adopted the Indian mode of trailing and scouting, and when we came on to Crooked river cached ourselves as well as we could in the brush and timber, and again sent out our scouts and lookouts, with the hope of finding a party small enough for us to attack. A few days passed, when White came in one evening and told us he had discovered quite a camp of Indians some miles above us, and he thought he could get us well up to them in the night, so that we could "clean it up" in the morning. This was good news to us, for things had been getting monotonous there for some days; so about midnight, having made all possible preparations, we started up the river "for blood." After we had traveled some miles White and

I left our horses with the boys and went ahead on foot, telling Hill to keep well behind us with the horses and follow along slowly. Some miles further up we found the Indians' camp, but a few hundred yards ahead of us; there were fifteen or twenty lodges (rather more than we wished). But we were resolved to give them a dose of their own medicine, and believed that if we succeeded in surprising them we could "pepper their soup" well and get away.' So after taking a good look at the lay of the surrounding land, and concluding on the best mode of approaching the encampment, we went back till we met the others of our party, and made known our plan of attack. We warned all the boys not to stop after the Indians got into the brush, for we didn't want any wounded comrades on our hands while so far away from a mining camp, with no mode of conveyance.

All being arranged, and future movements well understood, we moved on up to a point of brush within a few hundred yards of the lodge, and impatiently awaited the appearance of day. We had not waited long till the gray light began to steal along the hills, then the bottom, and every minute object could be more plainly seen. Smoke from the wick-i-ups and the sight of an Indian or two warned us that the time for action had arrived. We slipped into our saddles, and, with a concerted yell, dashed our horses against the lodges, firing at everything that moved, then circling and shooting as the Indians rushed out of their lodges. This was a complete surprise party, and for some time we had it our own way. As the hosts were not prepared to entertain us, we furnished the music and refreshments; they partook of the latter and danced to the former.

Chapter Fourteen

But pretty soon they gained the bush and commenced reciprocating. This we failed to appreciate; so we hastened to the bald hills, then circled around to our pack-animals and back to the hills again. The Indians were by this time thoroughly aware of our presence in their vicinity, and we could see small parties of them on the high hills around us watching our movements and dashing here and there in all directions.

Crossing a rivulet, we watered our horses and filled our canteens with water, then rode boldly to the top of a hill that had plenty of rocks and a few stunted trees on its summit. Here we unsaddled our horses and prepared our breakfast. After breakfasting some of us lay down to sleep, while others watched the movements of the Indians.

Along in the afternoon some of them ventured a little too close to our encampment, but a few well-aimed shots persuaded them to keep at a more respectful distance, which they maintained during the rest of the day. Night coming on, we stationed our men so as to watch all points of the compass; for we well knew that the Indians would signal to each other their whereabouts soon after dark. This they do by making balls of dry grass, and pitch from the pine-trees, setting them on fire and throwing them into the air from the summits of prominent hills; these are answered from hill to hill. As I had learned these signals years before, I hoped to find out where the main body of the Indians were.

Soon after dark one of the boys, who was looking in the direction of the place we had left on Crooked river that morning, called my attention to a bright light that flashed up in that quarter. I told the others to watch closely in the other directions and see the signal answered.

In a moment we saw two or three balls of fire flash up in the direction of Canyon City. This was all we wanted to find out, and satisfied us that the main body of the Indians had got between us and Canyon City, so as to ambush us if we attempted to return to that place — which we had no idea of doing yet awhile. So we saddled up and quietly rode back to Crooked river, and followed up the stream for some miles, then camped in the bushes till morning.

At daybreak we were again on our horses, and going toward the Malheur.

This morning, as we were quietly trotting along, we came suddenly upon a band of Indians. We met as we were crossing the sharp point of hill, and were within fifty yards of them before either party was aware of the proximity of the other.

At first sight our rifles commenced cracking. Our numbers were about equal, but we got the first shot. We dashed at them, and they didn't stop to count noses, but wheeled, and with their whips urged their ponies toward some brush about a mile away.

Our horses being the fastest, we kept up with them, and as we were not "out for our health," but rather wished to earn our wages, I may be pardoned for intimating that their number was considerably reduced before they reached the brush. There we left them, and pushed on our way for several miles.

We soon discovered that the Indians were again collecting round us in large numbers, and we were fully aware that they were aroused to desperation, and that nothing but the coolest management and watchfulness would save our scalps. To be caught in a position which would necessitate our running our horses down would prove disastrous to us. So, again we selected an eminence, and after watering our horses and filling our canteens at a little creek, we fortified, put our horses in a sheltered place, and cooked and ate a bite.

During the afternoon the Indians attacked us, but they soon found out that we couldn't be routed, and that they were "wasting their sweetness on the desert air," so they contented themselves with surrounding and watching us, knowing that we couldn't remain where we were without water for any great length of time.

This was a little more than we had bargained for. We spent the remainder of our time in planning a scheme for escape. It was finally determined that White and I should, after all was in readiness, mount our horses and dash

100

noisily down a slope to Crooked river, cross over through the bushes, then, if we had succeeded in eluding the Indians, make our way down to our camp of the night before, and await the coming of the rest of the party. As soon as we started, Hill and the rest of the party were to quietly move down a gulch and make their way as best they could by another route to the same point. In case we heard any firing in their direction we were to get to the main body as soon as possible.

White and myself had the best horses in the outfit, and it would have worried a good racehorse to beat either of them in a long race; so, after maturing our plans and studying the ground to be ridden over by each party, we made our preparations and awaited the coming of the night, all realizing that to-night it was "neck or nothing" with us; and that nothing but the coolest and most daring moves would extricate us from our peril; for peril it was, as we all knew; and all were fully determined to escape and "make it hot" for the redskins if attacked.

Darkness came on — and it was intensely dark. Our party being ready to start down the gulch, away went White and I. It was so dark that we couldn't see each other when a few yards apart. I dashed straight for the river, down the sloping hill with White close after me, our horses "doing their level best." On and down we went. Flashing past some mounted Indians, we exchanged a few shots, but it was too dark for either side to take aim or shoot with any degree of certainty, and, of course, this was a waste of ammunition. On we went, pursued by a yelling horde, who were shooting at us as they came on; but their bullets were as dangerous to themselves as to us in the darkness. They soon contented themselves with following us as fast as their ponies could carry them; but, as our horses made two feet to their one, we soon had considerable territory between us and them.

Coming to the stream, we crossed over and dashed down on the other side some miles; then, stopping occasionally to listen, and hearing nothing but distant yells in the quarter from which we had come, we became satisfied that they had discontinued the pursuit, or were following very slowly, and so we recrossed the stream, and, getting off our horses, led them slowly along for some distance, listening to learn if the Indians were after Hill's party. Everything being quiet in the direction from which we expected Hill and the rest of the boys to come, we felt sure that our ruse had worked as well as we could have wished, and, on consultation, we concluded we could strike across the country and intercept Hill's party, as we were sure the Indians could not follow us in the dark; so we mounted and trotted forward, laying our course to intercept them. We knew we were well ahead of them; for they would travel slowly, and as silently as possible, unless they were attacked or pursued, which latter, we were confident, was not the case, for we had heard no shooting or yelling in their direction.

We moved on swiftly and silently till we thought we were near the line of their march; then walked our horses, and, with strained ears, listened for any sound that would indicate their whereabouts. Soon we heard the footsteps of approaching horses.

After listening closely for a few moments, we were satisfied Hill's party was coming, though it might be Indians, for no other than the sound of the horses' feet could be heard; and if it was Indians and we were discovered, we would have another run for it, and a stray shot might stop either of us. I said to White, "The boys know your coyote bark; give them a specimen of your powers." The still night air was pierced by the shrill sharp bark of a coyote, which sounded so natural that I, who well knew it came from White's lips, found myself looking around for a prairie wolf.

The noise of the advancing footsteps ceased — again the sharp laughing bark; a moment later we heard the seeming whinney of a horse. Again the coyote, answered by the horse.

This assured us that it was Hill's party, so we trotted forward toward them, and a moment later heard the welcome hail, "Who comes there?" our answer being, "Hunter and White." We were soon shaking hands with them, Captain Hill especially, who by this time had gained the confidence of our men, he being a really brave fellow, at least.

All together again, we trotted briskly along for seven or eight hours putting some thirty miles between us and our last camping place, then stopped near the river till morning, to let our tired horses rest and eat and drink. As soon as it was clearly light we went back from the stream up a steep gulch and into some timber that crowned the ridge. This took us some miles from the river or creek; and here we again went into camp, proposing to pass the day there, unless the Indians persuaded us to move again.

After eating our breakfast White proposed that eight or ten of us should go back two or three miles on the trail we had come, conceal ourselves near it, and await the coming of the Indians if they were following us (and we believed they were). So we left Captain Hill and five men to look after our horses and the camp, while the other ten, headed by White and myself started back on our trail down the gulch or canyon. After going some three miles we found a suitable place to form an ambush; dividing our party, White with four of the boys took one side of the gulch, and I, with the other four, the other side. Concealing ourselves behind convenient rocks and trees, we lay down to await the coming of any one on our trail. There we lay watching till well into the after part of the day, when a low hiss warned all that some one was coming. We were all out of sight in a second, and as still as death. Soon we saw three Indians on foot cautiously following our trail up the gulch, and directly afterwards we saw thirty or forty others following slowly on horseback, some hundreds of yards behind.

It had been already arranged that in such a case those in the lead should be allowed to pass before we opened fire, and none of us were to show ourselves or shoot until I gave the signal. So we allowed the three footmen to pass on, which they did very slowly, watching the footprints of our horses.

Soon the mounted Indians came up, and just as they were about to pass we opened fire on them. Crack, crack went our rifles, ten speaking at once; then out whipped our deadly revolvers, speaking their pieces. Several Indians and horses went down at the first fire, but still the deadly fire continued from rock and tree on either side of them. This proved more than the nerves of the "noble red man" could stand, and without hardly exchanging a shot they retreated back down the gulch. The three that we had allowed to pass on foot took to the hills, firing at us as they ran, from tree to tree, and from rock to rock, finally making their escape. One of our boys was slightly wounded in the left arm, but the wound was so slight that it was deemed of no consequence.

Five dead Indians and several killed and wounded ponies remained between our two fires, and we had positive evidence that other ponies had carried off some very sick Indians.

We watched the trails till about dark, and as we saw no prospect of another audience we returned to the camp, told our little story, dressed our little wound, ate a hearty supper, posted a strong guard and got to our little beds, for we had decided to remain here till morning at all hazards.

The night passed without any alarm, and after partaking of an early breakfast we concluded to remain where we were for a day or two unless we were molested, and to send out scouts to ascertain the movements of our sneaking foe. White and myself being very tired, Capt. Hill, with four of the boys, went down the gulch to guard the trails, and two or three of the others went in the other direction and stationed themselves on elevated points as lookouts. At night all came in reporting having seen no Indians. So, as the night previous, we stationed our guards, and had a quiet night of it. The same mode of procedure was followed the next day, varied by a change of those on guard. In the afternoon White and two others went up the divide and killed three deer (game was plenty there). To say this was a welcome addition to our larder would be unnecessary. That night we all made a hearty meal of the venison.

As our stock of meats was running low, we determined to remain where we were and send out a party the next day to kill and bring in as many as they could, the meat of which we proposed to jerk for future use. Next morning, all being quiet, we arranged a signal to recall us to camp in case it was about to be attacked during our absence. This signal was to be the firing of a lot of pitch-wood and green boughs, prepared for the purpose, that would make such a dense smoke as to be easily seen and recognized by us.

White and I selected five of the best shots in the party, and started up into the hills or mountains after game.

I was convinced that the Indian scouts were watching our movements, and told the boys to keep a sharp lookout for skulking Indians, and that we had better keep well together, to be ready to help each other in case there should be need of it. After traveling two or three miles we found quite a drove of black-tailed deer. Getting within good rifle-range, we brought down four fine ones at the first round, and two more before they got out of gunshot.

We went up, separated, and were busy cutting open our deer, when bang! — whizz! — crack! — came three or four shots from behind some trees, some three hundred yards away, the bullets whistling uncomfortably near our ears. To grasp our trusty rifles and jump behind trees was the act we performed in much less time than it takes me to tell it; then silence reigned for awhile. White and I happened to be pretty close together, and were both of the opinion that there were but a few Indians in the party that had fired on us. We called to the other five to lie low and watch the point of timber from which we had been fired at, and we would drop back down the hill, crawl around and force the Indians from their cover. So, back and around we went, the others firing from time to time, as did the Indians, at long range. Soon White and I worked our way to their rear and into good range of the timber. We crawled up behind a large log, and soon my rifle spoke, and an Indian yelled and pitched forward on to his face. This told the Indians that they were taken "aback," and three or four of them sprang from behind their trees and made off; but one of them Had made only three or four jumps when White's gun rang a death-note; an Indian's heels flew into the air — another *good* Indian.

We followed them up, jumping from tree to tree, till we were satisfied they had escaped; then we returned to the dead Indians, secured what ammunition they had, broke their guns — as we had no use for such as they used — and went back to our dead deer. This time we were more careful, and placed two men out to guard us from an unexpected attack.

After getting our deer ready we carried them to camp as fast as we could, and arriving there safely, told of our adventure and narrow escape. This warned all of us of the jeopardy we were in when we carelessly allowed ourselves to be taken unawares while in the vicinity of these marauding Indians — in fact within their country.

The rest of that day and the next day was consumed in preparing our venison for future use.

On the night of that day we determined to again visit Crooked river. Our horses were comparatively fresh, and after mounting we pushed forward. Reaching the stream we turned our course up, passed our former scene of action, and when it was nearly morning we found ourselves in a well-sheltered place, in thick brush on the bank of the stream. Here we dismounted and let our animals feast on the rich bottom-grass, while the most of us slept some.

After daylight we were soon aware that the Indians were fully posted on our movements, as the hills around us were decked with them. So we concluded to move on toward the Malheur regardless of their "funny business," and on we went at our leisure, keeping pretty well away from the brush, with one or two men well in front as an advance scout. Thus we slowly moved along till nightfall, then selecting a good place, we again encamped, put out our guards, and remained over night without molestation.

The next day we worked similarly, but traveled only ten or twelve miles until we again went into camp.

We were satisfied that the Indians were watching us closely, and that at the first opportunity they would deal us a stinging, if not a fatal blow. But the opportunity we didn't propose to give, if it was in our power to prevent it. So, awhile after dark we mounted and took our back-trail to or past our camp of the night before. This only took two or three hours' time, and we again camped near the bushes, tying our horses — leaving the saddles on, and putting our guards near the trails; for we believed the Indians were following us constantly and in large numbers, and that there were as many or more in front of us, for the purpose of making a concerted attack on us as soon as they thought there was a chance of success. One of our objects in watching the trail was to learn, if possible, how many there were trailing us, and, if there were not too many of them, to attack them suddenly. On the contrary, if their number should prove too great, we would remount and be off as fast as possible.

Just before day our watchmen saw about a hundred mounted Indians pass. As soon as they were well out of hearing we mounted, having on consultation concluded that it would not be safe to "tackle" so large a party, especially when we knew they were prepared for us. Silently and swiftly we counter-marched, believing that all - or nearly all - of our Indian hosts were behind us.

We pushed on rapidly during the rest of the night and till nine or ten o'clock the next day when we went into camp, having found a convenient place, or one that we deemed secure. Here we remained some days, closely watching the movements of our foe, and as closely watched by them. We often sent out scouts to try and find small parties of the Indians that we dared "tackle." Bach night we could see by their signal-fires where the main body of the scoundrels were.

It was now a game of "hide and seek" with both the Indians and ourselves, and continued so for some weeks, as the Indians had become as wary as we. At times we exchanged shots at a long distance. We changed our camping-place almost daily, sometimes in one direction, sometimes another.

Finally, our provision and ammunition running low, we determined to try for Canyon City; and this we believed would be a critical move, as we feared the Indians would divine our intentions, ambush the trails and waylay us.

After dark one night we lightened our packs of all superfluous articles, and at the word, started at a ratling pace, taxing our horses to their utmost speed and endurance during the entire night, and well on to the noon of the following day, when we stopped for a short time to let our tired horses rest and feed, and partook of such provisions as we had left ourselves. After a few hours we again mounted and went, never drawing rein till we had put over a hundred miles between us and the camp we had left the night before.

Then we camped, fearing no further danger from the noble sons of the forest that we thought we had "left in the shade."

Our camp was at the edge of a mountain meadow. These are formed, as old timers believe, by beaver-dams and by drift wood gorging at the lower end of a broad space between footbills, deadening the current and consequently securing a deposit of soil from the adjacent hills. The small stream maintains for the most part its channel under this unsubstantial deposit, and in places very deep holes are found full of sparkling water and abounding with mountain trout from three inches to a foot in length. But as I am not preaching geology, I will relate that we found several pools, or holes, and some of the men "lured the wiley trout" with success that would have gladdened the hearts of men less hungry than we.

This must have been the place we read of where it took two men to unhook the fish as fast as one could catch them. We had fish for supper and fish for breakfast, and, although it was not lent, we had fish for dinner, because our loaves were few.

A few days afterward we reached Canyon City, without further adventure, where we were well received, feted, paid off, and discharged.

Chapter Fifteen

In a short time after our disbandment, I took leave of Bill White for the last time. Years afterward I learned that he had returned to the Willamette valley, married and settled down to farming. The small-pox broke out in his neighborhood, and the people being unable to procure nurses who would risk nursing those afflicted with this loathsome disease, White, in the nobleness of his heart, and with his old time self-sacrificing spirit, volunteered as a nurse for the afflicted; contracted the disease, and died of it soon afterward.

And so this old timer laid down his life, after passing through many dangers and trials, but his memory remained with his old comrades, never to be effaced while life lasts. And when they heard of his untimely end, they realized that this last sacrifice was the crowning act of a life of heroism.

Poor Bill! Your cheek has for the last time turned pale as you have gazed upon wounded, dying, and dead comrades; your fiery eyes are closed. Your nervous grasp has been returned for the last time; your lips have littered the last war-cry; you have issued your last cheering words of command that inspired your comrades to acts of daring, in the defense of the weak and unprotected.

I then entered into a co-partnership with one Doctor Price, by buying into a mining claim; took charge of the outfit and ran it, making considerable money. But my mind would revert to the dear ones that I had laid in the silent graves. I became restless and weary of this plodding life, and longed for excitement of some kind to detract my thoughts from the past with its bright morning and dear recollections. So I sold out to my partner, and mounting my trusty horse started for Boise and other newly discovered mining camps in Idaho. Reaching this basin I found one of my elder brothers engaged in mining near Placerville. Within a few days I struck good diggings and settled down to work for a short time. Soon after I arrived in camp, my brother sold out and returned to Shoalwater Bay.

Here I will relate an anecdote to illustrate the way miners would hide their wealth. It appears that a short time before I came to the camp my brother had buried near his cabin some $2,500 in gold dust. He had sold out, and was awaiting his pay when I arrived in camp. Shortly after he got the money for his claim, and one morning came to where I was working and said: "Come, George! I have got my money and have bought a horse, and am all ready to start for home to see Sally (his wife). Come, and see me off!" We went to the cabin and fixed up the money he had just received for his claim in purses, putting the purses in a belt that was made for the purpose. Then he said: "Now I'll go and raise my 'dead man'" (meaning the money he had buried), and, taking a sluice-fork, he went out. After he had been gone for some time he returned, with the sweat pouring from his brow, saying; "I have been robbed!"

I asked him how that was, and he said: "I buried my money at the end of that log, just as day was breaking one morning, and came and got a pan of ashes and threw them on the spot to mark it. Just afterward a man came along inquiring for a stray horse; he must have been watching me, and has come in the night and dug it up; for I have dug all around where I buried it, and it ain't there."

Finally, I prevailed on him to show me where he had buried it, though he said, "It's no use — it's gone! Do you think I'm a fool, or crazy, that I do not know where I put my money?" I believed he had made a mistake, but he wouldn't have it so, saying: "If you can find it, you may have it." He pointed to a part of a tree that had been cut down and the top used for wood. This tree, or log, lay with the butt toward the cabin; he said he had buried the dust in a can about ten feet from the top-end of this log, afterward returning with the ashes and throwing them over the place.

"Did you find the ashes when you came in search of the can?" I asked. He said, "Yes." I saw at a glance that he had made a thorough search at the end of this log; but, on glancing around, I saw another similar log some distance away with its top-end pointing toward the cabin, and went to it, my brother asking if I supposed he was such a fool as not to know at which log he had buried the can? "Don't know yet," said I, as I measured off about ten feet from the end of the log. One or two scrapes with the sluice-fork uncovered the can; and, as I lifted it out, its heft assured me that it contained gold-dust. I said: "Here, John, is your gold." "No!" said he; "that's not mine; I buried my dust at the end of the other log;" but, after awhile, he was convinced it was his, and concluded that after burying it he had forgotten which log it was near, while going to the cabin for the ashes, which he had thrown at the end of the wrong one, and thus "lost the combination of his safe."

Left alone among strangers, the spirit of wandering soon took hold of me again. Thinking to allay this mania, I concluded one morning to visit a neighboring town (Centreville) some ten miles distant.

On my arrival at Centreville, almost the first man I met was an old Masonic friend, named Owsley, a good physician, who had come to this camp some time before. On meeting and exchanging greetings, Owsley said, "You are, above all others, the very man I am glad to meet just now."

Thinking the doctor was probably "short," I put my hand to my pocket; seeing my move he said, "No, George, not that! The facts are that a man has died in a cabin just out of town leaving a wife and three small children entirely destitute, and far from their home and friends." He told me the man's name was Slade, and that he was from Yreka, California; that he had come into the camp a few weeks before, with a yoke of oxen and a light wagon, taking sick, he had sold the team and wagon, and consumed the proceeds in providing for his family while he was sick, finally dying, leaving the family destitute as before stated. That Slade had made himself known to him as a Master Mason, and had given him his Masonic pin, and the name and number of his Lodge, and requested him to do all in his power to assist the family; that he (Owsley) had attended Slade during his sickness.

"Now," said the doctor, "You are fertile in resources and a good worker, and you must help me out." I said, "Let us visit the cabin;" we did so, and I found the distressed family in a miner's cabin which was built of logs, the door was of split boards or shakes; in one corner was a fire-place and chimney of sticks and mud, posts had been driven into the ground, and on these had been made a platform of poles, over which was strewed fir boughs, making a regular miner's bunk. Lying on one of these bunks, with a few blankets under him, I saw what was left of Slade, while sitting around the fire were the sorrowing widow and children and Mrs. Dr. Owsley.

After taking a good look at the corpse, I said, "Doctor there seems something familiar to me in that countenance, and if I had seen the man in health I should probably have known him." As I said this I felt a hand laid lightly on my arm, and turning, I saw Mrs. Slade standing beside me. "Is not this George Hunter?" she asked; I answered "Yes!" And she asked, "Did you not know William Slade who used to edit the Yreka paper years ago?" I answered, "Yes! and you were Miss Brown, of Jacksonville; quite a young girl, when I saw you last!" She said, "Yes;" then pointing to her dead husband, said "George, this and these dear children are all that is left me in this wide world, and God only knows what will become of them and me for I am entirely without means, even to bury my poor dead husband, much less to clothe and feed my children." The tears streamed down her wan cheeks as she said this.

I took her hand and said: "Mrs. Slade, do not distress yourself about financial affairs; you have sufficient to do to comfort these poor orphan children; leave the rest to the doctor and myself, and rest assured that all will be done for your husband that you could wish, and you and your children will be cared for. There are hundreds of big, warm hearts near you, and when they are made aware of your troubles, they will sympathize with and assist you and yours to their utmost ability."

She replied, "The doctor has already assured me of these things; but I can only realize that I am left alone with these poor children and this my dead husband."

Then, dropping on to her knees, and laying her weary head on the un-throbbing breast of him who had been her stay and support, she cried, "Alone! Oh, God, all alone!"

Well, this was too much for me, an old timer. After wringing Mrs. Owsley's hand and kissing the babies, I hurriedly left the cabin, as I feared that if I remained longer I might "slop over" myself. Owsley followed me. Nothing was said till we reached the upper end of Main street. Here we concluded to part, each taking a side of the street in search of "Brothers" belonging to our fraternity.

I will try to describe my progress which, I presume, was duplicated by the doctor. The first house I visited was a large saloon, wherein were several "moneyed" tables around which were many miners, packers and others, engaged in "fighting the tiger" and similar games. It was "chips for dust" and "dust for chips" all around the hall. I approached the bar and ordered something, at the same time — in my own way — inviting as many other fellows to join me as stood in need of refreshments, thus soon attracting the attention of many of those present. Among them was Joe Oldham, a brother of the famed Sim Oldham, of California.

Joe was a tall, straight, fine-looking man — a sporting man by profession, and a saloonkeeper. He approached me with the others, and stepping aside asked me, if I wished to speak with them. I replied: "Yes. Upon my arrival in this place an hour or so ago, I met Doctor Owsley, a Brother, who informed me that he had been attending professionally upon a Brother who had recently arrived from Yreka, and that the patient died during the previous night, leaving his widow and three small children destitute and friendless in a cabin near by. Now, the doctor and myself are looking for Brothers, and we hope those we find will seek for others, and meet us in some hall here, where I will institute a Lodge of Instruction (or Investigation), when we will proceed to give the deceased a decent interment, and provide for the widow and orphans."

Oldham and myself then went to a store and ordered such things as were required for the immediate use of the family. Then we interested some sporting-women, who repaired to the cabin and sewed for the family, closing their houses till after the funeral. There were no other women near at this time, except Mrs. Owsley and the broken-down and grief-stricken widow.

For the rest of the day and night the hunt for Brothers went bravely on throughout the surrounding camps. There were no lodges in these camps as yet.

Burial of Slade in Boise Basin

The next morning at ten o'clock a saloonkeeper stopped his business and gave, us the use of his house to arrange matters in. There we met, some eighty odd Brothers, dressed in woolen shirts and patched pants.

After making the necessary examinations, we "clothed" ourselves in white pocket handkerchiefs in lieu of the proper aprons, and repaired to the cabin. We had prepared as good a coffin as could be gotten up in such a place, and the family were dressed in appropriate mourning.

Forming in procession, we repaired to an adjacent mound and there gave our Brother the usual Masonic burial, with all of its rites, etc.

Then we returned to our improvised hall, placed a table in the centre of the room with gold scales, a blower and a purse on it, stating that all Brothers had been made aware of the destitute circumstances of the widow and orphans, and asked that all would perform their duty. We then formed in line and marched around the hall; as a Brother came up to the table he would select a weight and balance it with gold dust, put the dust in the purse and move on, giving place to another. Oldham marched immediately in front of me, and as he came to the table, he pulled out a purse of some hundreds of dollars; carefully untied it, then poured the contents into the blower, shook the purse and dropped it on the dust, turned and said as he shook my hand — the tears trinkling off his long mustache, "Brother George, we can do something to atone for our cussedness, can't we?"

This settled it; I did not take time to untie my purse; my eyes being rather dim at the time; I suppose caused by' a bad cold that I had contracted a short time before. I just dropped what I had and passed on, as many others did. Suffice it to say, that on all being weighed, we found after paying all the expenses, we had a purse that we presented to the widow of nearly three thousand dollars. This purse, Owsley, Oldham, and myself were delegated to carry to the widow, which we did, and upon our presenting it to her she utterly refused to take it as she said it was too much to accept from strangers. But after we had explained that if she did not take and use the money for herself and children we would be forced to appoint guardians for the children, who would take and care for them and that which was donated to and for them, their use and benefit; our arguments prevailed and she accepted the generous aid, and within a few days started in the care of a Brother for her distant home and friends.

I tell this as another illustration of the generosity of old timers, and I have no idea that the same thing could be accomplished among any other class of men in any country, unless it would be for the benefit of the widow and orphans of some dead millionaire; and not then, unless it could be voted out of the public coffers that had been filled by hard earnings of the working class.

Soon after this, I returned to Placerville and my claim, more restless than ever. Sold out, bought two teams and started with ten or twelve passengers, for the Snake river diggings.

We followed up the Snake river some hundreds of miles and across the

Rocky mountains. At last as we could not hear anything more of the location of these mines we became satisfied that the rumors we had heard applied to the Stinking water mines, in Montana. These mines were on Black Alder creek or Stinking water. Upon said creek are located the towns Virginia City and Nevada City. The stream empties into the Beaver head, and this was a rich paying camp. More of this camp anon.

On arriving at this conclusion, and winter coming on, we turned and started for Salt Lake, for winter quarters. Soon the snow became deep, and to reach Salt Lake we were forced in many places to shovel snow to get our teams through the drifts. Being wet and cold, day after day, I took a severe cold, which resulted finally in mountain or lung fever.

On reaching Farmington, a town near Salt Lake City, I had become so ill that I could not bear the jolt of the wagon, and upon our going into camp one evening I asked our boys to go to a house near by, a long low adobe building, and see if the owner would not allow me to stay over night, and if I was not better the next morning remain with him until my friends could reach Camp Douglass (near Salt Lake City), and send out a doctor. And until I got able to be moved on to the city or the camp.

To ask was to be received, I was assisted into the house, and furnished a bed. I had a purse of gold dust of some twelve hundred dollars with me, which I placed under my pillow. On lying down I told a young man, a brother Mason, that if I was not better next morning, he should take my teams on to Salt Lake City, and put the horses on a ranch, go himself to Camp Douglass, and send an army doctor out to me. As I had heard so much of Mormons I was not willing to trust myself to a Mormon doctor's care.

When morning came I was out of my head, so my instructions were carried out, and the next evening Dr. Williams of General Connor's division, which was garrisoning Camp Douglass at this time, came out to see me; finding me, as he said, in a critical condition. He gave me the medicines needed and gave instructions to the nurses that attended me.

Taking my pocket book with him, in which were some letters and other papers that would enable him to commune with my friends if occasion should require, he returned to his post.

The name of the family that I stopped with was Dixon. Dixon had three wives and several grown daughters, among whom was one named Samantha, a young widow, who had two children. She was divorced from her husband; cause, cruel treatment. I call Samantha's name, because she was my principal nurse throughout my stay with this pleasant family, though all of them were kindness itself. On my return to consciousness I found that Samantha had taken my purse and put it away, as she said there were so many strangers coming to see me, she didn't deem it safe where I had put it. She had told the doctor what she had done. From the hour that I was taken to the house there was not any length of time but there was a woman sitting at the bedside, ready to respond to my slightest request. As I grew better I used to remonstrate, telling them I could call if I required anything. They said it took one or more of them continually to sew for the family, and they could do so there as well as anywhere. Many were the pleasant hours I passed conversing with these friendly women. The elder ladies would read the book of Mormon, and the account of what they called "the death of the martyr" — Joe Smith, the Mormon prophet — while tears trinkled down their cheeks. Samantha would, hour after hour, tell me of Mormon beliefs, and the goodness of "Brother Brigham," as she called him.

At one time I asked her what was the cause of her separation from her husband. (I had before this told her of my misfortune in losing my wife and child, which I suppose placed us on a more friendly footing than we would have been otherwise.) She said: "My husband and I lived together pleasantly until he took another wife. His latter wife was a young Danish woman. She would tell our husband stories about me, and finally alienated him and his love from me and my children. Things grew worse and worse, until he struck me, which led me to apply for a divorce."

Then I said: "You certainly do not believe in polygamy." She said: "All men are not alike, 'Brother Brigham,' on our being brought before him, told, my husband that a man that would abuse his first wife was not fit to have a second one, and that he would give me a divorce, together with the one-half of the property. My husband could take the other half of our property and his 'sealed wife,' with the assurance that he could never have another woman bound to him so long 'as the last wife lived.'" She said that she was as firm a believer in the Mormon faith as ever. In these friendly discourses I passed the tedious time, until I could be removed to Camp Douglass.

Upon taking leave of this Mormon family I tendered them pay, which Dixon firmly refused, saying that it was part of the Mormon religion to take care of the sick. Seeing that it was useless to argue with him, I took a friendly leave of this people, and when the holidays came around I remunerated them, to some extent, with presents for the family.

Arriving at Camp Douglass I made my temporary home with an ex-Mormon family by the name of Morris — the widow of Morris, the "dissenter," who had been killed the winter before. While here, I from day to day went to the city, about a mile distant, and there' made the acquaintance of another Mormon family, by the name of Cabbel. Cabbel was an old man, a New Yorker, who had been in Salt Lake City some two years. He being a brother Mason, a warm friendship sprung up between us. I used frequently to take meals with his hospitable family when I was in town.

On my arrival at the city I purchased a season ticket for the theatre, and, being a great lover of the drama, I would at all hazards attend each night. This resulted in a severe cold and a relapse. On again calling Doctor Williams, he ordered me to the hospital, which was full of sick soldiers. Some three or four days after my admission to the hospital, I saw a white head bobbing by the side of Doctor Williams, coming toward my cot. This proved to be Brother Cabbel, who said, when he came up to me: "My wife and the girls have been telling me for a day or so that you were sick again, and would not give me any peace until I came up to see after you." He continued: "I have a sleigh outside and plenty of wraps, and I am going to take you home with me. Mother is outside."

Doctor Williams assured me that this was the best thing that I could do. As there were so many sick and dying in the hospital, I couldn't receive the care I required where I was; that it was nursing I needed more than anything else; that he could visit me as often as it would be necessary in the city, as well as in the camp. So, I was taken to the home of this kind Mormon, and nursed into good health. As I had been led to believe Mormons all to be devils from what I had read and heard, the kind treatment that I had received at their hands caused me to believe that the devil was not nearly so black as he had been represented to be.

A short time after I had fully recovered I sold my teams, and engaged to carry the express to East Bannack and Virginia City, Montana, which I did in company with another man. The snow was deep when we started for Box-elder, some forty miles out from the city. This far we drove a stage, and from thence carried the mailmatter in *par flèches,* or pouches made of rawhide, hung on pack-saddles, and lashed fast with ropes.

Upon my taking leave of Doctor Williams and the Cabbels and Dixons, I could not help thinking that there were good people among all classes — Mormons, Catholics, Protestants, miners, soldiers, and even harlots, and that God in his goodness would not refuse such His free and full pardon for offenses, more or less of which others' acts, or circumstances, had forced upon them; and that He would, for the good they had done, welcome them to that home "not made with hands, eternal in the heavens."

As I close this, an old Californian by the name of White, who has been reading as I was writing, tells the following story, which illustrates my ideas more forcibly than I can write them.

As White tells it, there was a very wicked man, he would swear, gamble and cheat, give to the widow and the poor, and comfort the orphan. Among the many charitable things done by him, he had given from a stone-quarry that belonged to him sufficient stone to build a church. When this man died, White says, he appeared before Saint Peter and the devil, who were weighing the good and bad deeds of newly arrived aspirants for heaven. White's man's turn coming, it was for awhile a "close shave." Peter would put into his side of the scale a good deed — the devil on his a bad one. On went the work, first one side up, then the other, as the good and bad deeds fell into the scales on their respective sides. The devil at last threw a bundle of the bad on his side, and down went the scale. All appeared lost, when Peter thought of the rock given to build the church. He threw the whole business on the scale! Up came the devil's, and down went Peter's side, not to be raised again. And so, another old timer was saved.

Chapter Sixteen

From Salt Lake City to East Bannack and thence to Virginia City, a distance of some four hundred miles, parallel with the Rocky mountains, which we crossed on the way. We made reasonable time, taking into consideration the snow and other obstructions.

At Virginia City or Stinking water we heard all about the Vigilantes' operations of the fall before.

It appears that one McGruder, of Lewiston, Idaho, had taken a pack-train from the latter place to Stinking water mines, taking with him some men from Lewiston.

On his (McGruder's) selling out his goods some of these men returned with him a part of the way. Reaching a lonely part of the mountains they killed McGruder in camp and one of them rode his favorite mule back to Lewiston. They went on to San Francisco where they were captured, brought back to Lewiston, tried and hung — except one Page who turned state's evidence. Page was killed some years after in a brawl.

There were many hung at East Bannack, Virginia City and Nevada City; among them, Sheriff Plummer, Boon Helm, Dutch Slade and several others.

Soon after my arrival I joined a party of eight, myself making the ninth, and started out prospecting.

We went down the Beaver Head and across the mountains, to the Prickly Pear country, east of where Helena now is. Nothing occurred worthy of note until we got into the Yellowstone country. Here we camped one night near a small stream, that cut a deep channel through the loose soil near a bluff. We had supper, then staked and hobbled our horses out to graze just under the bluff, then lay down for the night.

As we had not seen any sign of Indians or heard of any hostilities we had no thought of danger. My bedfellow was one Raymond if I remember; we were sleeping in our blankets as were the rest, around our camp-fire. Just as day was breaking we were all aroused by the firing of guns and the yells of Indians from the top of the bluff. I said "all;" but Raymond, poor fellow, was just being awakened, as a rifle-ball killed him by my side as we lay in our blankets.

I felt a sharp sting in my thigh. It required but a glance to take in the situation. Hurriedly we tumbled the grub, blankets and saddles into the bed of the creek which protected us from the fire from the bluff above. Myself and one other, after a hurried consultation with the others, concluded to get the horses, as it would be sure death to be left afoot. Directing the others to keep up a brisk fire at the top of the bluff, we, when all was ready, started and ran as fast as we could to our horses, cut the picket ropes and hobbles; my comrade mounted the bell horse, I another, whipping the others ahead of us; we dashed away keeping well under the bluff for some distance and until we were assured we were out of range of the guns on the cliff, then we made for the gulch, and in to the deep cut, then led them up to our camp where we had left the rest of the party. We dragged the remains of our dead companion into the gulch and buried him under some rocks and gravel. Another victim of the "noble red man's" hospitality; another old timer had "passed in his checks;" another daring, brave and energetic frontiersman had sunk his last prospect hole, and without a moment's time allowed him to implore the aid or forgiveness of God, was cut down in the bloom of youth, and hurried to that "undiscovered country." No relative stood near to close his dying eyes. As he had nothing upon his person that gave us the address of his family or friends, and we were not sure that we had even his right name, we had no means of communicating with his kindred and friends, and as many pioneers had been and many more were, we left him in an unknown grave, saddled up and started away, following the gulch or ravine some distance; then we struck across the country, on our return to Stinking water. Getting eight or ten miles from the place of attack, we came to a small stream of cool water, and as we had not seen anything of the Indians following us, I got off my horse and told the others I would look after my pet. Pulling off my boot I found it and the sock saturated with blood which had flown from a deep flesh wound in my thigh. This was the first intimation any of the others had of my being hurt. As it was not painful, I wrapped some pieces of cloth around the leg, then saturated it with cold water. We filled our canteens and moved on. As we now had evidence of the hostilities of the Indians, we made the best time we could for Virginia City. As I kept the wound in my thigh wet with cold water, and a small piece of rusty bacon thrust into the openings to keep them from healing too soon, I suffered but little inconvenience during our return trip.

Upon our return to Black Alder, or Stinking water I engaged in mining. Hiring out to a party of eleven men to run a drain-race to their claim under the stream.

After working a couple of months I started one day down a shaft to see some timbers put in, when the rope gave way, and I fell some thirty feet to the bottom, bruising me up very severely. This laid me up for some weeks.

Just at this time a man came along with whom I had got acquainted at Camp Douglass, by the name of Doc Vanvalsey. "Van," as he was called, was an old 'forty-niner. He had passed through many hardships, and led a wandering life, and at last found himself at Salt Lake City, flat broke. Being too proud to beg, he enlisted in Connor's division at Camp Douglass. A warm friendship had sprung up between Van and myself while I was at Salt Lake, he being a brother Mason. Some time after I left Salt Lake he had a difficulty with a young "doughboy" infantry lieutenant, finally ending his relations with Uncle Samuel's business man by striking him on the head with the hilt of his saber. He then sprang on to his cavalry horse and skipped for a more healthy camp. After getting well away he left his horse and saber to be returned to his Captain (Smith), got in with some teamsters, and came on to Virginia City, where he heard that he could find me, and made his appearance at the cabin where I was lying at the time bruised and broken from my recent fall. He told me all about his trouble. I called the foreman of the company (the Nevada Company) to me and related Van's story to him, and he repeated it to the others of the company. Van was sure there were soldiers following him under command of the lieutenant that he had polished off with his saber, and said he was not at all anxious to return to Camp Douglass, as they had a bad "breast complaint" there, and the pills they prescribed for the complaint he had been attacked with would prove very hard to digest; so he preferred to stay where he was. All of the company being Masons instead of soldiers, and being in need of workmen, they hired Van to run a car in the drifts; and, as his clothes were much like those worn by soldiers, and quite unfit for underground work, he borrowed a suit from one of the boys and repaired to the drifts; and so great was his *care for the interests of his employers* that he never left the drifts from daylight till dark.

Soon after Van's appearance Captain Smith came up to our camp. He had heard of me as Van had. Smith, in conversation with me, said: "Hunter, we heard of Van's coming up this creek; and I believe, as does the lieutenant, that you know where Van is. That is your business; but I'm afraid it would go hard with Van if he was caught; and this lieutenant will catch him, if Van hasn't some good friend that will help him out of the country." The captain took dinner with us, shook hands, and returned to Virginia City, where a detachment was camped on the watch for Van.

A few days later, four of the company sold out to their partners, and I with them determined to start for Fisherville, a new mining-camp, struck on Studhorse creek in British Columbia, some five hundred miles distant.

These four men's names were Brents, Roarer and two Scott brothers. The Scott brothers and Brents repaired to town to purchase horses for the trip. We would require for the trip five riding-horses and three or four for packing; but as they had a chance to buy in a lot cheap, they took all the party had, which was six riding-horses with riding-saddles, and five others, with *aparajos* for packing. The same party that sold them this outfit having a large supply of guns and pistols, they bought one of each for each of the five of us, and were presented with an extra gun and revolver, as a mark of great respect, from the gentleman they had bought of.

On their return with the horses and an entire outfit to last the party to Kootenia or Fishers, the weather being warm, we concluded to go a short distance that night.

Just as we were shaking hands with our other friends, Van said, that as we had an extra horse, saddle, gun and pistol, and as he had never been in "Her Majesty's possessions," he believed he would accompany us. We having plenty of grub, and Van being a thorough good fellow, we could not find it in our hearts to refuse his slight request.

All being ready, we took leave of our friends, and rode swiftly away in the dark for the new *Eldorado*.

Near morning we reached Beaver Head, rested a short time, and then went on our way from day to day; crossed the Big Hole river, and on to the head of Deer Lodge river, passing on down this stream to near the mouth of Little Blackfoot, or near Grant's place, where we stopped a day to fish and rest.

Evening came, and just as we were sitting down to supper, Captain Smith came riding up to us, and after giving and receiving friendly salutations, dismounted, sat down and partook of our meal. He told us that he had come in company with "our" lieutenant, and that he was encamped a mile or so above Grant's, on the Deer Lodge; that he (Smith) had come on ahead to see after provisions, etc., at Grant's, and hearing of us and our camp, concluded to come on and see us before he returned to his camp.

Smith didn't appear to recognize Van. We were careless in those days, and didn't introduce him — in fact, I don't think it was expected.

After we had finished our supper, the captain said he would return to his command, and if we did not start too early in the morning, he would join us, and most likely keep company with us for some time.

We told him we thought most likely we would move on that night, as the mosquitoes were not as bad in the night as they were in the daytime. He said the lieutenant had frequently suggested the same thing, but he was not fond of nightrides, and should not attempt one for a few days if he could help it. He then bid us good night. We were soon on the road, and making good time. This was the last we heard of our soldier-friends.

Day after day we kept on our journey, passing Hellgate and the old mission on the Jocko, and on to Flathead lake. Here we again stopped for a few days, fishing and hunting and letting our horses rest, as we had traveled rather fast for some days. At this lake the Pen d'Oreille river or Clark's Fork of the Columbia takes its source. The river is about two hundred yards wide at the outlet of the lake, runs calmly for a few hundred yards, then goes bounding over rocks forming pools as it passes down the rapids, for a half a mile or so, and here we had some of the finest trout fishing that I ever had in my life, these trout were of the species known as salmon or lake trout, weighing from one to ten pounds. After enjoying ourselves here, we started around the lake following its margin until we reached its northern boundary where we left it and struck out across the tobacco plains; going north to the Kootenia river following up this stream to the mouth of Studhorse creek then up the latter to Fisherville, our final destination.

This newly discovered camp was a flourishing one. This trip I reckon as the most miserable of my life, on account of the mosquitoes and horse flies. In fact there were multiplied acres of them, and they would hit a person "business end foremost" every time, and "stick to him like a brother" or hard luck in a played out mining camp.

The reader will draw some idea of the misery these pests can inflict, when I say that they would measure a foot to the square inch, if condensed. We were compelled to build "smudges" or smokes with logs fired and covered with green bushes and dirt. Our horses would come and stand for hours with their heads over these "smudges," to get a little relief from these bloodthirsty "varmints."

To make a long story short, I had rather preside over a Democratic convention, assembled in a non-prohibition town on the Fourth of July, than interview the Kootenia mosquitoes and horse flies for an hour in the summer time (never wintered in Kootenia, can't say what they do then).

On our arrival at Fisherville, we engaged in prospecting and mining.

About this time Mr. Haines, the English gold commissioner arrived in the camp (these mines were within "Her Majesty's" dominions). The miners, assembled here, were mostly Irishmen and Danes.

Soon I struck what is known among miners as a "rim-rock" claim, some two hundred yards up the side of the mountain from the creek. I carried the "pay dirt" in a flour sack on my back down to the water where I washed it out in a rocker. My partners were opening a claim on the creek about half a mile up the creek. I had been carrying and washing dirt from this rim-rock claim for some weeks, and had excavated quite a hole. While at work I usually laid my belt and revolver on a rock in this hole. One day as I was working away cleaning up some bed-rock, I heard a voice near me ask, "What are yes doin' here?"

Looking up, I saw a large Irishman standing at the edge of my drift or hole, "Trying to make a grub stake," I replied. He asked, "Do yes know ye're on me claim?" I said, "No, I do not." He said, "Ye air, 'niff yes don't git off d___n quick I'll put a head on yes."

I tried to argue the point but it was no go, and at last, as he was about to come into the hole where I was, I thinking there was not room there for two of us, as he was a large man, picked up my pistol and informed him of my opinion. This was probably what he wanted me to do, for he said as he started for town, "I'll tache yes to dhraw a ghun an a man in this country, be gad I'll sind yes te the coal mines."

I replied, "If you fool around here I'll send you to a ____ sight warmer climate than British Columbia." Shortly after this he returned with a man who informed me that he was a constable, and that he arrested me for drawing an unlawful weapon on one of "Her Majesty's" subjects.

I asked permission to go past my cabin, which he allowed me to do. At the cabin I found my comrades and told them what was up. They all took their arms and accompanied us to the Commissioner's office. On making our appearance Haines exclaimed, "What! What! Gentlemen, do you not know that in Her Majesty's dominions, it is not allowable to carry weapons? I said, "yes;" in a civilized country, where the laws can protect her subjects, or those tarrying in her territory. And if you, Mr. Commissioner, will say that you can protect us in our rights, under your British laws, we will deposit our guns and pistols with you till we are ready to leave the camp." This seemed to please him (for we tendered our guns and pistols). He called up my case. The

Irishman had engaged a lawyer to prosecute me, but Haines asked me, "Have you a license to mine in British Columbia?" Upon my saying "yes," and producing my certificate, he asked his clerk if it was on record. After looking over his books the clerk said "yes."

Then I was asked: "Have you recorded the ground you were at work on?" Again I replied in the affirmative, and produced my receipt, which agreed with the records. Haines "rendered his verdict" promptly, paying no attention to the attempts of the attorney to plead, other than to tell him that if he had any law to cite him to, he would consider it; otherwise, if he attempted to interrupt the proceedings again, he would fine him for contempt.

The Commissioner's verdict was a fine of twenty-five pounds on the Irishman for trespassing upon and molesting a "subject" on his own premises, and then he said to me: "If you had shot him down, you could not have been hurt for it; for any English subject has a right to protect his own castle, and a miner's claim is his castle."

We found this man Haines to be a pleasant and just man, and the other party became quite friendly. I write the above to illustrate the rigid manner in which the British laws are enforced, even in distant mining camps.

Shortly after this I, in company with two of my partners, went north to Finley creek, some fifty miles, prospecting; prospects being poor, we sold out on our return, took leave of Doc Vanvalsey, and started for Walla Walla for winter-quarters, Van having intimated that her Majesty's dominions were, he thought, far more healthy for him than any part of the United States would be.

We left him with provisions sufficient to last him through the winter. Took the horses and as I said, started for Walla Walla; and perhaps, "The land of soft weather, pretty girls, woolen socks, and big red apples.

As the reader may not understand the "red apple" quotation, I will, to enable him to "catch on," quote from the descriptions given of the Willamette valley by learned writers.

The Willamette valley was the first settled portion of Oregon. In using this word "Oregon," I mean Oregon as it was, at the time that Webster Tyler and others strove to force what is now Oregon and Washington, upon "His Majesty, the king of Great Britain and Ireland," to prevent which, Doctor Whitman made his arduous, perilous, and solitary journey across the continent, as related in another chapter. It is now a remarkable fruit producing country, a damp country, a muddy country, a wonderfully productive country, where the "gentle zephyrs sob and sigh," about forty to the mile, through the saplings which are about six feet in diameter and three hundred feet high, for at least nine months in the year; where the thermometer scarcely ever reaches 90 F.H. (I mean Fahrenheit, not "feet high;") and seldom condescends to nothing, O or zero as yon folks call it. A country now fast becoming largely populated by a sweat-fearing people; a well watered country. Its streams having their sources in the high mountains that are capped with snow, summer and winter, go laughing down the rugged mountain sides, through deep and dark canyons, over rapids and gigantic falls; and on through the beautiful valleys that comprise the great Willamette. Seldom disturbed except by the silvery trout or festive salmon; seldom used for any purpose other than driving machinery or washing. The male portion of the inhabitants have very little idea of the soft or hard qualities of Oregon water, as it is hard to get them to "sample" anything so thin. Finally, a country noted for health, wealth, pretty girls, high mountains, beautiful valleys, big salmon, productive soil, mild climate, misty winters, navigable streams, big waterfalls, many Republicans, (white-washed by Cleveland in later days) energetic business men, coal beds, iron veins, mineral waters — would quote more, but fear I'll be accused of being an emigrant drummer, so refrain, and close these "explanatory notes" on red apples.

Quotation, P. S. As pretty girls are quoted, and it is generally understood that the "dear creatures" usually finish their epistles with a postscript, and their P. S.'s are usually the best part of their letters, I will try to ingratiate myself into their confidence with my postscript by mentioning the woolen sock business. Oregon furnished the California miners with a superior article of socks that were supposed to have been knit by the nimble fingers of Oregon's rosy cheeked and beautiful daughters.

I should have quoted stockings, as well as socks, but the miners of California, were mostly male-men who voted the "Old Time Whig," laterally called the Republican ticket, there being but few Democrats, and some of these oddities wore socks.

Have heard that the Oregon ladies wore stockings! don't know, and as stockings are not quoted in the foregoing indenture, will stay with my socks in this my P. S.

But to my story. Off we went, everything going as smooth and joyous as marriage bells. By the way, I have often asked myself why "bells" are mentioned instead of the newly wedded pair, as there is usually a ring to each of them (no malice intended, have "been there myself").

My verdict on this marriage bells business would be something the same as that of the Dutchman. He was elected a Justice of the Peace, in the State of Maine, after the Prohibition law took effect.

Three men were brought before him on a charge of drunkenness, the day after he had qualified. John being the first arraigned, "His Honor" asked, "Veil, you vas drunk, aind it!" John pleaded guilty. "Vot you drinks?" John said "Whisky." "Veil dot ish pad; I finds you dwenty-fife tollars und gost." Then Henry came up. "Veil, Heinery, you vas drunk too, don't he?" "Yes!" said Henry. "Veil, vot you drinks?" "Gin," was the answer. "Ish dot so? das ish petter. I finds you youst fifteen tollars und gosts." Then Jacob came up. "Veil, Yawcob, You vas drunk too, don't it?" Jacob pleaded as did his brother before him. "Veil, Yawcob, vot you drinks?" "Peach brandy and honey," was the answer. "Ish dot so? Dot vas goot, I drinks him mineself somedimes. I finds you youst notting at all und gost." So would I fine them "Youst notting at all und gost." (Bells and marriages I mean, not the men that were with me.)

Pursuing our course, nothing worthy of note occurred as we journeyed from day to day, up the Moyea and over to the Kootenia river, stopping occasionally with packers. On these occasions story-telling was in order for mutual entertainment and amusement. On one of these occasions a packer told the following about an Irish cook he had with him on one of his trips. He said that all of his men were "putting up jobs" on Pat for the purpose of hearing him talk, as he was a very witty fellow.

At one time they got Pat on to a bucking cayuse. Upon starting, the horse made one or two jumps, when off went Pat over the horse's head, alighting on his feet astride the bridle-reins, the horse's head drawn in close proximity to the seat of his pants. Someone laughingly exclaimed, "Pat, you can't ride a bit!" Pat replied: "The divil I can't a bit! Oi can roide d__n close to a bit, d'ye moind?"

Another told of a Boston man who stopped with him over night on the trail. This was Boston's first experience in the West. The cook seeing Boston watching him while he was cooking supper, sang out to one of the packers, "Give me a sweat-cloth to mix the bread on." All knowing that the cook was about to perpetrate a joke, a sweat-cloth was handed to him. After getting his sack of flour ready, he spread down the sweat-cloth near it, then dexterously exchanged it for the piece of duck-cloth, carried for the purpose of mixing bread on, and slipped the sweat-cloth to one side while Boston's head was turned. Boston asked the cook if he always used those cloths to make bread on. "Yes," Cooky replied, with the countenance of a saint. Soon supper was called; Boston sat down; the bread was passed around, Boston saying, he "seldom ever ate bread," wouldn't touch it until the owner told him, and showed him — after they had enjoyed a laugh — the cloth they carried for the purpose, and explained how the cook had made the exchange for his benefit. The explanation had the effect of changing Boston's habits, as he ate more bread than all the packers put together. He said he supposed the reason was that he had never before eaten bread that was made on a "manta."

Chapter Seventeen

From Kootenia we traveled through a broken and heavily timbered country southwesterly across Pack river and to the Semiackateen crossing of the Pen d'Oreille, at the foot of the lake; thence to the old crossing of the Spokane, about twelve miles above the falls; thence to the old crossing of Snake river, at the mouth of the Tukanon; and thence to Walla Walla.

Arriving at Walla Walla, I found my sister and brother-in-law, who had been living there a year or so, and I concluded to remain there for a time.

Winship, my brother-in-law, owned a pack-train, which I took charge of and was arranging to load for a trip to Boise, when Winship died, leaving my sister a widow with three children. I remained, and assisted her in settling up his business, then bought an interest in the pack-train, made one trip to Boise with it, and returned and laid the train up for the winter near Walla Walla.

Walla Walla was a lively place in those days. The valley was commencing to be farmed on a small scale, and two or three flour-mills had been erected. It was the winter-quarters for the most of the packers and teamsters, and was full of miners, packers, bull-whackers, mule-skinners, stockmen, sporting-men, etc., intermingled with a good sprinkling of roughs and cut-throats who had been driven out of other localities and came there to winter. To say that it was a pretty hard place at that time, is "hitting it" easy enough. "A man for breakfast" was not an uncommon morning salutation. Men were "held up," shot, stabbed, slung-shotted, clubbed, or "doped," very frequently, and the perpetrators of these jokes were in no way delicate in approaching their victims. Finally, in the early spring, the more honorable of the citizens and sojourners took the law in their own hands, and "cleaned up" the town and valley. These were denominated the "Walla Walla Vigilantes of 1864." There were some errors committed by them; they did some bad things; but I believe they thought they had cause for every movement. Their peremptory workings soon struck terror, or death, to the lawless, resulting.in great good.

In the spring of '64 I started with the train for Boise. The renegade Indians (mostly Bannacks) and the road agents (white renegades and highwaymen) that infested the Powder River and Burnt River sections were quite sportive in those days, stopping travelers, robbing stages and stealing animals, and now and then leaving a corpse in some isolated camp for a change. But stampeding and running off pack-animals seemed to be their main infatuation, which forced the packers to guard their animals closely at night while passing through that portion of the country. To give an illustration, I will relate that one night our train, with a number of others, was encamped on Burnt river. During the night an attempt was made to stampede the trains, but the animals were too well guarded. The night was dark, and those making the attempt were close to the animals when discovered. Our herdsmen, or savinaros, fired a few shots at them, mounted the riding and bell-horses, circled around and came into camp. All the other animals followed the bells — no loss at this time. Next morning we examined the ground where our herd had been approached; some blood was found on the grass, also a cap made from the mane of a black horse (this is done by stripping the skin from the top of the neck of a black-maned horse and stitching the ends together like a hat-band). This, when worn on the head of a man, resembles the long, straight, black hair of an Indian. This was evidence conclusive that the attempted stampede of the night before had been made by white men, and that they had got slightly demoralized.

In those ante-railroad days, when placer mines were found in nearly every prominent canyon in the mountains of eastern Oregon, Idaho and Montana, stages were run to all the mining towns which a wagon could reach, carrying

Holding up the stage by road agents - to the front

Wells, Fargo & Co.'s express, the U. S. mails, and passengers. Portland then being the supply depot and metropolis for the whole of the country named. These stage coaches, "mud-wagons," "gerkeys" (in fact anything that run on wheels, and had thorough-brace attachments, was called a stage) used to go eastward with a heavy merchandise express and light-pursed passengers, returning as a rule with "well-heeled" passengers and a heavy "dust" express. Though the west-bound passengers were provided with shooting irons as well as dust, and Wells, Fargo & Co.'s box was generally covered by a resolute man, who always had a quick-acting double-barreled "cannon" in his lap, which "cannon" (or express gun) was half filled with powder and buckshot, still the festive road agent would now and then join forces with one or more of his pals and "hold up" a west-bound stage, just for a picnic. The stage drivers were not generally the owners of the stages, horses, or the treasure in the box, but were salaried at from $75 to $150 per month, according to the route, teams, and speed they were expected to make, nothing in the contracts requiring them to drive over two or three cocked guns which had vigorous men at the other end of them, and as they had adopted the motto, "Better be called a coward, than a corpse," they usually made it a point to stop and rest their teams when they discovered that kind of a hedge in front of them; and the express messenger, if he allowed his "cannon" to go off at all, generally went off the coach himself at the same time. Then the driver, not being otherwise engaged at the moment, would comply with a husky request to "Throw out that box," and as a usual thing the obstructions would be removed and the stage would move on and make up the lost time. But sometimes the frisky fellows who stood behind the obstructions mentioned manifested a more inquisitive disposition, and would request the passengers to alight and form in line, *à la* military, for their inspection, which request the passengers (being tired of sitting in the coach) would eagerly comply with. While the commander held them at "attention" with a large-bored gun, his subordinates would thoroughly inspect their purses and jewelry, generally retaining such 'as "contraband." If the load was heavy they would authorize the otherwise unoccupied driver to throw off the mail sacks, take his passengers aboard and proceed on his way, while they inspected the mail bags and express box in some cool retreat.

This sort of a variety finally grew tiresome to the proprietors of the stage lines, as well as to Wells, Fargo & Co., and strenuous restrictive, mandatory and captivating measures were agreed upon between the aforementioned companies and the sheriffs of the different counties through which the stages were being run, to abate the nuisance.

In one instance, on The Dalles and Canyon City road, the stage was robbed, and subsequently two or three local stock raisers — one of whom owned a large amount of live stock — were arrested, indicted for the crime, tried, and (I think two of them) convicted and sent to the penitentiary, where they had served the State for about four years, when one "Doc" Phelps — who had in the meantime come to Dayton, W. T., loomed up with plenty of money and a stock of goods, married a nice young lady and finally settled down to farming — was arrested by Dr. Boyd (a special deputy U. S. Marshal who had been working into the merits of the case), and taken to Portland, where he confessed the "whole works" and gave the names of the guilty parties. Of course those in prison were released, but their property had all been expended during their trials. The State and U. S. Government refused to, and have never been caused to reimburse them for the losses they had innocently sustained or the humiliation and hardships they had wrongfully been compelled to endure. Phelps got part of the "swag," and having turned State's evidence, is, of course, Scott free, while his Pal is serving out a life sentence in San Quentin for another crime.

This kind of justice (?) led to the formation of impromptu vigilance committees all over the country, and now-a-days there are few stages robbed (in fact few are worth robbing). I knew of many instances of stages having been robbed, but time has effaced the most of the circumstances from my memory.

At another time I was encamped at New York ranch, on Burnt River, when a plucky fight was made between two sheriffs and two boys, who had stolen some horses — at least the owners had not consented to their taking them away. The sheriffs had followed, and found them that night lying in their blankets in the sage-brush, near the express ranch, a mile or so below my camp. Coming upon them suddenly, they pulled down the blankets, when the boys went to shooting. As there have been many versions of this affair, I will only say that at its close one sheriff was dead and the other badly wounded; one dead boy and one wounded, who was sent to the penitentiary for a long term. The wounded sheriff recovered, and the boy was some years afterward pardoned by the Governor of Oregon. He (the boy) still lives in this country, and is noted for his hospitality and genteel behavior among gentlemen, as he also is for the pluck and daring which he has shown on several occasions since his release in different personal encounters with men equally ready with "popguns." Once or twice it was announced through the Western press that he had been killed, but he continues to show up. I am informed that in his last fracas, while unarmed and making some purchases in a store, he kept walking toward the revolver that some one had pointed toward him, and, after it had emitted its last charge — others having taken effect in his anatomy — he did no more than to take the gun away from the man and arrest him. On another occasion he got into a difficulty with a sporting-man in Eastern Oregon. Both "pulled" at close quarters, and emptied their revolvers at each other, each shot taking effect, but neither of them hit the "bull's-eye." Both men were carried off by friends, and laid up under the care of the "man with the corking-iron," who managed to "stop the leakage." They were "on dock" for some weeks, and it was given out that they had each "pulled" for the last time, and must lower their flags to that "grim man with the crooked scythe." (Why the picture of a beautiful woman should be placed in front of that of the man with a scythe, and he counting the ringlets of her hair, is more than most old timers are able to explain.) While they lay at death's door, messages were being sent hourly from one to the other, bearing tokens of friendly feeling and anxiety for each other's recovery. Finally, they both recovered, and that settled* the matter between them. At another time this party prevented the robbery of a train on the Northern Pacific road by his timely appearance and plucky resistance. (I have called no names, because some of the parties are alive, and I have not asked their consent.)

Another incident of those days: On one of my trips I and my partner, Fult Johnson, remained a few days at East Bannack — or Idaho City — to settle up some business from the previous fall, sending our train out in charge of a hired man, keeping our saddle-horses and one mule with us (the mule to pack our grub and blankets). While here we fell in with a wealthy teamster named Bigsby, who owned several mule-teams that were freighting from Umatilla to Boise Basin. He had remained behind his teams for the same purpose that we had stopped behind the train, and having kept his saddle-horse to ride out, not liking to risk his dust and himself on the stage, induced us to remain over one day, so that he could accompany us back to Walla Walla. Reaching Boise City on our return homeward, we were solicited to stop over night, that two other gentlemen might join us. One of these was a tinner who had recently sold out his business and was about starting to his home in the States, via Walla Walla, Portland and 'Frisco. The other was a Jewish merchant by the name of Marks, who was on his way to 'Frisco to buy his spring stock. Each of the party carried a large sum of money. As we neared the Burnt River country we were frequently hearing of stages and trains having been stopped and robbed by the road-agents, and the further we went the oftener we heard such stories, and the more "shaky" grew the nerves of those in our party. One day, while riding up the Burnt River canyon, Johnson and I noticed that the other three had dropped back and were apparently engaged in an earnest conversation. This continued for some miles. Finally Bigsby rode up to us and asked what amount of money we had with us. After some jocular bantering we told him. He said, "I thought as much." Then he asked, "How much money do you suppose we represent, or that the five of us have with us?" I named what I supposed to be a reasonable amount. Then he gave me their "figures," which proved a much greater amount than I had imagined could possibly be in the possession of our party. They had "figured the thing down fine," and this figuring, taken with the reports we were constantly hearing from those we met, made them still more "shaky." It was generally believed that many of the ranchers or residents along this road were "mixed up with the gang," and "in with the swag." As Bigsby, Marks and the tinner had been stopping at houses over night and getting their meals there, while Johnson and myself camped out and stayed near the animals, it was concluded, after long consultation, that going to these houses with cantinas heavy with gold-dust was not a very safe procedure, as it could be plainly seen in handling them that they contained considerable wealth. Finally, on nearing Straw ranch, we arranged that Johnson and I should go ahead, and, as usual, make camp, the others to drop in later, talk with us awhile, leave their cantinas in our care, and then go to the ranch and stay there over night. In accordance with this programme, when Johnson and I got near the Straw ranch we turned a few hundred feet away from the trails to the brush that grew along the river, and went into camp. After unsaddling I spread out some blankets as though I was making my bed. While I was doing this the other three came up and engaged me in a loud conversation, at the same time dropping their cantinas, which contained nearly all the money they had with them, into the blanket. As I was holding a blanket in my hand at the time, I happened to spread it over them. After a short talk they bid us good night and went to the house for their night's entertainment. As soon as it became dark Johnson went out to stake our animals on good grass; I remained in camp and soon had the money belonging to the whole five of us cached in the brush, marking the place. Johnson returning, we ate our suppers and retired to our blankets, laying an "express-gun" (short shotgun with a large bore, which was usually loaded with a double dose of buck shot, for the benefit of whosoever might attempt to interrupt the progress of the "old-fashioned stage coach" or the returning "freighter") on each side of us. The moon shone brightly, and along toward morning I awoke and saw a man coming up the road on foot, he passed on, and was gone some time when he returned, but in returning he had left the road and came between the bushes where we lay and the road. In less than an hour he came again, this time following close along the edge of the brush. Being sure it was the same man, I was satisfied that he was trying to locate our "roosting place" for the purpose of leading others to it, so I awoke Johnson, and when the walker had got within a few steps of where we were lying, close to and in the shade of the brush, where he had not yet discovered us, I covered him with a shotgun and asked him if he wasn't lost, suggesting that he had passed our camp at least twice before within a short time. He said he thought he had got turned around, but was confident he could find his way now. I differed with him in this, and, at my peremptory suggestion, he took a seat on our *aparajos* "to await the dawning of the day," I having informed him that it would be more healthy for him if he refrained from making any unusual sign or sound, and that we would have a cup of coffee pretty soon. It occurs to me now that the muzzle of the shotgun wasn't pointed away from him, and, if my memory serves me both the hammers were up. Johnson was soon at work building a fire to prepare the coffee. I in the meantime was paying every attention to our guest, who had shown by his actions that he could hardly resist such a pressing invitation. The way of the gun didn't change, and he kept his seat. When the fire commenced burning brightly we could see a brace of revolvers and a knife in his belt. He had proven to be a very pleasant fellow from the time he took his seat. He laughed and joked, while looking down the barrels of the shotgun, as coolly as though he was calculating the size and number of the "puncturing pellets" it might contain. Just as it became broad daylight our three comrades came to camp, loaded with crackers, sardines, butter, and a large black bottle supposed to contain the "pure, unadulterated Democracy." Upon seeing our visitor, it would have been an easy matter to have "knocked their eyes off with a club." Bigsbee said, "Hunter, I see you have company?" The "company" answered, "Yes, I have found him to be the most hospitable man it was ever my good luck to run against." It being daytime we felt ourselves comparatively out of danger, and all of us took breakfast, our newly made friend being the most jovial of all.

After eating he took a good pull at the black bottle, bid us good bye, wished us a safe journey, and started back down the road which I had first seen him coming up. Our horses were soon ready, when we "raised the caches" and started. After we had traveled a few miles we were overtaken by a man who was riding a very fine horse. After he had talked with us a short time, he signified a wish to speak to me in private! So he and I dropped back behind the others and he said to me, "Your party has a large amount of money with it! you have made a scratch, and you had better skip mighty lively, for you mightn't do so well next time." Like a fool, I asked him what he meant. He answered "No matter, you fellers had better travel, and I don't wish to be seen in your company; and as I am in somewhat of a hurry to reach Auburn, I must bid you a good day." And he started off at a lively gait, up a ravine in the direction of the place he mentioned.

When I came up with the party, they asked, "What did that man want?" I replied, "It was a little matter of business. But," said I, "I'm in a great hurry to get to Walla Walla. Our animals had a good rest last night, and there will be plenty left, when they are dead, and I guess we'd better hurry!"

Well, we traveled, and arrived at our destination, perhaps worse scared than hurt. The vigilantes "cleaned out" that country subsequently.

We took another partner in with us, named Stephen Allen. Allen had lost his wife some time before, and his daughter Elizabeth (or Libby, as she was called), with her baby brother, were left in the care of my sister. But, having obtained Libby's consent, I thought I was the most capable of caring for her; so I married her. Shortly after being married, I, in company with my father-in-law and another partner and our packers, were on the trails to Boise and had encamped for a night at Washoe springs, on Snake river, at which place many other pack-trains and some ox-teams were also camped, as this was a favorite camping place. In all there were forty or fifty packers and teamsters assembled.

Just after we had turned out our stock, and while we were arranging cargo and *aparajos,* an expressman rode up; as I was acquainted with him. He said, "Here, Hunter, is something that will interest you;" handing me a newspaper that was dressed in mourning. At a glance, I saw that it contained an account of the assassination of President Lincoln, and, at an exclamation from me, all gathered around the cargo on which I had seated myself and requested me to read aloud so that all could hear, as none of them had heard of this. I proceeded to read the account as published; and, when I had finished, a man who owned an ox-team threw his hat in the air and shouted, "Hurrah for the man that killed him! I'd like a steak out of the old s_ of a ____ for my supper, or of any man that sympathizes with him."

For a minute all were painfully still. I supposed some Republican would take up this challenge, but all seemed too much stunned to do so. At last I sprung from the cargo; and to my saddle where my pistol was in my holster; jerked it out and cocking it, told him I would give him just half a minute to take that back and apologize to the gentlemen present; and that it had been my experience, that a man who wanted to eat steaks from a murdered man, had not the grit to attempt to cut one from a live one. A hasty glance told him, that if he hadn't become tired of living, he had better "crawfish," and apologize, which he did in good shape and then walked off to his wagon.

Then I found that nearly all were ready to lynch him, as the most of those present were Republicans; and, as an old friend of mine put it, "blamed black" at that. This will give the reader some idea of how the news of President Lincoln's assassination was received in many places in Oregon and Washington.

Chapter Eighteen

Late in the fall of 1864 I sent the train to Blackfoot in charge of Allen and Johnson, I remaining with the family at Walla Walla. They made the trip to Bear gulch, in Montana. On their return they followed the Pen d'Oreille lake trails, and in the severe snowstorm they lost forty-seven animals on the trail near Pack river, and finally arrived at Old Fort Taylor, at the mouth of Tukanon, on Snake river, with the remnant of the train. As I had heard of their trouble, I took two large train horses that I had, and packed one of them with clothing, boots, and a supply of provisions, and started in a storm to meet them. I had about fifty miles to go across the rolling hills by trails. When I had made about thirty miles, I came to a wayside place, called "Dobson & McKay's Ranch," the last house I would pass till I arrived at the mouth of the Tukanon. It was just night, and blowing a gale. The snow was about eighteen inches deep. It had snowed about a foot, then thawed some, turned cold, and crusted; then six or seven inches of fresh snow had fallen on this crust, and the air was full of snow. On my arrival at this ranch, I put up my horses, had supper, and was ready to turn into my blankets, when a pack-train came in from Tukanon. The men told me that Allen and Johnson were coming behind, and undoubtedly couldn't make it with their worn-out animals. I at once resaddled and packed up, and started in the storm to meet them. There were thirty or forty packers at this ranch, who assured me that no man could make the Tukanon in such a storm in the night. The snow had drifted in the trails so that it was impossible to follow them; and they said that no one but a fool or a madman would undertake it. This made no difference to me. I told them I should try it, at least; and I did. As soon as I got to the corner of a fence that surrounded a small piece of land, I found that it was out of the question for me to follow the trails; so I left them to my right, and, keeping the wind to my back, strove to travel parallel with them. By walking and leading my horses I knew I could tell if I came to the trails, as the crust had been broken by the trains recently passing.

I plodded my way for an hour or so, then turned to my right, keeping the wind on my shoulder, and in a short time found the trails, then left them as before. These maneuvers I kept up for hour after hour, and until I had made fully ten miles, when, while looking for the trail, I heard a noise which I supposed to come from some wild animal. Peering into the darkness, and through the driving snow, 'I saw what I supposed to be a wolf or mountain lion (cougar); I stepped to my saddle-horse, took my pistol out of my hostler, and was about to fire, when the thought occurred to me to "hallo" before shooting. I did so, and to my surprise was answered by a man's voice near by. I recognized the voice as that of my father-in-law and partner. It was his horse I had seen, and the noise I had heard was the whinny of the horse.

I found Allen sitting on the mechillas of his saddle, exhausted, while the horse had given out. Examining his feet, I found they were not frozen, but his boots were so worn that they were filled with snow around his socks. I strove to put on him an extra pair that I had brought along, but he was so chilled that he couldn't help me.

I caught up a blanket and wrapped strips of it around his feet, put over them my own buffalo over-shoes, then helped him mount my riding-horse and started back for Dobson & McKay's ranch. Knowing my horses would follow the trails when headed for home, I followed on foot, whipping Allen's worn-out horse along. In a short time, Allen declared he couldn't stand it any longer, but must get off and walk. I helped him off, when he staggered a few steps and fell, saying he could not walk. Then came the "tug of war;" as he was a man that weighed over 200 pounds, and was so badly chilled that he could not help himself a particle, it proved to be quite a job for me to help him on to the horse again. I finally succeeded; then I wound blankets around him, and tied them and him to the saddle; took the bridle off the horse; took out a flask of brandy that I had brought along, and had him drink all he could of it, as I told him he would stay where he was till we reached the ranch. He thought I would freeze myself, as I had but thin calf boots on my feet after giving him my overshoes. I told him I could make it by keeping close up to the horses which broke the trails, and kept the wind off me to some extent.

The wind and snow cut like a knife, but by running, whipping, and taking an occasional pull at the flask, I got along finely. I gave Allen a "dose" semi-occasionally. In the course of an hour Allen said he was warm, and would get off and walk, and let me ride awhile; but I thought I wouldn't trust him off again, and I knew that if I stopped running and walking, I would soon chill so that I wouldn't be able to help either of us; so on he staid till we reached the ranch, which we did near morning. On our arrival at the ranch, we awoke the proprietor, who took care of our stock, and we sat down by the stove. Some one of the packers asked Allen where he was from, and he told them Tuka-non. They asked if he had met a man riding a large horse. He, not thinking of me, replied no. The packer said, "Well, I pity that d___d fool!" Being told at the breakfast table, that I was the person he had spoken of, he said he had no apology to offer for his past remarks, as he believed no one but a fool or an idiot could have done what I did in such a storm and night.

I accepted the apology, for I could plainly see by the countenances of most of those present that they indorsed his sentiments, and that in declining the apology, I was liable to get a worse instead of a better one. Next day, the storm having abated, I went on to Tukanon with the provisions and clothing for our men, Allen going with the others to Walla Walla, where I arrived soon afterward with the train, a Chinook wind having taken the snow off.

The next spring we bought some more horses and mules, and Allen re-turned to Blackfoot, where he opened a trading-post, leaving Johnson to run the business at that end of the route. He made a few trips that summer and fall, I remaining at Walla Walla. Winter coming on, he wintered the train at Horse prairie (or Horse plain), in Montana. The next spring he went out pro-specting with others, struck a prospect in the mountains north of Pen d' Oreille lake, named the creek "Libby" for his daughter (my wife). He came down to the Pen d'Oreille with our animals for supplies and tools to work with, and on his return, in company with three or four others, was killed by a marauding band of Indians, as were all of his comrades except a man named Joe Herrin, who was shot through the breast. He crawled off and hid in a drift till after the Indians left, then crawled out and kept himself secreted for twenty-one days on this wild mountain-stream, living on huckleberries, until a search-party came out and found him. They had left eight men in the camp when they went out, and had got within a few miles of the camp on their re-turn, when they were ambushed. The other eight men heard the firing and came out, and told what they believed, which afterward proved to be true, except that Herrin was not killed.

Upon this news arriving at Walla Walla, I, in company with my brother Wil-liam and three others, started for the scene, about 300 miles distant. We had with us a man who had served throughout the Rebellion as a rebel officer. He was a large man, and about thirty years of age. His name was Robinson. An-other's name was Thompson, and the other's Dougett. Robinson was the life of the party. He told stories of his services and adventures during the Rebel-lion in which he had taken part, picturing himself throughout as a very nerv-ous man. So much did he do this, that my brother, Dougett and Thompson had concluded that he was a consummate coward, and intimated as much to him on more than one occasion. He would laugh it off. We traveled as rapidly as possible across the country to Spokane, and on to the Semiackiteen crossing of the Pen d'Oreille; across Pack river and to the Kootenia river, then followed up this stream to the mouth of Libby creek. Here we had to swim our horses, and construct a raft of logs on which to carry over our provisions, guns, saddles, etc.

The timber was thick on the opposite side of the river, and we suspected there might be Indians in it awaiting us; so we concluded it best for two or three of us to go over first on the raft, and the others to remain watching, and covering us with their guns; then, if all was safe, to swim the horses over.

My brother and myself volunteered to go over on the raft, as we had had experience on water, and were good swimmers, knowing that if we were fired upon we would have to take to the water, Robinson was asked to go on the raft with us, but positively refused to do so, for he said he was sure that the timber on the opposite side was full of Indians, and he had too much respect for his hide to risk it in any such a way; but he would come over with the horses, when we ascertained for a fact that there were no Indians on the other side. He went out on the flat to look after the horses. Just as my brother and I were pushing the raft out into the water we heard a whoop and a splash near us. A moment later we saw an auburn head pop up some hundreds of feet out in the river, and start for the other shore. It was Robinson; swimming overhanded, his head and shoulders protruding out of the water, and by the time we had our raft well out in the stream he was running through the woods on the other side, naked, and making them ring with his yells. He was at the shore to assist us in landing the raft, then into the river and across again, and assisting the others in swimming the horses over. He said he "got scared," and couldn't help swimming over, fearing we might leave him. From this time on no one accused him of cowardice, no matter what stories he told of his exploits, but we were sure that whatever part he played in the late "unpleasantness" on the Potomac was a brave and generous one to his comrades.

We went on up Libby creek to the scene of the massacre of Allen and his party and found Allen's grave where the Indians had laid him after killing him. It had been fixed up subsequently by his comrades. And as it was out of the question for me to bring his remains out to Walla Walla for more decent interment, we left him in his lonely grave on the creek he had named for his loved daughter, my wife —

Brave Allen! in your mountain grave asleep,
    Wild animals are your only bards;
Your children far distant away, do weep
    For their murdered father. Oh! God! 'tis hard
To be doubly orphan'd by a murderer's hand,
    Left alone, penniless, and deeply in debt,
As they mourn for their murdered in a far-off land, —
    They are taught to believe they will meet him yet!

133

From the scene of the massacre we went on up Libby creek to what was called "Discovery," where a great many men had assembled, as the news had spread far and wide; and it was supposed that Libby creek was a rich camp. Here I stayed a few days; but, realizing that my family, as well as my little orphan brother-in-law were wholly dependent upon me, I had to make my stay short. I was told by Herrin — the man who was wounded, and escaped from the Indians — that six or seven of the Indians had ferried them across the Kootenia river; came to the camp the night preceding the massacre; took supper with them, and told them that the Blackfeet were near them; that they were bad, and would kill them (meaning Allen's party). After dark they started for their camp, as they said; but, getting off a little distance, took cover behind trees and opened fire on the camp. Allen and his comrades took to trees and returned the fire with two shotguns and their pistols. Firing was kept up till nearly morning. Lacking and Herrin frequently urged Allen to escape in the night up the creek to the rest of the party, which they could easily have done in the darkness; but Allen said: "No; I'd rather die than return to my partners and children without a cent, and tell them I had run and left all we had." Near morning the Indians drew off, as all believed, and the little party were packing up, after it became light. As Allen and Herrin were putting a whipsaw on to the last animal a sudden fire was opened on them from the trees near by. At the first volley Allen fell dead, and Herrin was wounded. The others ran away, but were followed by the Indians, and killed some distance off. While the Indians were after the others, Herrin crawled off and hid under a drift, as before related; saw the Indians bury Allen, and destroy what property they didn't take away. The remains of the others were left where they fell, a prey to the wolves; and the first parties who came in after the tragedy found and buried some portions of their remains.

Thus another party of hardy pioneers and miners, after overcoming many hardships, sufferings, and terrible privations, were cowardly butchered by the "noble red man" — the wards of our government — far from their homes and friends. Another sacrifice had been made; more brave men had laid down their lives while striving to open and develop our new country and our mines. Afterward these Indians were followed to British Columbia. The British authorities turned them over to the miners, who brought them back across the line, and — well, they contracted a "bad neck disease," as Artemus Ward used to say. More *good* Indians.

I returned to Walla Walla to my family, and six or seven thousand dollars of indebtedness, without a dollar to cover the amount. By the assistance of Baker & Boyer of Walla Walla, who were my principal creditors, I bought a blacksmith shop (my father was a blacksmith), and, as this was a good trade in those days, I was enabled within a few years to liquidate the most of my indebtedness. Then I traded my property for a ranch, and tried to make a farmer of myself. After getting eighty acres in cultivation, I was offered a good price for it, so I sold it, and finished paying myself out of debt. There being but few settlers, and plenty of good land thirty miles northeast of Walla Walla, I removed to the front. Near what is now the thriving town of Dayton I took up a ranch, and proceeded to put it in shape. I landed on this claim in November, with my wife, four children, and a little brother-in-law, an old wagon, a crippled horse, a Cayuse (Indian) mare, a two-year-old filly, a set of tools, and about three hundred dollars in cash. Out of debt and as happy as a millionaire, I got a few teams to haul the logs from the mountains, ten or twelve miles distant, and with these built a cabin fourteen by sixteen feet in size, and settled down, "a bloated land-owner."

Having nothing in particular to do at home this winter, I traveled on foot through the snow and mud and sold trees for a nurseryman. In the spring I engaged in blacksmithing and improving my farm, and I made a good one of it, if it was Northern Pacific land.

Chapter Nineteen

Those who located on the rich farming lands in the vicinity of Dayton were poor — very poor. Yet they possessed the gift of stick-to-it-a-tiveness, as a ride through that section will prove to you. Money being very scarce, they had to figure closely to make both ends meet and improve their lands.

While I was thus engaged in brain and muscular work, I attended the organization of the Dayton Grange of the Patrons of Husbandry, and became Master of the Grange.

Soon afterward I assisted in organizing the State Grange of Oregon and Washington, where I was made its lecturer; but, as the Patrons were too poor to pay my expenses in the field, and as I was poor indeed, I failed to make many speeches in their behalf, which was, probably, the cause of their somewhat long success. I had also been appointed a deputy under Mr. Clarke, the First Master of the State Grange. I went to work, and in mid-winter made more Patrons and established more subordinate lodges than all the other deputies in the field. Some of the would-be leaders concluded that I was too industrious, and I was brought up for trial on three counts: First, for charging too much for organizing subordinate lodges; second, for telling a sister that a demit had been granted her; and, third, for being a grossly immoral character.

As to the first accusation, I proved that I had never charged a cent, but had accepted such sum as was voted to me by the lodge I organized.

To the second charge I pleaded guilty of having told the sister that the grange had granted her a demit; and an examination of the secretary's books showed that she had been granted a demit, but the secretary had failed to notify her of the fact.

To the third charge not a voice claimed that they had ever seen or known of any "gross immorality," or of my having been disorderly, or other than gentlemanly in my deportment. But, on the other hand, they had seen my persecutors so drunk that they were laid on the "cooler" tired.

The result was, that instead of working for nothing and boarding myself, I was made their agent at $75 per month and expenses paid, and was authorized to build a $10,000 flour-mill, and to build warehouses at the mouth of Tukanon at a cost of $6,000 more, which I did. Finally my wages were raised.

While I was building the first warehouse for the grangers at Grange City (as we had christened the site of old Fort Taylor) I had in my employ as man of all work an auburn-haired "cuss" who, like many other pioneers, had seen better days, and was now "clear down at the heels." He was about twenty-eight years old, very talkative, and a fine book-keeper; I shall call him "Rook" for short as I don't wish to give him away among friends. As the reader has already been told, I never had any educational advantages, so I made use of Rook's talent, and he taught me how to keep my books. He told a good story sometimes of his adventures, scrapes and experience, especially alluding to his fighting qualifications. He being red-headed, and as men with "carrotty" hair are generally supposed to be bad, we treated Rook with the utmost respect for a long time, and by our general comportment gave him to understand that we believed every word he said.

Among other stories he told for our entertainment and terror was, that once in his life he found himself in the city of Portland, flat broke (this we were eager to believe but dared not say so) and that he went to work as a longshoreman and was soon transferred to a barge of which George Sampson was captain. Once when they were being towed to Astoria with a load of wheat, our sorrel-topped friend got it into his head that he knew more than his captain, which led them into a discussion, and finally, as Rook told it, he "pulled his derringer," and stuck it to Samp's ear, whereupon the captain apologized. Rook said he had earned all the money he needed, so he resigned when they got into port. I had about a dozen men working on the building at the time and they all believed this to be about a fair statement of the affair.

A few days after he had related this adventure, we discovered smoke rising over the low hills down the river, indicating the approach of the first steamboat of the season. As I had never had any experience in forwarding or shipping, and knew that Rook was a first-class business man, I proposed to use his talent some more on this occasion, and asked him to superintend the shipment of the first load for my enlightenment.

We stood on the bank as the boat neared us. And as she swung in close to the landing the captain asked me how many tons I would have for him to take on his down trip. I told him, and he steamed on up the stream, when Rook poked me in the ribs and said, "George, do you see that fellow on the bow, with the long black beard?" "Yes," I answered, "What of him?" "Why, that's Sampson." "What, the fellow you made apologize on the barge that time?" "Yes," said he, "Bet ye'r life that's him." I made no remarks; neither did any of the rest of the men who had heard what Rook told. But I couldn't help thinking that Rook was a better judge of the man than I was, for I should never have thought of shoving a pistol into his face on short acquaintance. However, this was all good so far. But the next day the boat returned and landed to take on the wheat and flour. As we had no wharf, they had to run the wheat up a gang-plank that was very steep for trucking. Sampson stood about midway of the run, and as the boys came along with their truck loads he would help them up by shoving on their loads. Rook being a great fellow for newspapers (he was reporter for several), took one of the trucks to run while the man he relieved went on board to hunt up some papers for him. I had been up in the office arranging receipts with the purser, and was standing just inside the companionway, when Rook passed Sampson, who was acting mate and pilot, and asked, "Sampson, do you think I can run one of these fellows?" The captain straightened himself to his full height (over six feet two), put his hand on his hip, and in a low, sarcastic tone said, "Well, if you can, you can do a d___d sight better than you did when you worked for me, sir." Rook went on; not another word was said.

The boat being loaded, steamed on down the river, her destination being Celilo. That night at supper Rook was dishing up one of his blood-and-thunder stories, and, just as he had got his man in a tight place, I imitated the whistle of a steamboat. He stopped, and looking me square in the eye, said, "You heard what Samp said to me, did you?" I said, "That's what I heard." "Well," said he, "you didn't hear me say anything back, did you?" I said, "No, not much." "Bet your last dollar," said he, "I'm better educated than to do that! Why, that long-legged, black-eyed son-of-a-sea-cook would have converted me into an angel before my wings had fairly sprouted." This part of his story we all endorsed.

At the time of building the warehouses mentioned above, we had among us one Joe Courtney (Colorado Joe), a naturally bright and musical fellow, and a clever fellow when out of liquor. Joe had been roving since he was a boy, and had gained considerable knowledge of the world. Although he was born and raised an American, he had, by association, adopted a vernacular peculiar to himself. [But here I must mention that, there being no houses near where we were at work, we had to camp out and do our own kitchen and chamber-work, and were short of dishes.] Joe drank his coffee out of a frying-pan. One evening, while we were partaking of our frugal meal, Rook asked Joe what made the scar under his eye. Joe said, as he passed the frying-pan, grasping it by the bowl instead of the handle: "Gimme s'more dat swill (coffee), 'n' I'll give ye all de fine p'ints 'bout dat optic." After swallowing half a pan of coffee he continued: "Ye see, I had a tie ticket on de C. P., from Colfax to Sacramento —" "What's a tie ticket, Joe?" "W'y, ye snide, dat means I wasn't flush, 'n' had to hit de ties wid my soles. Wa'l, I uz stampin' along, 'n' purty soon I sees a passel o' biscuit shooters (girls) playin' dis yer Injin billiards, whar dey punch de ball wid a mall, 'n' I skinned over de fence 'n' sot down on de root o' de tree to larn de game. Wa'l, purty soon one o' dem caliker-kivered hairpins knocks a ball close to me, 'n' den nudder un picks up 'er ball 'n' comes 'n' freezes it ont' de fust un, 'n' puts 'er foot on't, den she tries to make a six quishin shot, but she miss-qued 'n' caromed on dis yer side-lamp o' mine wid 'er mall." "What did you do, Joe?" "Me? Wa'l, 'bout the fust thing I done uz to dig de ground out'n m'ears 'n' eyes 'n' git up; den I tole dat she-rooster if I didn't know no more 'bout dat game'n she did, I'd rack my cue."

At that time the mouth of Tukanon was the the handiest and nearest shipping point for Columbia County and the western portion of what is now Garfield County; and the building of warehouses at this point (which we christened Grange City, the night we arrived there to commence work) was regarded at the time as an experiment. But it was believed that it would lead to the navigation of Snake river for at least nine months in the year whereas previously boats had only been run during the high water — about three months in the. year.

The hopes of those who started the enterprise were fully realized, and it was soon demonstrated that instead of three months, the river could be navigated for nine or ten months, and instead of 120-ton boats those of 450 tons capacity could be run a part of the time, and were used until the O. R. & N. Co.'s railroad was completed to Riparia, above the most dangerous of the rapids. Then the road having tapped the grain-producing section — which had theretofore been tributary to Grange City — and furnished more rapid transit to the same points, virtually killed the river trade for a distance of over two hundred miles. About half a million bushels of grain is annually shipped by this railroad, which is raised in the section for which Grange City was formerly the only accessible shipping point. But of course the country has made rapid strides in development since the advent of the railroad.

While canvassing among the grangers and business men of the section named, for means with which to build the first warehouse at Grange City, in 1875, and since then — as I have had occasion to pass over different portions of this country and visit the thriving towns — I couldn't help noticing the changes that have taken place since the Indian war of 1855-56, where, but a few years before, we volunteers while marching in phalanx, had "kept a weather eye out" for the fiendish redskin, and where, six years afterward, the tired foot-traveler rolled himself up in his blankets for a night's quiet slumber alone, we used to keep out pickets and a double guard while dressing wounds and burying comrades — the victims of the "noble red man," as the latter-day Indian-loving cranks are pleased to call them. The "arid wastes" were soon known as the "elysian fields of the stock raiser," and later the cow and sheep retreated before the plow and the barbed wire fence. Homes and hamlets now dot the once arid wastes, and when this country is thoroughly advertised every acre of it will be utilized and made to yield good profits to the thousands of husbandmen who are now awaiting tangible proofs of its remarkable resources and its health-giving climate.

The remnants of the different Indian tribes have profited by experience, and are gradually adopting the ways of the "Bostons," to their own advancement and comfort and the peace and dignity of these United States and Territories.

The old maxim, "Spare the rod, and spoil the child," is, I am happy to know, fast getting into disuse among all nations and races; but it frequently comes handy, and should be "filed away for future reference." Even at this writing I imagine that Uncle Sam ought to keep it in sight.

Until the fall or winter of 1862 the greater portion of Idaho and all of eastern Oregon was embraced in the County of Wasco, State of Oregon, with the county seat at The Dalles, and men lived for years here who had to send 500 miles for their mail, and also traveled that distance to vote. Now there are ten counties in eastern Oregon and five in that portion of Idaho which was taken from Wasco County, and at each session of the respective Legislatures new counties are formed, and the post-offices are only ten or fifteen miles apart. I mention these points as suggestive of the development which has just commenced. Being more familiar with eastern Washington, I give more proofs of our civilization.

Chapter Twenty

This brings me down to the Nez Perce Indian War of 1877.

Early in the summer of 1877 the news was hurriedly passed through the eastern part of Washington Territory — which had for twenty-one years been a peaceful country — that the Nez Perce Indians, who had hitherto been friendly and courteous to the whites, had gone on the warpath in the northern portion of our neighboring Territory of Idaho, and their terrible war-whoop was resounding throughout Camas prairie and adjacent sections. The rusty scalping knife was performing its awful work. The partially civilized "noble red man" had doffed his religion and clothed himself in all the regalia and colors of his species. With his natural fiendishness and treachery, he had gone forth with gun and torch, and was killing, ravishing, burning or destroying every person or thing he found in his path. The few settlers of that portion of the country who had not been killed had collected at either Mt. Idaho or Grangeville, at the edges of Camas prairie, and fortified themselves as best they could. Many defenseless settlers with their wives and children had been ruthlessly murdered before they had time to avoid their danger.

It appears that Joseph, the head war-chief of the Nez Perces, had, on taking the war-path, planned the murder of the settlers on Camas prairie, Salmon river and White Bird creek (the latter named for one of the war-chiefs). When this news reached Dayton, the county seat of Columbia County, W. T., a company of forty-five young men was immediately organized, elected their officers, and sent for me, for they had made me their captain. They said they would go to the assistance of the north Idaho people if I would lead them.

When this transpired I was some forty miles away, attending to some business for the Patrons of Husbandry; and had not heard of the outbreak until the messenger met me one morning about 8 o'clock. Together we hastened to Dayton, arriving there about 3 P.M., where we found the boys rushing around, securing horses and other things needed for the trip.

On my arrival I was warmly received by all. The command was tendered me, and I accepted it. It took us but a short time to secure horses, saddles, and the other articles required; for I told the boys I was sure that the government officers would be glad to receive and arm us. Late in the evening we moved out about seven miles, and encamped near my farm for the night. I visited my wife and family and took leave of them. The following morning we resumed our march for Lewiston, 55 miles east, where we arrived that night.

The next morning I tendered our services to Colonel Spurgeon, the representative of the government there, General O. O. Howard, the commander of the Department of the Columbia, having gone to the front, leaving Colonel Spurgeon to forward men and supplies, as fast as they arrived at Lewiston, by steamer or otherwise.

On presenting myself to the colonel I was received in a most courteous manner. He asked me whether I wished to cooperate with the United States troops, or go independently. I told him I was not able to arm, equip and maintain forty-five men in the field, nor were any of my command able to do so; that I proposed to attach my company to General Howard's forces, and to operate in accordance with his orders, and requested him to fit out my company. He said General Howard would be glad to have us with him, and that within a day or two he would have plenty of needle-guns and ammunition up from Fort Vancouver; that on their arrival he wished that I, with my command, would escort some army-officers up to General Howard on Camas prairie.

There had come to Lewiston, from Pomeroy (a small town, twenty-five miles east of Dayton) a company of about twenty-five men, under command of one Elliott as captain, and E. T. Wilson as lieutenant. This company proposed to act independently of the United States troops, and had asked Colonel Spurgeon for arms before I reached Lewiston with my command. On my arrival some of the men wished to consolidate, but the scheme failed. This gave the mischief-maker an opportunity and pretext for causing trouble. Of this trouble I shall speak more fully at the proper time. The evening after my arrival Colonel Spurgeon requested me to furnish a guide for a party of United States officers who wished to visit Lapwai, some twelve miles distant. As it was believed there were Indians all round and through the country, they thought it best to go at night. I told the colonel that I would go myself. About dark five or six officers, the colonel among the rest, assembled at the hotel at which I stopped. When my horse was brought to me the colonel asked: "Had you not better take one of our cavalry horses? We in all likelihood will have to ride fast, and may be attacked, and that small horse of yours will not be able to keep up." I thanked him, and said I thought the little horse would do. This small horse was a half-blood "Rifleman," as white as a snowball, and a

The scout and his little wonder

perfect beauty; could run like the wind and had the endurance of a grey-hound, but he wouldn't have weighed over 950 pounds, and as he stood alongside of the powerful cavalry horses he looked like a poor excuse to cope with those to be ridden by the officers, so far as speed and endurance were concerned.

All being ready, we started, riding in couples. The officer riding by my side proffered me a cigar, which I accepted. Dropping my bridle-reins over the horn of my saddle, I struck a match and was lighting my cigar, when my horse saw a pool of water ahead of us in the road, and as quick as a flash he was fifty feet from the road, and as quickly back by the side of the officer's horse. This was an old prank of his, and from long riding him I was used to his pranks. I had put in almost all my lifetime riding wild or tricky horses, hence he never shook me in the saddle. As I paid no attention to this little joke, Colonel Spurgeon remarked, "I see we have ridden a little ourself." "A little," was my reply. On over the high and almost level table-lands that lie southeast of Lewiston we rode at a rapid pace, and until we came to Lapwai creek, a mile below the fort. Here, as we had a level and smooth bottom be-fore us, I proposed that we speed our horses. All agreed, and away we went. At the first jump "Whitey" took the lead, and rapidly left the party behind. On reaching the fort, we transacted such business as the officers came for. We remounted, and on our way back to Lewiston the officers were admiring my small horse. They said he was a "little wonder." I told them if we got into a fight, they would find that the Indians had hundreds of "little wonders," and a whole army of squaws and boys to bring up fresh "wonders" to replace those tired and crippled. The most — if not all — of these officers had served through the rebellion, but this was their first Indian campaign, and they were anxious to have me tell them of my former adventures on the frontier. They had been told of many of them before I reached Lewiston.

Thus we rode along in pleasant converse, exchanging experiences; I telling of frontier-life — they of the many battles in which they had taken part dur-ing the great rebellion.

I must say that a more sociable party than these gentlemen made, it was never my pleasure to pass a night in the saddle with.

On the arrival of the steamer, my company was armed with 50-calibre needle-guns, and furnished sufficient rations to last them to Camas prairie.

We started on a forced march for the front immediately, in company with a small body of mounted soldiers and officers, among the latter being Captain (now Major) Babbitt of the Ordnance department. We moved on as swiftly as possible to Lapwai, and thence up and over Craig's mountain. As the snow was fast going off these mountains, the swales and flats were very miry on the Camas prairie side. This part of the route we traveled in the night and in a snowstorm. While crossing a swale about eight miles west of the Cotton-wood House, at the edge of Camas prairie, word was passed along the line to the front where I was riding that some of the men in the rear had mired their

horses and were calling for help. I halted the command, and quickly returning, found that Major Babbitt's horse — a heavy one — had mired down, and
in floundering around had rolled completely over his rider before he could
extricate himself from the saddle. We soon had man and horse out of the
mire. The major was severely bruised, wet to the skin, and a perfect mud-
ball. I consoled him by saying I was glad it was he instead of I, as he could
report the damage done "in action," and draw a new suit; while had it been I,
it would have made a total wreck of me, as I had no "changes" with me and
no *fat uncle* to draw on. Again we mounted, and in company with the major I
soon regained the front. As the majoz was chilled through and badly hurt,
and it was storming — half snow and half rain — I saw that we must get him
to a place where he could rest, warm and dry himself. Taking a few men with
me I turned the command over to my lieutenant (Watrous), and we pushed
on for the Cottonwood House, some miles ahead, leaving the rest of the
command to follow as fast as they could, encumbered as they were with
pack-animals loaded with provisions, ammunition, camp equipage, etc. We
reached the house, having to carry the major the last mile or two, or support
him on his horse. On our arrival we soon had a roaring fire and got the major
in a comfortable place; then I went out, stationed my pickets, and anxiously
awaited the arrival of the rest of the command, as we were now on the
ground of the first demonstrated outbreak, later the scene of battles by both
soldiers and volunteers. Some time after our arrival they all came in, tired,
hungry and wet. The rear-guard reported that they had seen a large body of
Indians on ponies in a gulch to the right of the road, about half a mile back. I
took a few of my best-mounted men, and went back, only to find a band of
Indian horses, quietly feeding in the gulch mentioned. Returning, we found
plenty of hay for our horses. We soon had a feast prepared that the tired and
hungry boys did full justice to, and even Uncle Sam's fat officers remarked
that they couldn't remember ever having eaten a meal they relished so much.

The rest of the night passed without incident worthy of note.

Early the next morning — Major Babbitt feeling able to ride — we crossed
the prairie, and over the hills, to the head of the White Bird creek where we
found soldiers under General Howard burying the remains of those who had
been killed a few days before, in Colonel Perry's command. It appears that
Colonel Perry, with his command, accompanied by a few citizens from Mt.
Idaho, had come on to White Bird creek to look after the hostiles, and were
found themselves by the Indians, who opening on them from the rock-
crowned mounds with so withering a fire that their ranks were decimated
like snow before a furnace.

To whirl, and retreat toward Mt. Idaho was the word. This, from the first
fire, was a complete stampede. The few survivors came straggling in, one by
one, after riding a distance of about twenty miles pursued by the now jubi-
lant savages, who overtook many, and quickly dispatched their victims, continuing the pursuit nearly to Grangeville.

Here Colonel Perry lost thirty-three of his command, killed on this retreat, and left the dead to the tender mercies of the hospitable wards of our government. The scene of battle, as I viewed it, showed that there had not been any stand made after they were attacked; as here and there would be found a dead soldier, who had been overtaken and killed. There were a few instances which proved that some of the soldiers, after being unhorsed, got to some rocks and made a gallant fight before they were finally dispatched, as the empty shells lying around their dead bodies testified.

These dead soldiers were buried where they had fallen, as they were not in a state to be moved to a more suitable burial ground.

About four o'clock we reached headquarters, on White Bird creek, General Howard having established his camp for the night on the bottom, in front of the brush. My command coming up, I moved past his left flank and into the brush. Finding a small glade free from brush, we commenced to unsaddle our tired animals, when an officer approached and inquired for Captain Hunter. I was pointed out to him as I was assisting in unpacking a horse. He rode up to me, and said it was the wish of General Howard that my company should take a position for the night on his extreme left, fronting the bushes. To receive orders was to obey them. Saddling up again, we moved out to the chosen ground, and were again preparing to relieve our horses of their loads and saddles, when the "one-armed hero of Gettysburg" rode up, accompanied by some of his officers, and asked for me. As I approached he introduced himself. I then reported myself and command, and formally tendered our services. He said he was glad to have us with his command; that he had heard of me as having had much experience in Indian warfare. He said he would designate Lieutenant Wood as the officer to supply the wants of my company.

He then asked my object in going into the brush to camp; I asked in return if he believed there was any likelihood of our being attacked during the night. He said he thought it more than likely. "If so," I said, "The Indians will be either in the brush or on those mounds, and I had much rather they would try to drive my command out of the brush than to have to drive them out."

The general frankly said: "I have not had much experience in Indian warfare. You can take up your quarters for the night wherever you choose. From what has been told me I have confidence in your judgment, and will leave the upper creek for your company to guard and protect. About sundown we will visit the outposts and see how they are arranged." Then, returning my salute, he rode back to his headquarters, accompanied by his officers. After preparing our camp I went out about half a mile to place picket guards on the upper creek. We dug a rifle-pit on the opposite side of the creek from the camp, on the side of a gulch. I gave the pickets their instructions, then went down the gulch, about half way to the creek, and posted three others. In the brush at the bottom of the creek I left three more.

Near sundown the general with his staff came to my camp. I joined them, and we visited the pickets. Reaching my first pickets the general asked one of the men what they would do in case of an attack on their post. The answer was, "Fire and retreat to the post below, where there are three others; and in case of firing on the creek, repair at once to the post attacked." We then visited those in the gulch, who said they were, on the arrival of those from above them, to fall back to the creek bottom, to the three there, and with them hold out as long as they could, or until the company came to their relief.

The general expressed himself as being well satisfied with the arrangements. The other side of the creek was left to the care of the soldiers, as was also the creek-bottom below the camps (the bluffs on each side being so steep and rugged, that we didn't fear an attack from there).

Nothing in particular occurred this night, except that a young lieutenant mistook one of his guards for an Indian and shot him, while out relieving the guard. I think he killed his man, but the full particulars I have forgotten.

This creek was the scene of most of the depredations of the outbreak. At this writing I am unable to give the names of any considerable number of the sufferers, but suffice it to say it was distressing to see the beautiful homes that had been destroyed, and their owners ruthlessly murdered at the hands of those they had fed and treated well on their visits.

Morning approaching, the command moved on for Salmon river, a few miles distant. Here I will state that on our coming up to headquarters we found Captain Tom Page in command of a small company of Walla Walla men. They had rendered valuable service to General Howard up to the time of our arrival. Captain Page was an old timer — one of the earliest settlers in the Walla Walla valley, well adapted to Indian warfare, and would have done good service if he had remained; but his command was mostly composed of business-men from Walla Walla, and could not well remain longer away. So, as it was believed that Howard had now a sufficient force to cope with the hostiles, his command was discharged, and he and they returned home.

As my command had been on a forced march from Lewiston to this place, we were left in camp for some hours, but the men becoming restless, I moved on to the front. We could see Indians on the opposite side of Salmon river, and it was believed that they were strongly fortified, and would give us battle upon our crossing the river. Reaching the summit of the high hills that overlooked the river, I dismounted my men, left a few in charge of the horses, and with the others ran swiftly down the steep hills to some cabins that had been built years before by miners. We then scouted up the river to where the White Bird trails struck it. Here I found Howard's headquarters already established, and was soon joined by those I had left in charge of the horses. Having obtained permission from General Howard, I, with a part of my company, went up the river a mile or two, to where one Mason and others had been killed and burned up in their cabins. My recollection is, that in all there were three killed and burned here. We collected all of the remains we could find (there was little left but the feet, which were incased in boots), and buried them. We found an old skiff that had been split in two, which we managed to patch up; then we made paddles out of boards, and I and one of the boys paddled it down the river to headquarters, the rest of the boys running along the bank, ready to cover us in case of an attack.

On reaching the main force I proposed to cross over the river and make a reconnaissance, but for some time was restrained by the general, who said it was too dangerous a mission for any one to undertake, until all could, cross.

Chapter Twenty-One

Upon consultation with General Howard, and after I had told him that I should like to know what was ahead of me, before attempting to cross my company (for, as we had but one small boat, we were liable to be cut off in detail on the other side). The general finally gave his consent for me to try it. I asked any one that wanted a little fun to accompany me on this little walk on the opposite side of the river; but as we could plainly see the smoke arising over the hills from the burning houses, some four miles distant, where it was believed the Indians were in force, not one of the men volunteered to accompany me.   There was a young man in my company by the name of John Long. He was stout and active, and I believed he would "stand fire," if necessary. He was first sergeant of the company. I told him that I might need at least one man on this scout, and I thought he could run as fast as I could; and it was my peremptory order that he should accompany me. "Well, captain," he replied, "I have told you that I would obey orders, and I'll go with you; but I don't hanker after the honor!"

We were about to step into the boat which had been manned by soldiers, to set us across the river, when a gentleman by the name of Randall, who had been looking after his stock and was now with the command, came up to me and said, "Captain Hunter, if I had a gun you shouldn't go on this scout with but one man."

A square look at him told me that he was a brave and cool man. I asked my orderly sergeant (Crawfood) to lend me his needle gun and belt for the evening, which he did. I handed the gun and belt to Randall, saying that I liked his looks, and would be glad of his company. Randall was afterwards captain of a small company of volunteers that was organized at Mt. Idaho. More of him later. Taking General Howard's field glass, we (Randall, Long and myself), was set over the river, and started up the side of the mountain toward the creek, where the smoke was curling up from the burning buildings.

Gaining a short distance from the river, I stopped by some rocks, and gave my directions for advancing and my plan of retreat in case of being attacked.

This was after we had studied the ground to be passed over ahead of us, and closely scoured every object that would secrete an Indian. I was to proceed ahead a few hundred yards, or till I could find another bunch of rocks; then stop, and scan everything ahead as well as each side of me. Randall and Long were to stay where they were, till I gave them the sign to advance,

which would be my rising and starting forward; then they were to move rapidly to the place last left by me, and lie down and stay there till I signaled
them to again move forward. In case of an attack, they were to stay where
they were till I reached them, when they were to retreat to the last place they
had made a pause at, and hold as before, I covering their retreat, and they in
turn covering mine; and so on till we reached the river bank again.

Slowly on we went as described, from cover to cover, for some two hours,
our every move being watched by General Howard's signal officer, who reported to him our progress, as we were in view of headquarters for some
miles as we proceeded. On reaching the summit, we stopped for some time,
closely scanning the bottom and burning house, we could see several beeves
as they lay, having just been killed, and meat stuck upon sticks, cooking before a fire, not far from the burning house. There was a small field near the
house in which was wheat and a fine garden growing; the wheat was just
heading out. As we could not see any Indians after scanning every object that
would cover a foe, with our glass, I raised and prepared to move down the
mountain to the field and cabin, turning to give some instructions to Randall
and Long. Long said, "Captain, you are spreading it on rather thick." I saw
from Long's and Randall's faces that they fully realized that this was a daring
and probably a foolhardy undertaking. I asked Randall, "If he were placed in
my position, whether he would return and report Indians from what we had
seen, or go at all hazards to the burning buildings; or, until we had actually
seen some of the hostiles, before we returned and made our report."

He said, "I would do as I know you are going to do; either know that there
are Indians there, or know that they have left." And I knew that he meant
what he said, so telling them to observe the same manner in moving, that
the}" had in coming up the hill, I started down to the creek, followed by Randall and Long as before. On my reaching the fence on the creek bottom, I signaled my two comrades to me, and told them I should go up to the burning
cabin and the brush, and pointed out the places where I should expect the
Indians to be concealed. Then I moved out of the range between them and
these points and walked cautiously toward the cabin; or, more properly
speaking, what was left of it. I passed the dead beeves and cooking meat; and
just as I was within a few yards of the burning cabin, something began to
move in the tall rye grass that was growing around a root-house near by. I
could see a black head raise slowly; and as this was the place I expected an
attack from, at the first shake of the grass and move of the black object, my
gun was to my shoulder, I took aim, but just as I was in the act of pulling the
trigger I saw that it was a black hog which had been lying in the grass, but
she didn't play hog worth a cent, and came near getting her head shot off, for
her lack of "hog manners." She had raised her head so slowly, that it appeared to me in every way like an Indian, cautiously preparing to shoot at me.

This episode convinced me that there were no Indians near at hand. So
calling to my comrades to run forward to the brush, I made a few jumps

when I was in the tall grass and soon moved from tree to tree, on the bottom — up and down the creek — which I continued to do till I was quite certain that the Indians had left. Their "sign" was very fresh, and everything went to prove that they had hastily left but a short time before we arrived.

We then went into the garden and filled our pocket-handkerchiefs with new potatoes and young onions. While we were in the garden we heard the reports of several gun shots, above us on the side of the mountain, which caused us to hurry to cover; and, as we had gained all the knowledge we had come in search of, and reached the place we started for, we returned to headquarters as cautiously as we had come.

The boat was waiting to carry us over, as we had been in plain sight for some time coming down the mountain side. On reaching headquarters, we were questioned by the general, who was very much surprised when we told him we had seen no Indians, for he as well as others at headquarters had heard shots in our direction while we were over the high ridge or mountain.

After giving a full report of what we had seen, I said (jokingly), "I knew there were no Indians over there, otherwise I shouldn't have gone!" There was a scout or two present; one of them asked me what I went for. I answered (as I presented the general with the handkerchief), "Knowing the general was fond of onions and new potatoes, I went over after some, there being no garden nearer." The general accepted the handkerchief, and a rather "loud smile" broke from the lips of all present. This scout put me on good terms with all of the army officers.

That evening I received the following from General Howard:

HEADQUARTERS DEPT. OF THE COLUMBIA
In the Field.
Camp Hodges, near Mouth of White Bird, I. T.,

June 29, 1877.

Special Field Order, No. 20.

Captain George Hunter, commanding Dayton Volunteers, will report with his company to Captain Marcus P. Miller, 4th Artillery, for duty.

By command of Brig.-Gen. Howard,
(Signed,) M. C. Wilkinson,
1st Lieut. 3rd Inf.,
Aid-de-Camp.

The next day was consumed in crossing the river, but as my company was first over, I received the following order:

Special Field Order, No. 22.

Captain George Hunter, commanding Dayton Volunteers, will, at 6 p. m. tomorrow, make a reconnoissance in the direction of Pittsburg Landing, and examine the country thoroughly as he proceeds, especially in the direction of Joseph's reported encampment.

By command of Brig. Gen. Howard,

(Signed,) M. C. Wilkinson,

Pursuant to this order I selected ten or twelve of my best mounted men, and, in company with a signal officer — furnished by the general to accompany this expedition — we pushed on up the mountain in the direction of Canoe Encampment. We found the mountain very steep and hard to climb. On reaching the summit, we soon struck Joseph's trail, which was broad and easily followed, as Joseph had hundreds of horses with him. These trails we followed some distance; then swung around, and returned by the way of Pittsburg Landing. Arriving at the summit of the mountain, we tried for some time to attract the attention of those at headquarters on Salmon river, twelve or fifteen miles away, but we failed to "catch their eye."

After fully satisfying ourselves that the Indians had gone toward Canoe Encampment — on Snake river — we returned, having traveled over forty miles over rough mountains, and the most of the way without a trail.

The next day, as I was in the lead with my company, on starting out to follow the Indians, General Howard said he would like to scout ahead with me; and, as the command was about ready to move we started on ahead. I had three or four of my men with me, and the general had two soldiers with him. It was storming, about half and half snow and rain. About eight miles from the river we came to where a house had been burned; the logs were yet on fire, making a good place to stop and warm.

As the general had told me he was expecting General Greene to come through on the trails from Boise, and hoped to meet and form a junction with him, I told the general whilst he was waiting the coming up of the command I would take one of his men and go a short distance ahead and see if I could find any indications of General Greene's approach. I, with the soldier, started up the mountain through the timber, and had not proceeded more than a couple of miles, when, on looking through the timber, we saw a large number of horses at the head of a gulch in the timber. These horses being quiet, I feared that it was a trap or ambush set by the Indians for our especial benefit.

Telling the soldier what my opinion was, and that General Howard was too far in advance of his command for safety, I requested him to return to the general and inform him of the suspicion I had regarding horses discovered, and to tell him that he had better fall back to the advancing command. The soldier started back at once, and after I thought he had had time to reach the general, I started through the horses on a run, determined to get the Indians after me, if there were any there. Then, as I was well mounted, I would make in the direction from which General Greene was supposed to be coming, thus giving our general time to reach the command. But, on my dashing among the horses, they "struck out," and I was satisfied there were no Indians near, and that these were mostly horses and mares which they probably couldn't well drive with them. By circling them around, I soon got them under control,

149

and drove them to where I had left General Howard — there being a good corral there.

Reaching there, and corralling the horses, I found General Howard sitting quietly by the fire in company with the other men, and coming up to him I asked:

"General, did you not get the word I sent back to you?" He said, "Yes. But, captain, you certainly would not do as you have advised me to do, would you?" I said: "Certainly not; for the command cannot well spare you, while I would not be missed except by my family and a few friends. Your past history is a sufficient guarantee of your bravery; but it doesn't warrant you in jeopardizing a life that is of great value to all, in making a scout that any one else could make as well; nor would it reflect credit on me, if I didn't do all in my power to prevent such a disaster." He said, "Captain, I fully appreciate your action; but I came out with you, and for the time *I am a scout, and I never forsake a comrade in danger.*"

Stepping to one side, I questioned one of the men who was with the general when the soldier that I sent back returned, asking him what the general said to my courier. He said that the general had asked, "Where is Captain Hunter?" and being told that I proposed to get the Indians after me, if there proved to be any, and give him time to get back to the command, he said: "Get your horses ready, and if we hear any shooting, we will go to the captain. He can't be left alone in this affair." And he quietly maintained his seat, until I came in with the horses as before stated. I relate this incident only as a matter of justice to the man I believe to be an able, brave and courteous officer. As the preceding pages show, I had served with General Lane, Bob Metcalf, Ben Wright, Nathan Olney, Colonel Kelley, and many other brave and efficient officers and frontiersmen, but I feel safe in saying, that I do not believe I ever served with or under the command of an abler general or a more pleasant and courteous gentleman in all my life. His actions were very severely criticised by the stay-at-home soldiers in the Northwest, who pronounced him slow in his movements, wanting in energy, and, lastly, as consuming too much time in his "devotions." But as I am well informed, the general had up to that time never had any experience in Indian warfare; had but few men, and nearly all he had at command had met with very disastrous defeat at the hands of the hostiles, and probably could not be depended upon; and to overtake the hostiles with infantry before they chose to be overtaken, on their own selected ground, no man of sense or experience would expect. To say that General Howard strained every nerve in this campaign to overtake and punish the hostiles with such soldiers as were available, is no more than just. The fact of his hiring every team that could be had to haul his weary infantry across Camas prairie, to enable him and his command to strike Joseph at Kamai, where he defeated him, and forced the Indians across the mountains into Montana, should be sufficient proof of his energy and determination.

It is true that Joseph was met at Big Hole by General Gibbons, who made a most gallant fight, and inflicted severe punishment on Joseph's band of hostiles, and not getting off "scott free" himself, drew off, satisfied for the time. But General Howard, like a sleuth-hound on Joseph's trail, came upon this battle field, and, without halting, kept on preying on his trail till Joseph was finally intercepted by General Miles in Eastern Montana, who captured him. General Howard "was in at the killing," proving that he had strained every nerve and taxed the strength and energies of his command to their utmost to overtake and punish the hostiles. I believe every man who has traveled over the rough trails followed by Howard on that occasion, will agree with me when I say, the only wonder was that he kept as close to Joseph as he did, and I will here say that those who accuse the general of being slow, and "spending too much time in praying," would themselves, in all likelihood, if they had been in his command, have put in all their time in praying to get out of the scrape and back to their distant growling posts.

But I must go back to my story, for it is not in my power to do the man Howard the justice due him for accepting the services of the volunteers, putting steamers on the rivers in the service of the government, as guard vessels, in the Nez Perce war as well as the Bannack war, thereby showing the croakers that he was not only willing but anxious to receive all the help he could get. He is certainly not to blame for the Government's failing to remunerate the volunteers as yet, whom he armed, fed, and, in some instances, clothed, during the troubles.

Chapter Twenty-Two

The command coming up, the horses I had captured were placed in charge of the proper parties, then General Howard ordered me to go with my company the nearest route to the trails of the hostiles on the top of the mountains. I told him I hadn't discovered any trail leading up the mountain, but as he had scouts with him who knew the country well, they could doubtless pilot us over the best route up the mountain and to the trails of the hostiles. He asked, "Can you find the trails of the hostiles?" "Certainly," I replied. "Then," said he, "Lead with your company, I can go where you can." This settled it. I took the straightest shoot I could up a spur of the mountain. On going a short distance my boys discovered a lot of Indian caches containing flour and other articles, together with wearing apparel made from dressed deer skins.

The route we had chosen up this spur of the mountain proved to be a hard one; but we toiled on, hour after hour, and finally reached the summit and struck the trails. We pushed on some fifteen miles, when, night coming on, we went into camp in a small bunch of timber near the trails. It was storming hard, snow and rain. After we had arranged camp and got good fires started, and I had placed my guards for the night, a courier came in and said it was the general's order that we fall back to him at the crest of the mountain we had climbed, and that he had been unable to get his artillery and provisions up the hill yet.

In a few moments my command was again in the saddle, and on the way back to headquarters through mud, snow and rain, with very little of the grumbling that would be expected among such a class of men under the circumstances.

About midnight we arrived at headquarters and found rousing log fires, built by the general's order for us to camp by (we had no tents). This act of kindness and forethought on the part of our general put all in good humor, and we fell to work making coffee, and preparing as good a meal as was possible under the circumstances. We carried ten days' rations on animals that belonged to our command, and while we were eating, one of the boys asked some of the regulars who had been building fires for us to take a cup of coffee with us, which invitation was gladly accepted, none of the command had eaten anything since morning and had no hope of getting anything to eat till next day noon, as they had not been able to get their packs up the mountain. There being some officers present, I told them my men would divide what rations they had with them for the regulars' supper, and we would soon get the train up the hill in the morning. The offer was quickly accepted, and we divided our rations with them gladly.

Early the next morning we got the quartermaster's stores up to camp. On their arrival I repaired to General Howard's tent and asked him for an order on the quartermaster for extra rations for my company. "Did you not draw the day before yesterday for ten days?" he asked. "Yes," I replied, "but, finding your soldiers out of provisions and supperless last night, we divided our rations with them." "That was very kind of your men," said he, "and I will go with you myself and see that you get extra rations." Accompanied by some other officers, he went with me to the quartermaster's tent. The quartermaster's name I have forgotten, and I don't care to recall it, but at our approach the general told him of our having divided our rations with the soldiers, and he should issue more to us. He stiffened up, and in a pompous tone of voice said to the general, "I will have to put a guard around your tent to keep these fellows away from you!"

I had heard of some scurrilous remarks that this same officer had made in presence of some of my men about the volunteers while we were climbing the mountain, and this insult added to that was a "lee-tle" too much for me, so I said: "I presume these people" (the volunteers) "are getting you a little nearer the hostiles than you want to be! I heard yesterday that you said, 'the volunteers didn't earn their salt.' Now, don't you think they'll fight if they get a chance?"

He, in his egotistical way, replied, "I don't think they will." I asked him, "can you fight a little; have you got a gun? If you have, get it, and I'll prove to you that there's at least one volunteer who will fight you." Then I gave him a "blessing" which he will probably remember during the rest of his days. Here the general interfered and gave peremptory orders for double extra rations for my command, and it was filled to the letter without further comment.

He was relieved that day by the general and sent back to Vancouver, I was informed. Probably he thought Vancouver a more healthy place for a man of his temperament; that he would be more capable of moving around down there than he would be in the presence of the cowardly (?) volunteers; that the government needed more clerks than valiant soldiers, This was the last I ever saw or heard of that kindly quartermaster.

It was also the only instance of ungentlemanly treatment I remember the volunteers receiving at the hands of any of the general officers. After we had gotten up the Quartermaster's stores and the artillery that morning, we took up the trails and followed the hostiles at our best speed. The trails led along the top of the mountain in the direction of Canoe Encampment, on Snake river. The summit of this mountain is comparatively level prairie, interspersed at points with timber. This is a grand grazing country. Thousands of broad acres of rich and abundant grass, with water plenty, furnish the finest of summer ranges, while the deep canyons, with little bottoms, rank with shrubbery and tall grasses, furnish food and shelter for cattle and horses during the winter season.

Toward night we camped on a small rivulet, nearly opposite the mouth of Rocky canyon. Just after forming our camp we received word by courier that Joseph had made a flank movement and swung around back to Camas prairie; that he then had Perry's and Whipple's commands surrounded near the Cottonwood House.

These were the troops that had been so roughly handled in the White Bird canyon. They had been sent back by General Howard from Salmon river for ammunition and supplies, and were attacked at the Cottonwood House, where brave young Lieutenant Raines lost his life. He was out with eight or ten men (soldiers), making a reconnaissance, and was cut off by the Indians, and the whole party killed after making a gallant fight.

This news resulted in my company of forty-five men and Captain McConville's company of fifteen Lewiston volunteers being sent on a forced march across the country by the way of Rocky canyon to the Cottonwood House, to the relief of Colonels Whipple and Perry. As the most of my command were young farmers who were needed at their homes to care for their crops, and Howard thought he had sufficient United States troops to cope with the hostiles, he sent an order by the men he dispatched for boats to cross us over Salmon river, from which order the following is an extract:

HEADQUARTERS DEPT. OF THE COLUMBIA

In the Field.

Camp Raines, Junction of Rocky Canyon and
Canoe Encampment Trail, I. T., July 4, 1877.

Special Field Order, No. 23.

The Commanding General of the Department takes this opportunity to convey to Captain George Hunter, and the individual members of his command, his thanks for the hearty, prompt and energetic manner in which they have responded to every call to duty during the period they have served in his command.

Often sent in the advance under the most trying circumstances, they have never failed to answer cheerfully to every demand to perilous duty.

By command of Brigadier-General Howard,

(Signed,) M. C. Wilkinson,
Aid-de-Camp.

Accompanying the foregoing was the following:

Special Order, No. 23.

Captain George Hunter, commanding company Dayton Volunteers, will proceed, *via* Rocky canyon, to Cottonwood, I. T., reporting, upon his arrival there, to the commanding officer.

As soon as his services can be dispensed with on reaching Lewiston, I. T., Captain Hunter, with his company, is hereby relieved from duty with this command.

(Signed as the foregoing.)

Receiving the above orders, McConville's company and mine (sixty-five men all told) made a forced march to Salmon river, opposite the mouth of Rocky canyon, and there camped for the night. The next morning the boats reached us about daylight, when we ferried our men and supplies over, swimming our horses, and pushed on over the mountain for Camas prairie. On the top of this mountain we met another courier, who stated that fighting was still going on at Cottonwood. So we hurried on to the prairie, where we stopped half an hour to rest our horses and partake of a lunch ourselves. From an adjacent hill we could see men riding back and forth near the Cottonwood. This assured us that the fight was still going on. Soon remounting, we rode across the level prairie as fast as our horses could stand it. At about sundown we were among the low mounds or hills a few miles from the Cottonwood House. Then, as we could not see any signs of the Indians, or hear any shooting, we concluded that they had drawn off to attack us, and were lying in concealment among these hills. We believed they could make it warm for us before we were able to reach the soldiers. Having arrived at this conclusion, we called in our advance-guards. I had told McConville I would do the scouting through these hills myself, and in case he was attacked he had better have our horses shot down, and use their bodies for breastworks, for they were so tired that it was almost impossible to get away from the Indians on them. The Indians would be mounted on fresh, fleet horses or ponies. All must make up their minds to either whip the Indians or themselves be killed to a man.

Captain McConville was an old soldier, but without experience in Indian warfare. He was a brave man and a good officer. He requested me in case of

154

an attack to return and assume command of our men. Getting ready to go forward, I told him to keep his men a few yards apart, and to move only as I should signal to him from time to time as I passed over the hills, and to always keep a good place in view whereat to make a stand and fight.

All being understood, I passed rapidly ahead, from mound to mound, closely examining the ground for evidences of the presence of Indians as I went, and signaling McConville as I proceeded over mound, hill, gulch and flat at as rapid a pace as my "Little Wonder" could carry me; and until in the fast gathering darkness I heard a loud voice saying, "Don't shoot at the man coming on that white horse, that is Captain Hunter — I know his riding." The sentence was hardly finished when I galloped up the slope, and into the midst of a squad of soldiers who were standing around a gatling-gun near some rifle-pits. I was soon grasping the hands of Major Babbitt and others.

This hill had been fortified with rifle-pits by the soldiers, who had defended and held it against Joseph's entire force for a day or two.

Captain McConville soon came up with our two commands. But our rejoicings at having gotten in so easily were soon turned to exclamations of sadness as we listened to the particulars of the gallant fight that had been made a few hours before our arrival by seventeen Mt. Idaho men.

As it was told to us, Captain Randall (the brave man who crossed Salmon river on the scout with me as before related) had returned to Mt. Idaho and organized a company of seventeen volunteers.

Hearing of the perilous position into which Colonels Perry and Whipple had placed themselves at Cottonwood, this brave little band started across the prairie in broad daylight to their relief.

They had got within a mile of the soldiers when they were suddenly attacked by a large number of Indians who were mounted on swift ponies. The Indians would circle around them in relays of fifty or sixty, firing on them as they passed. The heroic seventeen were soon dismounted and down behind their dead or dying horses returning the fire with their repeating rifles and revolvers, with a cool bravery that was never surpassed, if equaled.

Brave Randall soon lay mortally wounded beside his dead horse; yet he coolly continued to give his orders and pour his deadly fire into the savage circle till he finally died while in the act of reloading his gun. Houser had been severely wounded in the first of the engagement, but he fought on like a lion at bay, not ceasing for a moment until the hostiles withdrew.

Young Fenn, son of Idaho's delegate to Congress, distinguished himself for cool bravery, as did all the rest. He received a "warm kiss from an Indian," as he afterwards expressed it, by a minie-ball grazing his lips and badly burning them. Captain Curley, Eph. Bunker and Major Geo. Shearer were among the rest, equally brave and determined in this affair, which was witnessed by the United States troops under the command of Colonel Perry, who was severely censured by the volunteers for not rushing to their relief. But there were many things for him to consider. The troops under him had been terribly cut to pieces but a short time previous, and it was doubtful if they would stand fire; and if he was defeated he might not be able to hold out till reinforced, which would entail the loss of the munitions and supplies which he was trying to take to General Howard. Not wishing to censure any one in this case, or to take part in the dispute, I will say that Geo. Shearer expressed something near my opinion when he exclaimed — as he viewed the situation from the hill where the soldiers were fortified, and took a quick look at the struggling seventeen, surrounded, as they were, by whirling, yelling, painted fiends, and then dashed down to their assistance — "The man who goes down there is a d___d fool, but he's a d___d coward if he don't!"

It was said by some that the soldiers did finally move to their assistance, while others say they did not.

The foregoing was written as it was related to me at the time, as nearly as I can recall it now. Possibly there are some points incorrectly stated; but some time in the future I hope to have the opportunity to write this up more fully and better.

It was believed that the Indians had seen me and the command approaching across the prairie, and that the warm reception they had received at the hands of the seventeen Mt. Idaho boys was a "pointer" to what they might expect at the hands of sixty-five men of similar habits. At least they drew off in the direction of the Kamai Reservation pretty soon. On the arrival of our two commands the boys were soon in camp and listening to different accounts of the happenings of the past few days at and near the Cottonwood House.

About this time a young man — hardly more than a boy — by the name of Bluitt was killed while out scouting with a comrade, but the circumstances I have forgotten, as they were only told to me.

The next morning I received orders to escort the dead and wounded of the brave seventeen across the prairie to Mt. Idaho. Fully expecting the Indians would give us battle when they saw us out in open ground, and as we had never tried our needle guns, I ordered my men to try them at a target. The boys moved out, and, to our utter astonishment, not one in twenty of our cartridges would fire, as one after another of the boys attempted to test their guns.

Then things began to "rumble," and the air was resonant with "cuss words" as we all began to realize the helpless condition we had unknowingly been in while making the dangerous and toilsome marches of the past few days, sometimes almost into the jaws of death, encumbered with heavy belts filled with worthless cartridges, which rendered our guns useless except as clubs, and only a portion of the command provided with small arms.

Major Babbitt, who had issued these cartridges to my men, being present, he at once had other cases brought out, opened and examined. He said there had been some damaged cartridges discovered before, and by accident we had got hold of some of them. We were all satisfied that it was an unintentional mistake, and could see that the officers who furnished them to us felt really worse about it than we did, as they fully realized that if we had been attacked during our forced march to their relief there would not have been a "grease spot" left of either McConville's or my own command to mark the spot where we fell. This incident I note to show that sometimes luck favors those who are unable to favor themselves. In other words, "a fool for luck!"

Being furnished with good cartridges, we started across to Mt. Idaho with the dead and wounded, arriving there without molestation. The next day we buried the dead.

As we were now away from the government troops, and were not likely to be able to rejoin them for some time, and the hostiles being near us, it was thought best to consolidate the Idaho and Washington volunteers and form a regiment, there being three companies of Idaho men; and one (my own) from Washington Territory. After some delay we effected an organization by electing Captain McConville, Colonel; myself Lieutenant-Colonel, and George Sears Major, of the 1st Regiment of Idaho and Washington Volunteers.

This necessitates an allusion to a very unpleasant circumstance that took place after this organization was perfected in which I was personally concerned.

The bickerings and jealousies so common to volunteer organizations now manifested themselves more prominently, and the ever-present mischief-maker and tale-bearer seized the opportunity to ply their vocations, which were managed so skillfully as to bring about a personal verbal encounter between E. T. Wilson (formerly lieutenant of the Pomeroy company, but now attached to Colonel McConville's company) and myself, which culminated in my receiving a pistol-shot wound in the shoulder and neck. Wilson surrendered himself to the civil authorities, and I was taken to the hospital for "repairs."

Wilson soon learned the actual facts in the matter over which the altercation took place, and sent me his explanation and apology, with the urgent request that he be allowed to nurse me, and do all in his power to repair the damage he had hastily done. When the time for his examination arrived, there being no prosecuting witness who chose to appear against him, he was discharged, and after remaining with me a few days returned to his command.

There are many versions of this affair, but as the matter has been adjusted between Wilson and myself — as we have since met, and are now on friendly terms, both regretting the unfortunate occurrence which was brought about by third parties, and both deem it a matter of the bygones — I shall pass it with the slightest mention that I feel justified in giving it in carrying out my promise to write in this book the events of my life.

The volunteers moved on in the direction of Kamai, under command of Colonel McConville, leaving me in the hospital among those who were suffering from wounds inflicted by the Indians.

Chapter Twenty-Three

Honorable L. P. Brown's hotel at Mt. Idaho was the hospital. Doctor Morris (now of Lewiston) was the physician in charge. The nurses were attentive, careful and kind, and the citizens of the place seemed to vie with each other in their attention to the wounded. Doctor Morris deserves special mention for his kindness and surgical skill; while Brown seemed worried for fear something might be left undone that might in some way lessen the sufferings of the wounded and the homeless.

I cannot find words to express the gratitude I feel toward those good people for the many kindnesses they showed me while I was an inmate of their hospital.

I conversed with many other of the inmates, and heard many sad and revolting accounts of the atrocities perpetrated by the Indians when they first demonstrated their "abilities" and "attainments." I shall mention a few as I can recall them to memory, though after a lapse of ten years my memory may be faulty in some instances. Mrs. Ben Norton, who was lying there with a gunshot-wound in each leg, related somewhat as follows:

About the first act of the Indians, at the outbreak, was the mortally wounding of Lew Day (an old timer in this country, and an old friend of mine), while he was traveling on the road near the Cottonwood House, of which her husband was the proprietor. Day managed to work his way to the Cottonwood House, where he reported the happening and probabilities to Ben Norton, who soon concluded to take his family and Day to Mt. Idaho, seventeen miles away, that being the nearest place of safety, where a doctor could be found to dress Day's wounds.

Norton's household consisted of Mrs. Norton, a little boy and Mrs. N.'s sister (a young lady), and, I believe, another woman with some children. There were also two or three men stopping with him at the time. I am not positive as to the latter statement. But, at any rate, Norton hastily hitched up a team and started with the wounded man and the women, accompanied by the men who happened to be there. It was afternoon when they started. The road, for the most part of the seventeen miles, lay across a level prairie, and they drove as fast as they could till they got within a few miles of Mt. Idaho, when the Indians came upon them. Then — as I understand it — they had a running fight for some distance, and until the Indians shot down one of the horses that was hitched to the wagon, and soon afterward killed the other. Thus the devoted party was left at the mercy of the inhuman butchers. Night came on, as though to draw a veil over the hellish work of these painted reservation pets of our government.

Norton was mortally wounded, and dying by the side of his brave, noble young wife, who had been shot through both legs. Their little boy made his escape in the darkness, and finally made his way to Grangeville and gave the alarm. Mrs. Norton's sister escaped on the prairie, and was found wandering

Pat Price exposes the cross

around the next day. Poor Lew Day, mortally wounded as he was — with one other man, I think — kept the Indians at bay till morning, when relief came from Mt. Idaho and Grangeville. Norton was dead, Day died in a day or two, and one of the other men was wounded and soon after died, and I believe one of them was killed there. Mrs. Norton finally recovered.

It would require a far more able pen than a rough old pioneer can command to portray the sufferings experienced by that little band on that occasion, even if I could recall all of the story told me by Mrs. Norton.

At about the time of the above-mentioned attack, a general attack was made upon the settlers along the White Bird and Salmon rivers, as alluded to in a previous chapter.

A recent chat with two or three of the parties who were conversant with occurrences at that time has refreshed my memory on one or two points.

Mrs. Osborne, whose husband was killed on the bar when Mason was killed, appeared at the residence of Mr. Cone, on Slate creek, three days afterward, with her little children. The only garments she had on were her stockings and chemise. She was covered with blood, and in every way gave evidence of having received the most inhuman treatment.

A friendly squaw, who, from her infatuation for gambling, was called To-lo (Chinook for "wager"), was, at the outbreak, furnished by Mr. Cone with a fine horse, and sent to Florence, a distance of twenty miles, for aid. She soon returned with seventeen men, who assisted Mr. Cone in building a stockade and remained with those who collected there till all danger had passed.

To-lo told of many of the Indian outrages, among the rest that of Mrs. Manuel. Manuel made his escape by getting into the brush and lying there for twelve or fifteen days, living on berries, and with the spear of an arrow still in his shoulder.

The Indians attacked Manuel's house and took all of his family prisoners, except Mrs. Manuel's father, who escaped to the brush on the river, and, lying there concealed, witnessed some of the atrocities perpetrated upon the family:

Mrs. Manuel and her children being captured, the Indians burned the house, killed her little boy, broke her baby girl's arm, and then Chief Joseph stabbed Mrs. Manuel to death because she resisted his infamous attack upon her person. Her remains were never found, but the little baby girl was found wandering around by an Irishman named Pat Price, who made a kind of a chair out of a box, put the child into it, swung it on his back and started for Mt. Idaho. Meeting a lot of Indians, who surrounded him, he opened his bosom, exposing a cross which had been pricked there, in India ink, and told them to kill him if they wanted to. Pat was a Catholic, as were many of the Indians, and he believes that the sight of the cross saved his own life and that of the child. At any rate, having exposed his breast with the cross on it, Joseph's men permitted him to pass, and didn't molest him in any way. And this brave fellow brought his little broken-armed charge safely to Mt. Idaho, having toiled over fifteen miles of mountain trail, burdened as before stated. The night after that massacre Mr. Baker (Mrs. Manuel's father) witnessed the Indians' war-dance, which was kept up nearly all night. Could the mind of man conceive of the feelings of that aged man as he lay there watching their fiendish jubilee over the remains of a loved daughter and a grandchild? Having every reason to believe the other child had met the same fate, as well as his son-in-law, conceive of him, if you can, lying, hour after hour, in close proximity to these red fiends, a silent witness of their imp-like dance, after (as he supposed) they had committed the last of his loved ones to torture and death, while at any time his slightest movement or the breaking of a twig might prove the signal for his death, either by the bullet, knife or torture.

There are few, if any, of the survivors of those scenes who doubt To-lo's story. Yet, the survivors of that band of fiends were returned to Kamai by the government some years later; I suppose, as a reminder to the widows and orphans of pioneers of the hospitality of the "noble" red man.

In this hospital I saw a child — a little girl — whose tongue an Indian had cut off because she was crying while seventeen other of these fiends incarnate were outraging her mother in her presence. I saw women whose husbands had been killed, and in many instances left to burn in their flame-begirdled houses while they were being outraged and otherwise tortured, and then turned loose to wander in their nakedness in search of a place of refuge, homeless and widowed. And now, ten years afterward, the blood rushes through my veins so fiercely that I can scarcely hold my pen while trying to convey to the reader a faint idea of the horrors of an Indian massacre; and I ask myself the question, why will those reared in peaceful homes, in the lap of luxury, far from danger, persist in writing and preaching pitying words and sentences about the lazy, skulking demons of the far west.

The survivors of this same band of fiends were a few years afterward returned to Kamai and their old haunts by our sympathetic Indian bureau, because their health was not good where they were (perhaps also as a reminder, to the widows and orphans of butchered pioneers, of the bounteous hospitality of our glorious government), and are now being fattened and clothed, at government expense, while the widows and orphans gaze on the sleek red pets, dressed in gorgeous red blankets and with painted faces; and their hearts (those of the widows and orphans, I mean) swell with patriotism as they contemplate the evidences of the gloriousness of our free and just government.

It is possible that in their dreams, in the "stilly hours of the night," they fancy they again hear the fiendish war-cry or see the glittering scalping knife gently drawn around the heads of fallen husbands and fathers, removing the locks they have so often fondly caressed; and with a shriek and a start they awake, to realize that "'twas but a dream" and that the same generous protectors (?) have been returned, to remind them of former kindnesses (?) received at their hands, thereby furnishing them a guarantee of future peace and protection.

Now, after the lapse of ten years, it seems to me that I can almost hear the baby whose tongue was cut off by these gentle protectors, as it tries to utter its evening prayer, including such supplications as these: "Give, oh, give me back those who outraged my mother, butchered and burned my father! Oh, thou mighty men who control the destinies of Indians, and ignore the white widows and orphans, left homeless, maimed and outraged, to wander in their nakedness to a place of safety or of death; oh, we pray thee, take them under thy protecting wing, furnish them and their children teachers, blankets and food; but do not, in your pity, assist the poor widows and orphans of your white brethren, left naked, heart-broken and far from their relatives; for we realize that it is far preferable to be tortured by educated Indians than to be killed by ignorant savages. Oh, give us back our Indians! Furnish them with reservations, schools, annuities, blacksmiths, carpenters, farmers, doctors and missionaries, that we may in the near future be exterminated in the most scientific manner, while our poor widowed and orphaned white trash are allowed to go to — (their neighbors for a home and assistance)." Let it be so recorded.

* * * * * *

Within a day or two the volunteers were attacked on a hill where they had made a stand, but the hostiles found them too strongly fortified, and drew off after having succeeded in capturing a number of our horses.

The ball had been extracted from my neck, and I was able to move around a little when the courier arrived at Mt. Idaho with this news. I proceeded forthwith to secure a sufficient number of horses to remount our men, and sent them to the command.

A day or two later a courier brought in word that the Indians had engaged General Howard in battle at Kamai, and that the volunteers had refused to assist him in the fight, and moved down to Clearwater on their side of the mountain, General Howard being on the opposite side of Clearwater from Mt. Idaho. When I heard this I induced a one-armed courier named George Greer to bring my horse to me, and to fill my canteen with water. Then we quietly left the hospital and Mt. Idaho, and went for the scene of battle as fast as we could, armed only with one old revolver between us. On going into the hospital I had loaned my gun and revolver to a party whom I believed could make better use of them in the field than I could in bed. Being both well mounted, we made good time, and arrived at Kamai just after Howard's cavalry and McConville's command, together with a few Indian scouts, had been repulsed on the Lo-lo trails.

I believe I have neglected to state heretofore that not all of the so-called Nez Perce Indians had joined Chief Joseph in his insurrection. There seemed to be a number of factions in that tribe, and many of their able-bodied men had either remained neutral during this trouble or had come out pronouncedly in favor of the whites, some having joined Howard, and done good work for him.

A few of these friendly Indians were killed or wounded in this affair, but I believe there were no other casualties on the part of the whites.

The volunteers and cavalry, having found the hostiles too well posted in the timber and brush, had returned to Kamai.

My first inquiry upon meeting General Howard was as to the conduct of the volunteers during the battle of Kamai, of which I had heard the uncomplimentary report at Mt. Idaho. He said there was no blame to be attached to McConville's command, that their showing themselves on the mountain was all that could be expected of them under the circumstances; for they, by their presence there, were attracting the attention of the hostiles to a certain extent, and preventing them from flanking Howard and returning to Camas prairie, where the people were now almost at their mercy. Besides, if McConville had attempted to come down to him with so small a body of men, the Indians would have undoubtedly cut him up badly. Finally, he said, that McConville had used good judgment, and done all that was necessary to be done on his side of the river.

Having subsequently made a thorough investigation of this matter, I am satisfied that Colonel McConville did a wise thing in keeping his command where he had posted them between the Indians and the Camas Prairie settlements; and judging from the hard fight that the Indians gave General Howard, who had artillery and a far greater number of troops than McConville had volunteers, I am sure that the latter would have been "handled without gloves, and knocked out in the first round," if they had attempted to go to Howard. His losses at the battle of Kamai I can't remember, but they were quite severe, as the well-filled hospital at Grangeville testified. Joseph's loss could not be ascertained, for — as is usual with the Indians — they quickly disposed of their dead and cached their wounded.

It was generally believed that most of the so-called friendly or neutral Indians, who had remained on their reservations since the outbreak, professing fealty to the whites, had lent Joseph a strong hand in this battle, and quietly returned to their homes when Joseph's people retreated toward the Lolo trails.

General Howard also told me that he had, just prior to my arrival, given Lieutenant Watrous permission to return with the Dayton volunteers to Mt. Idaho for me, and then to go home with us, as our term of service had expired, and all the volunteers would be relieved, he now having, as he believed, sufficient regular forces to drive the hostiles out of Idaho; and other large commands were marching from the eastward to intercept them on the other side of the mountains, all of which proved to be true, as before stated.

At his peremptory command (or request) I remained with General Howard over night, he having had good bed made up for me in his own tent. My company had already been discharged and was on the way to Mt. Idaho after me, while I was riding to the front on a different route. The next morning, as my fast ride had greatly irritated the wounds in my shoulder and neck, leaving them in a bad condition, the general sent me in an ambulance to Fort Lapwai, with two officers to accompany me. The journey occupied nearly two days.

At Lapwai I procured a horse, and rode on to Lewiston in company with a friend. That night I suffered much from my wounds, as riding in the hot sun had greatly inflamed them; but the careful attention which Madame French, of the Hotel de France, bestowed on me, enabled me to soon proceed homeward by stage.

Chapter Twenty-Four

Reaching home, I was shelved for some weeks (experimenting with probing irons and healing plasters), but, under the skillful nursing and care of my wife, I recovered from my wounds, and came out slightly disfigured but "still in the ring," and had the pleasure of again meeting most of the men who had so gallantly served with and under me.

They had returned to their homes, and their several occupations, and were pursuing their different vocations — seemingly not realizing that they were heroes, that although they had passed through the greater portion of an active and ferocious Indian campaign, and came out almost unscathed, they still had afforded succor, quietude and peace of mind to the greatly imperiled citizens and their families as well as to some beleaguered troops.

Perhaps it would not be out of place for me, at this writing, to say that while these brave fellows were under my command, they cheerfully obeyed my every order, or command, without regard to their personal sufferings, from cold, wet or hunger; or the peril they might undergo, in so doing, and did so cheerfully. And now, after the lapse of ten years, I reckon them all as being among my very best friends. What I say of my own company is equally true of the Idaho boys who were in our regiment, always responsive, willing and prompt. And all of them are entitled to much better treatment than they have received at the hands of our government.

Ten years have elapsed since they performed the services exacted of them by the general commanding (an agent of the government), who has, both verbally and in writing, acknowledged the services, rendered at the time they were most needed, as is heretofore shown in these pages. Yet, not one dollar of indemnity or remuneration has either of them received as a token of the recognition by the government of their prompt efforts to protect the weak and defenseless in response to the request and written command of its agent, the commanding general.

Then, too, they furnished their own horses, clothing and equipments, and, in many instances, their own arms and ammunition, much of which proved a total loss to them while acting under orders, and for which they have never been remunerated. The citizens of North Idaho, who had been induced to cross the continent, thereby enduring hardship, toil and privation, and at fearful cost in the early days, to settle in, and commence developing that beautiful portion of the northwest, in the full belief that the government had subdued the murderous hand of the savage and would protect them in the peaceful occupation of their new-made homes, have not as yet received a cent of indemnity for the loss of stock, buildings and other improvements sustained by them, or those upon whom they were dependent, at the hands of these wards of our rich and powerful nation.

While the volunteers and soldiers of other wars and insurrections have been paid, and well paid, for the time they served, and if by chance they were from any cause partially disabled, by wound or disease, they are well pensioned, as are also their widows and orphans after their demise, and the people of the States have been indemnified for all the damage they sustained by virtue of any incursion or raid, and even the citizens of Oregon, for losses sustained in the Bannack war of 1878.

I believe I am warranted in saying that it is a shame and an outrage on the enterprising pioneers of our territories that the representative men of our country should allow themselves to overlook, or ignore, the very righteous claims of the sufferers from such unexpected uprisings, and those of their brave fellow-citizens who, regardless of their own welfare and prosperity, rushed peremptorily to arrest the fiendish hand of those government pets, and protect the remnant of once happy and prosperous families.

'Tis true that the "remnant" is usually small after such raids, and, as a rule, had it not been for the timely interference of volunteers, there would have been no remnant at all!

And I must say, further, that to my personal knowledge not an Indian outrage has occurred on the Pacific Coast during the past thirty-five years but what the volunteers afforded the first succor and relief to those endangered.

Indians, unlike foreign nations, neglect to announce through all the leading newspapers that they intend to declare war, but they leave that matter to those who unexpectedly come upon the ashes or embers of the happy home of the previous day, and while gazing at the remains of friends around are aroused by the soul-piercing cry of a wandering infant, the only remnant.

No horse too fast to carry that news! None too fast to spread it! As the courier is dashing through some little village, burg or hamlet, he is unduly stopped by those who saw him approaching, who inhale the exhaust from the lungs of his panting horse while listening to his brief but blood-curdling story. And as the horse bounds on towards the nearest post or telegraph station, with rowels deeply inserted in his bloody sides, the cry goes up, re-echoing in the heavens, "Boys, get your guns, and come a runnin'; there's women and children in peril!" Then come the volunteers, in "one time and four motions" — hear it! mount! travel! fight! And that's what they do, without awaiting orders from any superiors. They rush to the scene of massacre and danger to the settler, and either peremptorily dispel the fiendish hell-hounds, or hold them in determined check until the courier has arrived at his destination. Orders and counter-orders are sent and repeated; a slow coach, hired at three prices, to transport officers, and the famous United States troops, by order of the Secretary of War, come "tramp, tramp, tramp," to the protection of loyal citizens after the work is done, and to coax the red-handed fiends back on to their reservations, with a new outfit of blankets, knives, beads, paint and government grub, while the tortured and suffering women and children are left unaided to rebuild their homes — once beautiful and happy — over ashes, which will forever be associated, in their minds, with the war-whoop and scalping knife.

Why not give to these women whose husbands were ruthlessly murdered — and in many instances before their very eyes, while they were undergoing tortures from which death would have been a welcome relief — left penniless and almost naked, all by the action of government wards; why not, I say, grant them a small pension, while you are voting from the overflowing government coffers princely sums to the widows of wealthy men who, for fame, plunged into the war and thought they did good service, were correspondingly well paid, not only during the war but during the rest of their lives — while the widows, the co-workers of the horny-handed pioneers are left to the charities of the survivors of their kind, with scarcely a voice raised among the representatives to plead the cause of those who were left "poor indeed." And if such move be made, hundreds stand ready to ridicule and ignore, while they are waiting for an opportunity to vote pensions to the widows of opulent and influential citizens, both civil and military.

What I say of these prime movers in the development of this glorious Northwest, is but a re-echo of the cry for succor and relief, which has been ringing from time to time, since the landing of the pilgrims at Plymouth, throughout the thirteen mother colonies, and westward as the frontiersman (The forerunner of the "Star of the Empire,") moved toward the setting sun, which cry is long unheeded by the sluggards, who follow twenty or thirty years in the wake of such men as Boone, Crawford, Kennon, Wetzel, Fremont, Carson, Meek, and Whitman, seeming to think that those who have subdued the savage and the native soil at first, ought to be able to maintain themselves, their families, and the widows and orphans of those of their fellows, who through the treachery of the viperous Indian, have fallen by the wayside and at the same time, help to pay munificent pensions to rich widows at fashionable resorts in states first developed under similar circumstances, and with similar sufferings.

But in the language of my tribe, "Nika cupet wa-wa" (I have spoken).

To give a faint description of Camas prairie, and its surroundings, may be proper here.

The prairie or basin is bordered on the west by Craig's mountain, north and east by other spurs of the Blue mountains, and south by Salmon river and its mountains; all of the mountains named being covered to a greater or less extent with fir, pine, and tamarack timber. Near its northwestern boundary runs the Clearwater river.

This beautiful basin is almost level for sixteen to twenty miles across, and about thirty miles long. Through it run several small creeks which form deep canyons as they approach either the Clearwater or Salmon rivers. The soil is a deep black muck capable of producing immense crops of wheat, oats, barley, fruit, and all but the most tender varieties of vegetables. Timothy grows to perfection, and immense crops of hay are raised.

Craig's mountain is covered with scattering timber, except where it dips northward toward Clearwater, where it is no more than a fertile, high-rolling prairie. For several miles across the top the land is rolling, being drained by numerous streams of clear cold water, abounding in trout that furnish the citizens of Lewiston, Mt. Idaho, and the surrounding country, such rare sport and "brain food," as is seldom equaled in any country. While in the timber are to be found thousands of deer and grouse, and not a few elk and bear. The cougar and mountain wolf semi-occasionally break the stillness of the peaceful air with their music. During the summer this mountain and basin form a panorama of beauty and loveliness that would gladden the eye and heart of any lover of sport, health and varied scenery. The mountain ranges to the south and east are very much similar to that just described, those near Salmon river being, as a rule, less timbered and more rugged.

Salmon river has for years been noted for the rich placer-mines along its banks and bars. Its mountains are also covered with a rich growth of nutritious grass, and are fast being covered with live-stock of all kinds.

Further east on the tributaries of this stream are located the very noted Florence, Oro Fino, Warren's, and many other mining-camps, which were struck in the sixties, and are still being worked by hundreds of miners, while innumerable veins of rich ore pierce the mountains and await the advent of railroads, as intimated in another chapter, which will furnish employment to thousands of men and millions of capital. They have room for miners, mechanics, stock-raisers, farmers, professional men, and a limited number of festive politicians. [Of the latter we would prefer Democrats, for there are plenty of Republicans there now.]

I might try in my feeble way to give a more extended description of that valuable region in the Northwest, but if the reader is at all anxious to know more of it, he should personally inspect it. So I will add, that several railroads are already within close proximity to it, and it only consumes four or five days of your time, and a matter of twenty to fifty dollars for expenses to visit it, while it took the most of those already there from four to six months of weary travel over scorching plains, rough mountains and rapid streams, to perform the journey to this land of promise, and those who lived to reach it found themselves loaded down with poverty and alkali-dust, which two latter acquirements have left my descriptive brain considerably muddled.

Chapter Twenty-Five

Having so far recovered from my wound as to be able to resume my storage and forwarding business, I removed my family to Grange City, and was devoting my time and attention to shipments, when General Howard came down the river on his way to hold a "wa-wa" (council) with the Palouses, a small tribe of Indians who, owing to their peaceful habits, had never been forced on to a reservation, and continued to live by themselves at the mouth of the Palouse river, nearly opposite my warehouses. I had become well acquainted with these Indians, especially with their head-chief Big Thunder. I had prevented them from taking part in the late Indian wars, and could converse with them quite fluently.

General Howard, being aware of these facts, requested me to accompany him and act as his interpreter, with which request I cheerfully complied.

Arriving at their headquarters, we met Big Thunder and the most of his head men in council.

Thunder told the general that their fathers had "lived and died here" (near the mouth of Palouse), and that none of his people had ever promised to go on to a reservation; but they wished to remain where they were, take up lands in severalty, and become the same as white men.

Howard told them that it was right to do so, and that was just what the great father at Washington wanted all Indians to do; and by so doing they would never be molested by the soldiers; and suggested that they should council with me from time to time, in making their locations and getting the numbers or description of the tracts which they wished to hold in severalty, and to gain such information as was necessary in conforming to the land laws.

Big Thunder then asked why Hunter could not be their chief, as he (Thunder) knew that when the Indians and whites went to war Hunter was always in the lead with the "Bostons" (meaning volunteers). He also said that he had been with Pu-pu-mox, and was wounded at the battle of Frenchtown in 1855; that Hunter was there with the "Bostons;" and that they (his people) had confidence in Hunter and would obey him.

General Howard responded: "That is the right mind. Colonel Hunter and you will never get into trouble with the white folks."

After some further talk the council adjourned. General Howard went his way toward his headquarters, and I returned to my warehouses and home.

The next morning, just as the sun was peeping over the tops of the high hills for which the lower two hundred miles of Snake river banks are famous, my wife saw Big Thunder approaching with about fifty of the head men of the Palouse tribe. She called to me to get up, saying she was fearful that there was something wrong with the Indians, judging from their number and appearance. Getting up, I went to the door where I met Big Thunder, he having caused the others to halt some distance away. I asked him the meaning of this demonstration with so many men. He said his people had held a big "wa-

I am made the White Chief of the Palouses

wa" the night before, and had made me their head chief, and that they had come over to inform me of the fact and to install me into office. He asked me if this was "my heart" (meaning could I act as their chief). I told him I would talk with him and them. So they formed a circle and seated themselves on the grass, when the chief informed me of their wishes, saying that I was elected head chief, Big Thunder second chief, and Hoo-sis-mox-mox (or old Charley) third in rank. I asked if this was the desire of all their people, and, if so, if they would mind me, and keep bad Indians away from them, or arrest and turn them over to the whites to be dealt with. To all of which they responded in the affirmative, adding that they would mind my words, and in all things obey me as being their white father.

After a "close wa-wa" (good talk), I formally accepted the position, and became an Indian chief, assuming (among my tribe) the title of "Timus Me-o-hut" (the White-Bearded Chief), and have ever since been designated by the different tribes of this portion of the country as "Timus, the White Chief of the Palouses."

Here I must say that during the ten years since that day they have faithfully kept their promise. And perhaps I will be pardoned for inserting some incidents regarding "my tribe."

Soon after I had accepted the chieftaincy some Indians broke into the Dayton Woolen Mills and stole a large lot of blankets and cloths. The sheriff of Columbia county, with a posse, followed their trails some thirty miles to where they found them encamped. Finding the Indians more inclined to fight than to return with them under arrest, and the posse being poorly armed and too few in number, the sheriff contented himself with securing a few of the stolen blankets and returning home without any Indians. Sometime afterwards a lot of my Indians (Palouses) happened to be in Dayton, when two of them were arrested as having been parties to the crime. One was named Mox-mox; the other's name I have forgotten. By their talk and threats the sheriff and others had succeeded in frightening these Indians very much — so much, in fact, that Mox-mox attempted to hang himself in the jail. The word soon reached the Palouses, when Big Thunder, Hoo-sis-mox-mox and others came to me and asked that I should look after the welfare of the accused. After a long talk I became satisfied that the Indians arrested would be able to clearly prove that they were not the guilty parties; so I accompanied Big Thunder and the others out to Dayton (twenty miles), and bailed the two out, they agreeing to appear in court on a certain day about three months hence. The bail was fixed at $600 each. I became surety for one and Big Thunder for the other.

Many of my "Boston-til-a-coms" (white friends) told me I would have that $600 to pay into court; but, to their surprise and my satisfaction, both of the bounden appeared promptly in court on the day set. The grand jury failed to find a true bill against them, and they were released and permitted to "go hence without day."

Subsequently Mox-mox made me a present of five ponies, in consideration of my services. This Mox-mox was a young man, weighed about 180 pounds, and was one of the most powerful men of the tribe. He came along one day in company with some other Indians, when I was in great need of manual assistance. I had about 7,000 tons of sacked wheat stored in my warehouse, and when navigation opened in the spring (when the river had raised so that boats could pass over the rapids below my warehouse), the O. S. N. Co. made it a point to have things rushed in order to get out what produce there was along the banks of Snake river before low water. At this season of the year it was almost impossible for me to secure help in this isolated place to handle the sacks of wheat required to load a steamboat that carried from 250 to 400 tons. But — as I had commenced to relate — Mox-mox came along when my men were well worn out. I explained my situation, and asked him to work awhile. He said, "All right," doffed his blanket, and with nothing on but his leggings, moccasins and breech-clout, went to work. During the day we loaded a steamboat with 400 tons of wheat, and just as she steamed out along came another that wanted 250 tons more. This was about dark; but at it we went. At that time hands were very scarce on the river, and the officers of the boats had to humor their deck-hands considerably; otherwise the hands would leave the boat without men enough to man her. I ran the sacks in a chute from the warehouse to the boat, a distance of about 200 feet. But when the river was high the incline, of course, was not so steep, and hardly sufficient to run the sacks to the boat. Hence, I had to raise the head of the chute in the warehouse and lower it at the foot to the deck of the boat to make the sacks run, thereby entailing on the deck-hands the necessity of stopping the sacks before they reached the deck, or pick them up off the deck to place them on the trucks, which they didn't like to do, and insisted that I should raise my end of the chute in the warehouse higher. This I declined to do, for, as I told them, it was much easier for them to lift the sacks a foot or two from the deck than for my tired men to lift them four or five feet in the warehouse. We worked on till midnight, the deck-hands doing lots of grumbling and very slow work. In a conversation with the captain he admitted that I was in the right, but said that if he took any part his hands would leave him; hence he must do the best he could.

After partaking of our midnight lunch I was talking with the mate on board, when, seeing no men at work on the boat, and hearing some loud talk in the warehouse, I hurriedly went up; finding the deck-hands in possession, and raising the chute, while my men were remonstrating. I stepped up and lowered the chute, telling them that their place was on the boat; at this one of them made a move as though he would attack me. I pulled a knife and ordered them out.

Mox-mox, seeing the motions, knew I was having trouble, though he couldn't understand our language. Dropping a sack of wheat, he jumped to his blanket and jerked out a knife that was fully a foot in length. Then, pushing me back, said in his native tongue, "Go away, Timus; I can kill them all." The boatmen hurriedly left, while he stood with that terrible knife poised and ready to strike "death to the dissenter" and we resumed work.

In a few minutes I wanted to go on board, and was getting into the chute to slide down, when my men cautioned me, as they feared the deckhands would attack me; but I slid down, and as I stopped among them they assisted me to my feet, seemingly in the best of humor; one of them remarking, "Egad, the oul' man's on it; an' so's the red divil up yander."

Things ran pleasantly the rest of the night. Mox-mox worked about fifty hours all told, and when I was going to pay him, he said he wanted about two dollars. But as he had done as much work as any man I had, and I was paying them fifty cents an hour, I counted him out twenty odd dollars in silver. He took two or three dollars of it and passed the rest back to me saying, "You are my chief, keep it." I made him understand that it was his money; but he would have me hold it for him, and he was over two years in drawing that money.

One day Big Thunder came and asked me to go with him and others of the tribe to find the "corners" and "lines," and generally assist them in locating and entering their lands in severalty at the local land-office at Colfax, about sixty miles distant. I told him I would go, but as I was now an Indian chief, he would have to furnish me with a horse and rig; and as that portion of the country was sparsely settled at that time, he would also have to board me on the route. He said that was correct, and that his people would see that I was mounted and fed as became the dignity of one filling so important a position.

Early one fine morning I crossed the river to the Palouse village, where I was received with all the pomp and ceremony due my dignified rank. They mounted me on a finely caparisoned and magnificent half-breed horse. I had brought along in my cantinas some crackers and cheese and a little salt. I put my cantinas over the horn of the saddle, and was soon on the way up the Palouse in company with Big Thunder and another Indian named Bones, all bound for the Colfax land-office. After a rapid ride of twenty miles over high and precipitous hills, we again came to the stream near where a cold spring-creek empties into it. Big Thunder asked me if I was fond of trout. Receiving an affirmative reply, he said, "I have a trap (a set-net) with me, and as it is about noon, we will catch some trout and have dinner." "All right," said I; "catch your fish." The two Indians dismounted and undressed; then, taking the net, one at each end, they waded out into the little stream up to their necks, I all the while remaining on my horse, watching the maneuvers of my adopted brothers. Big Thunder said, "Timus, kishkish!" (white chief, drive). It being a very warm day, I was anxious to take a plunge into the cool stream, but I realized the full dignity of my position; so I said, "I am head-chief now, and you agreed to furnish the food on this mission." "But," said he, "it requires both of us to hold the trap, and you must drive the fish." I jokingly argued with them a few moments, and then asked Thunder if he had a sister. "Yes," he replied. "Then," said I, "I'll kish-kish if you will give her to me." He soon saw the joke, and said, "Good, kish-kish." In a moment I was off the horse and into the water head foremost, splashing, diving and swimming around, creating enough commotion to drive a pious trout up Jacob's ladder. Raising the net, we found two fine trout in it that would each weigh about a pound.

Thunder then said we would go up a few hundred yards, to where some other springs came in, and catch enough for supper and breakfast. Remounting, we went up to the springs. Being again asked to "kish-kish," I again demurred, saying our contract only covered one drive. Big Thunder settled the matter by raising two fingers, and saying, "Timus, two sisters; kish-kish." "The more the merrier," said I, and into the water I went again to earn the other sister. This time we had good success, and got all the trout we desired. We cooked some for dinner, and rode on till near nightfall, camped, and the next morning rode into Colfax, transacted our business and returned.

Arriving at the Palouse encampment, Big Thunder told all the Indians of our bargain, and then said to me, "There's my two sisters; take them along!" As I had one wife and plenty of family across the river, and had not understood any polygamous clause in the obligation I had taken as chief, I declined with thanks. I relate the foregoing to show that the Indian, like the white man, can enjoy a joke with those in whom he has confidence.

At another time some of the young Indians had procured whisky, got drunk, and threatened to kill some white men. Big Thunder sent for me. Arriving near their camp, some white men warned me not to go further, as the Indians had threatened my life. But I went over, alone, and directly to the chief's lodge, where I found nearly the whole tribe assembled, many of the young men being in war paint.

The leading men shook hands with me, but most of the young men kept aloof. One (Cuscus by name, the son of an old chief) came forward, spoke of his troubles, and offered me his hand. I declined to take it, and told him I was ashamed of him, and if he kept on he would cause the whole tribe — men, women and children — to be killed; that if he would go and wash off his paint I would shake hands, and we would have a talk, when if I found they were suffering a wrong, I would have it righted; that I didn't fear any of them; that he, as well as the rest, had agreed to mind me, and he should. He said, "Good; nika pot-lum" (I am drunk). Then he, with the others who were painted, went out, washed off their paint and returned. I remained and talked with them for some hours, then left them in good humor. This Cus-cus was a c-u-s-s-"cus," and was subsequently killed by a white man whom he and one or two other drunken Indians attacked on the road. All of the tribe said he ought to have been killed, for he had become "hi-as cul-tus" (very bad) through drink.

Later, while I was in the legislative council at Olympia, a disease broke out in Dayton which — after much wrangling and newspaper discussion among the doctors, and after hundreds of the citizens had exposed themselves to it while doing the "good Samaritan" act, was pronounced smallpox in a virulent

173

form, from which — if my memory serves me — some twenty died, and three or four times as many suffered its loathsome attack. Incidentally I will say that the hitherto prosperous, beautiful and attractive little city was quarantined some forty days, which gave it a disastrous back set, from which it has not fully recovered to this day.

Excuse me — I was writing of "my tribe." Some of the Palouses were encamped near Dayton, and their squaws (clootch-men) were doing the washing for some of the families, whereby they contracted the disease. As soon as they were made aware of the nature of the infection they started for home, and having to pass my residence en route, made as wide a detour from the house as they could on the creek bottom. One old Indian rode up within hailing distance of the house, and calling to my wife, told her the Indians had the smallpox, and advised her not to allow any Indian to come near the house.

After that, chief Big Thunder, although he had not been exposed to the disease, would come within a few hundred yards of the house, and make known to my wife by shouts and signs what little article he wanted; which she would carry out away from the house, and leave; then he would come and get it.

This old Indian (Big Thunder) died at his home in 1885, of consumption, from which disease all of his large family had preceded him to the happy hunting ground. Soon after his death a delegation of Palouses called on me and asked that I appoint a man to fill the "vacant chair;" or, more properly, to cover the space at his end of the circle in council. I named Hoo-sis-mox-mox (sorrel top) as successor to the position left vacant by Big Thunder's demise.

These Indians have, as a rule, entered lands in severalty; have good teams, harness, wagons, plows and other agricultural implements; raise wheat, oats, barley, potatoes and other vegetables; and for several years have proven themselves an industrious class. Up to the time of this writing they make it a point to visit me every few days, or as often as anything transpires in which they wish to understand the laws of the country (Boston Momock). Knowing as I do that they have full faith and confidence in me, I cannot help manifesting some interest in their welfare; and although all classes of Indians are treacherous from instinct, and especially so when intoxicated, I believe that in case of an Indian outbreak in any portion of the Northwest I could go into their camps and make every mother's son of them who is capable of bearing arms accompany me, and work and fight to their utmost ability in defense of the whites, notwithstanding the former friendly relations existing between them and the hostiles. On the other hand, I know from the long and somewhat vivacious experience I have had with the numerous tribes, and a close study of their tactics, that in case the Palouses should from any cause conclude to avenge their imaginary wrongs against the whites, I would be the first victim of their scalping knives. In such cases Indians always make it a point to first annihilate those of whom they entertain the most fear; and these fellows are fully aware that I will do my best to bring them to justice for every misdemeanor.

Chapter Twenty-Six

I must relate a little incident — or story — of the palmy days of mining excitements, which many of the old settlers in the Walla Walla country will remember.

Toward the latter end of those days one Robinson came to Walla Walla and exhibited specimens of some very rich quartz, which he said he had taken from a ledge or lode that he had discovered in the Coeur d'Alene mountains, about two hundred miles northeast of Walla Walla. He said he would show the ledge for a nominal bonus if a company could be made up to work it. Soon a lot of old timers, lured by the remarkable richness of the specimens and the gorgeous descriptions of the lode given by Robinson, made up a company, paid him a good bonus, fitted Robinson and themselves out in good shape, and with him went on a "wild-goose chase" three or four hundred miles up into the mountains, and followed him around till they became satisfied that he was bilking them, when they commenced talking, "hang him." The talk became so loud, that he took occasion one fine morning to skip, leaving them to pilot themselves home — sadder but wiser men.

The next heard of Robinson he was in Boston, Mass., where he again placed his specimens on exhibition, and soon raised a large company which advanced him a good bonus and paid his way to Walla Walla. Bach was bound under oath to keep silent as to their mission and purposes. Here they bought a complete outfit for exploring and developing mines, and made their way to the Coeur d'Alenes, where a repetition of the experience of the Walla Walla party awaited them.

Next Robinson turned up at Cincinnati, Ohio, where he worked the same maneuvers that he had in Boston. A large party was formed, a bonus put up, and the location of the mine remained unknown. Robinson again left them and this was the last heard of him.

He was loudly denounced as being a fraud, but since the remarkable discoveries in the Coeur d'Alenes I am inclined to the belief that Robinson was acting in good faith; that he had found a very rich vein of ore near where the rich veins have been discovered during the past three years (for that is the district he led the parties to); that if either of the parties had been more patient, and not so quick to talk "bilk" and "hang," the rich mining-district of Coeur d'Alene would have been developed years ago.

I hardly think that Robinson's rich find has yet been rediscovered, for new lodes are being discovered all the time, and some are very rich. Many instances are known of rich mines having been discovered in the mountains by parties who became bewildered after leaving them, and who subsequently searched for months before they found them again, and in many instances they never have found them.

That the mountains of Oregon, Washington, Idaho and Montana are rich in ores and placers, has been already demonstrated; and it is believed, by those

175

best informed and most capable to judge of such matters, that discoveries have only begun, and the lodes already found have not been prospected sufficiently to give an idea of their richness.

But now that railroads are piercing these mountains, and machinery can be brought in, development will proceed much more rapidly, and in a year or two we will astonish the mining world, for we have all the timber, coal, water and other facilities for working them cheaply.

It has already been proven that richly paying gold and silver lodes exist in the mountains near the Colville river, in Northeastern Washington; ore is already being shipped from there by wagon 80 miles to Spokane, thence by rail 2,000 miles, at great expense, to refining or reduction works, and even then it pays well to work it. Capital and machinery will cause hundreds of lodes to be worked there, where now there are but two or three.

The Okanagon district, near the British line, between the Columbia river and the Cascade mountains, embraces a large scope of country, that has as yet been prospected but very little, yet a large number of rich lodes have been discovered there. West and southwest from there the Cascade range is proven to abound in rich ores, both gold, silver, copper and iron; coal and granite are also found there in large quantities, and several placer mines have been worked for years.

The Coeur d'Alene mountains have proven to be rich in ores, placers, mica, marble, etc., all over, only a few areas as yet being worked, owing to the lack of transportation facilities.

The Blue mountains have also proven to be streaked with ledges for hundreds of miles which will be developed during the next decade, or as soon as moneyed men can get freights at living rates and miners' wages come below $3.50 per day.

The energetic railroad construction now going on, with the hundreds of feeders contemplated, warrant me in the prediction that, within five years, our freight rates will be reduced at least fifty per cent. While it cost $155 per ton to ship a small quartz mill into the Blue mountains from Portland twelve years ago, the same would now cost but about $20 per ton.

The same may be said of what are called the Salmon River mountains, between Snake river and Clearwater, the connecting link between the Blue and the Coeur d'Alene mountains, wherein were made the marvelous discoveries of placer mines in the years 1861-2 and 3. Hundreds of good paying ore veins and placer diggings have been discovered there that will be developed soon, for there are two railroads already headed toward them.

Thousands of acres of placer grounds that will pay from $3 to $6 per day to the man, lie there unmolested because of the cost of living, and the freight rate on the necessary tools, machinery, etc. The best of the ground was worked when wages was from $6 to $15 per day, when flour was worth from 25 cents to $1 a pound; a pair of gum boots were worth $50, and everything else in proportion. And at those rates several men lost their lives or were badly frozen, while coming out on foot late in the fall, carrying their blankets and 20 to 100 pounds of "Salmon River dust" (a by-word originated on account of the dust being poor) to the man, the result of a season's work.

From the south fork of the John Day river to the Snake river, a distance of about 250 miles, along the Blue mountain range, placers were worked out and abandoned under much the same circumstances. Though not at so much cost, and yielding less, but they had to be abandoned when the owners couldn't realize $5 per day to the hands. For everything had to be done by hand as it takes capital to build ditches, flumes, penstocks, hydraulic pipes, etc., when freights rate at $200 per ton from the foundry to the mine.

All along the Columbia river and Snake river Chinamen are working the bars with the primitive shovel, pan and rocker, and making from seventy-five cents to $4 per day to the hand; and with proper machinery these bars could be made to pay handsomely.

Remember I am only hinting at the mining resources of the great Columbia basin (The Inland Empire) that must of necessity pay tribute to the farmer, the stock-raiser, and the fruit-raiser, who is wise enough to locate in this productive and healthy country. Why, the peach-growers along Snake river, so renowned for producing the finest quality of that most delicious fruit, have to watch their orchards to keep the Chinamen from working the ground for gold.

I make these digressions not as a scientist, mining expert, or speculator in mining ground, or "feet," but, having adopted this portion of the United States for my final home (no reference to things spiritual) and knowing whereof I speak, and believing that I may benefit some of my readers by writing a few hints of the advantages this country offers to those who wish to change their location, I just put them in for a change; for it would require an abler party than I and a much larger book than this, to impart any adequate idea of our mining prospects.

Having incidentally mentioned the fact of some of the first miners at Florence having frozen to death, while attempting to reach their homes in the Willamette valley, during what has ever since been mentioned as "the hard winter" ('61 and '62), and having since conversed with a survivor of one of the parties, I deem it proper to write a brief sketch of Moody's story, as told to me:

"My name is W. A. Moody; I was born in Illinois on the 6th day of July, 1831. Am a carpenter and joiner by trade, and have raised a large family. Crossed the plains to Oregon in '52; arriving late, I passed that winter at The Dalles; engaged in building steamboats at Celilo in '53; and moved my family to Portland in '54; in '55 I removed to Corvallis; thence to Brownsville in '56; thence to Eugene City; where I resided ten years.

"Hearing of the remarkable gold discoveries on Salmon river in '61, I determined to try my fortune in those mines, and started for Florence rather late in the season. Failing to reach Florence, I stopped at Walla Walla and built the first flour mill there for H. P. Isaacs. On the 3rd day of January, 1862, the Columbia river being frozen over, I started in company with ten miners, who came just down from Salmon river and were on their way to their homes in the Willamette valley, carrying from twenty to eighty pounds of gold dust each. The stage company had agreed to put us through to The Dalles in two days, but we were five days in reaching the John Days river, forty-five miles from The Dalles. Here we found nine other miners awaiting an opportunity to cross, as the river was so full of ice that the ferry-boat couldn't be run. The snow was three and a half feet deep, on a level all around us. Here we lay for five days, having only nineteen pounds of flour and a beef hide for the whole twenty of us to subsist on. On the sixth day eleven of us, including Wells, Fargo & Co.'s Express messenger, crossed John Days river, in a swing we had constructed and attached to the ferry rope, or cable. Having succeeded in getting over the river, we found it would be impossible to proceed through the deep snow, carrying all the money we had along with us. So Jack James (Wells, Fargo's man) concluded to stop there with another man in a tent, and the most of us left the bulk of our dust with them.

"Being joined by the ferry-man (Pat Davis), we eleven men started at sunrise, on the 13th day of January, to make the journey of forty-five miles on foot, without snow shoes; and while the thermometer ranged from 40 to 50 degrees below zero. Marion Olphin acted as guide, but the snow was so deep that we had to break the trail "turn about." Olphin being short in stature could not break trails at all; and found it so difficult and laborious to keep stride with the rest of the party that he gave out about eight o'clock that night. One Doc Gay and myself, being old friends of Olphin, we assisted him along, till he froze to death. His last words being, 'I could die more contentedly if I only knew that my wife, on Willow creek, had a sack of flour.'

"The ten men remaining formed a circle and, having scraped the snow, away, we wrapped him in my overcoat and laid his remains there on the bare ground, covered them with snow and left him in his snowy sepulchre, alone on the hill, six miles from where we had started eighteen hours before. Slowly and sadly we worked our way along, for about a mile, when we discovered that Pat Davis, the ferry-man was freezing. We assisted him along, as we had Olphin, for about half an hour when he died, and the remaining nine buried him as we had Olphin. Then moved on, being now without a guide, for two or three hours, when Wm. Riddle fell dead and was buried by the remaining eight, as the others had been. Soon after this we became bewildered and lost, but continued to move along till McDonald expired; and was buried by the seven of us left alive. About ten o'clock the next day, a New York man, whose name I have forgotten, was buried by the remaining six who as yet retained their right minds. Next we left one Duffy, who lagged behind and fell; but the other five dared not return to bury him. The next to fall was one Jagger, a son-in-law of R. R. Thompson, of Portland. He was left unburied by the remaining four, about eight miles from the Deschutes river, 23 miles from The

Dalles, on our second night out. Next we left Johnson Mulkey of Benton county, Oregon, about four miles from the Deschutes. He was not yet dead as we moved away from him.

"On the morning of the third day, we left another man dead. Doc Gay and myself came in sight of the house at the Deschutes ferry, which we reached about eleven o'clock, and sent a man back with a mule. He found Mulkey alive, but completely exhausted and sitting on his blanket. He brought him in, but the large amount of gold dust, which he carried in a belt around his waist, had so chilled and irritated that portion of his body that mortification set in, and he died two days afterward. When we arrived at Deschutes, we found Doctors McAteeney and Shields there, who amputated my badly frozen feet at the instep, and gave me such attention as it was possible for them to do. We laid there five days when we were hauled to The Dalles in sleighs belonging to the O. S. N. Co. (now the O. R. & N. Co.) Jagger's body was brought in on a board drawn by a mule. It was frozen stiff and was taken to Portland for interment. James, the express man, came in with the gold dust all right and it was turned over to the relatives of the deceased.

"When we arrived at The Dalles Dr. Dennison, a friend and brother Mason of Gay, gave up his office to his brother and his best friend, and performed many acts of kindness which, I believe, was the main reason that both of our lives were saved; for we suffered terribly for weeks. I was afterward presented with a fine new overcoat by Olphin's brother, to replace the one I had used for a winding-sheet when we placed his dead brother in his grave of snow."

Chapter Twenty-Seven

I bought the warehouses and conducted the business myself for some years. While occupied in this business I took part in several elections.

At one time I received a letter from an old friend, a Democrat (with which party I had been doing my voting), asking me to accept the nomination to represent the Democrats of Columbia county in their territorial convention soon to assemble at Vancouver, and give him my support for his nomination for Delegate to Congress.

In accordance with this friend's request, I attended the county convention. My name was submitted, when a violent Secession Democrat rose to his feet, and in an eloquent speech said, among other things: "Mr. Chairman! George Washington was a Democrat, and that's the kind of a Democrat I am" (slapping himself on the breast). After detonating about that Democrat Washington awhile, he said, "Thomas Jefferson was a Democrat, and that's the kind of a Democrat I am" (again clapping his hand on to his Democratic breast). He then mentioned others, and finally Jeff Davis, "But I am no such a Democrat as is this man Hunter — one day with the Democrats and the next lending his aid to the Republicans" (meaning that I was and had been a strong Union man). After a lengthy and eloquent effort he took his seat, when I arose, only to be rapped down by the chair (the chairman had been a major in the Confederate army during the rebellion, and it was thought they had put up a job to sit down on me). At the sound of the gavel down I went, but up again as quickly. "Bang" came the gavel, and down came I again. This pantomime was repeated several times, and finally I asked: "Mr. Chairman, why do you pound that table so? It certainly has not harmed you." He replied, "I don't want any disturbance in this meeting." I said: "I certainly have not done or said anything that would have a tendency to disturb the peace and harmony of this meeting, as I had not said a word when you sounded the gavel. My standing in the party has been violently assailed by the gentleman, and I demand an opportunity to defend it; and if the chair will not allow me sufficient time to do so, I shall appeal to the house."

Then a cry went up "Go on, Hunter, go on!" "Yes, boys," said I, "it's always go on and never go back with me."

Then addressing the chairman and the gentlemen present, I said, "The gentleman has told you that George Washington was a Democrat, and that was the kind of a Democrat he was. Well, I was glad to hear that the father of his country was a Democrat; but, as I never had any personal acquaintance with that great man, I am not prepared to vouch for the assertion. But I imagine I can almost see the hero as he strove to rally his disheartened militia, at Brandy wine; as he stood in his boat while crossing the frozen Delaware, leading his weary, bleeding-footed soldiers to Valley Forge, with Burgoyne, surrounded by such men as Green, Lee, Lafayette, Tom Paine, and Benedict Arnold; can see him as he finally lay on his death-bed, and can hear him whisper to those near him to catch the dying words of the man that was first in war, first in peace and first in the hearts of his countrymen: 'Guard well the Constitution; remember the Declaration of the Independence of the United States, as it was signed by the fifty-six heroes of the thirteen colonies; and last, but not least, guard well the emblem of the free, and never allow it to be lowered, unless with honor to your homes and your country.'

"The gentleman says, that Jefferson Davis was a Democrat, and that's the kind of a Democrat he is. Well, the first, Washington, fought seven long years to establish the independence of these United States: the other, for four long years, strove to destroy the principles inculcated by Washington, at a cost of thousands of lives and millions of money. While I believe that the South suffered many hardships and was unjustly treated, I don't believe Jefferson Davis was warranted in striving to destroy the best government that the sun ever shone upon. And as I have been twitted of having used a musket to keep the old flag from being disgracefully lowered, I will say, that if my old father of seventy years should so far forget his Democratic teachings as to attempt to tear it down, and trail it in the dust at my feet, I fear that I might forget which one of the Democratic boys I was, and bend my musket over his head.

"If these are not Democratic sentiments, there is not a drop coursing through my veins."

I took my seat and was chosen delegate by acclamation, thereby proving that Washington (Davis!) and your humble servant were all Democrats.

I took five or six proxies from my own and adjacent counties, which caused the office-seekers to recognize my importance.

On my arrival at Vancouver, I underwent the usual amount of "button-holing," and the convention was organized. Two prominent lawyers from the Sound counties (counties along and near Puget Sound, west of the Cascade range of mountains) aspired to the delegateship, and my friend became "shaky," and requested me not to place his name before the convention to have him "slaughtered," for we both well knew that unless we secured some support from the western counties, he could not be nominated.

I told him I didn't think all was yet lost. When a short recess was taken for dinner, I went into a house where the "pure democracy" was dispensed. I met one of the Sound candidates, took him to one side, and held a short conversation with him. I saw that the other candidate from the Sound was watching us closely, whereupon I shook the hand of the one I was talking with, went up and "took something," and started for the hotel.

Shortly I was joined by the other candidate, and asked what the first was talking to me about. I told him, "business matters." He said: "That scrub sha'n't steal a march on me. Now, Hunter, you want Caton nominated, and it will come better for some one from west of the mountains to put his name before the convention, than for one from your own side to do so; and, if you will allow me, I will propose his name and you can second it, and we will down W___." I assured him that if he would do so he would confer a great favor on both Caton and myself, and I would gladly reciprocate, at any time, when called upon.

This being settled, I soon joined my friend Caton, and we went to dinner, when I told him what I had done, and for him to be ready to "spread himself" on receiving the nomination. He was skeptical. But when the meeting was again called to order, the Sound candidate arose and "moved" that the rules be suspended, and that the Honorable N. T. Caton, of Walla Walla, be declared the unanimous choice of the convention for Delegate to Congress. It is needless to say that I seconded the motion in due time. The motion prevailed.

Soon I could see some very dark looks among the Sound members.

I was nominated for Brigadier-General of the Militia (as a reward). I suppose they wanted me elected to this position as there was not a cent in it; and they were in hopes we would soon have a war, and they would have the satisfaction of getting one killed.

That evening, after the convention had adjourned, my friend Caton and myself stepped in to the side door of a billiard room, in which nearly all the members were congratulating each other on the results of the day when the Sound candidate W___ said to the other S___ C___ "You have raised the devil.

You have let that bunch-grass granger come down here and run the whole caboodle of us." As none of them had noticed Caton and myself, up to this time, I stepped forward and asked all hands to take a — (smoke). None had time to refuse; and as the joke was too good, they all acquiesced in the opinion that I would make a royal "Gigadier Brindler" for the Territory of Washington (and I would if there had not been so many Republican votes polled at the ensuing election).

My friend Caton and myself had the pleasure of knowing, after the election, that we were very badly beaten. But we consoled ourselves with the idea that the Republicans had made as great a mistake in electing their candidates as did our convention in making their nominations.

For, whereas, we had been inflicted on the "dear people" only during a two months' campaign, the Republican nominees would hang on two years longer. And meantime we could advocate "reform," and urge the grangers and "sand-loters," to exercise better judgment in the future in casting their votes, and confirming party nomination,, especially the Republicans.

On the evening of election day we were all aware that our county ticket was badly beaten. The editor of the Democratic county paper who had been on the ticket for the school superintendency, took the bits in his teeth, rushed to his sanctum sanctorum and "set up" a flaming Salt river editorial, "To get ahead of the Republican paper," he said. I happened in, and looking over his "proof," I saw a lawyer, Baker by name, mentioned in association with those of the candidates who were defeated; and as I knew the "Judge" had not been a candidate, I supposed it to have been a typographical error, and so informed Mr. Abbott, the editor. "But," said Abbott, "there is the fun in it. When Baker sees that, he will kick like a mule, and after we have had our fun out of him I will change it in the galley!"

Slipping the proof in my pocket I went out as soon as I could, and around to Baker's office, and said to him as I pointed to that sentence, "See, what that old villain has said about you." The "Judge" read it clear through, laughing heartily all the while. When he had finished, I asked, "Why don't you get mad?" "At what," he asked. I said, "Your name is mentioned in that article, and you are not a candidate. "Oh!" said he, "That's all right, I enjoy being in with the boys." Then I told him for what purpose Abbott had put his name in with the others, and asked him if he wasn't a pretty good actor. "Bet your life," said he.

Then we put up a job on Mr. Abbott, I was to have a number of men in the office, to enjoy the fun when Baker would come in as mad as a wet hen, and demand that his name be taken out of that article forthwith. "But," said Baker, "You fellows must keep an eye on the old fellow, for he might try to hurt me, he's not to be fooled with too much." We assured the "Judge" that we would look out for that, and would "gobble" Abbott if our prank worked.

In a few minutes we had a large number of gentlemen present in the office on one pretext or another, when in came the "Judge'" in an apparent frenzy of passion, with the paper in his hand, and, pointing to the piece, said: "Abbott, who authorized you to use my name in that manner?" Abbott attempted to explain, but Baker could out-talk him, and finally he went back into his hip pocket for his supposed pistol, exclaimed in apparent passion, "Take it out, and quickly at that."

Abbott saw the move, turned white, jerked open a drawer and grabbed for a pistol, but quick as his move was, there were some quicker, for four or five of us grabbed him and whirled him around and around the room, while every one present was laughing as loud as they could.

Abbott soon tumbled to the joke and said, "Good, boys come and smile; I have been an editor nearly all my life, but this is the most damnable prank I ever had played on me." Thus ended my "military career" for that time.

About this time another laughable circumstance occurred, the sequel to what came near proving a very serious affair. The major, whom I mentioned as being chairman of the county convention, and an ex-rebel surgeon, known as Doctor Henrahan, got into a dispute, when the doctor broke his cane over the major's head.

The next day the major was sitting by his door with his rifle awaiting the coming along of the doctor. He said he would shoot him. Some of the doctor's friends knowing of the fact, told the doctor, and he sent for me and two others of his friends. After talking the matter over the doctor admitted that they were both under the influence of liquor at the time of the striking, and said he was willing to make reparation to the major; that we could see the major and arrange a meeting between them, either friendly or otherwise, as occasion required. He said he would leave the matter entirely in my hands to arrange for a fight or an apology as I thought best.

We then went to the major and told him he should not shoot the doctor down while the doctor was unarmed, but we would arrange a meeting, and if he chose a friend, I, with the doctor, would meet him and his friend, and if we could not satisfy him with apologies, we would fight it out. This proposition was accepted. He named his friend, and the friend and I selected an undertaker's shop as the place of meeting. The principals were to come unarmed, but the friends should bring revolvers along, and when they failed to settle the matter with words, they could resort to a harsher method. They were both brave men, and had fought their men in former days.

Bringing them together, we seated each upon a coffin, and gave the doctor the first opportunity to speak. He said: "Major, I have none but the kindliest feelings toward you. It was not me that did what was done last evening, it was whisky. I hope you will forgive me, and I will make good any damages which you have sustained at my hands." Williams said: "Doctor, I accept your apology on one consideration: You must bring and give to me the pieces of the cane you broke over my head, and give me your word of honor that you will not carry a cane for a year."

I knew that the doctor would not do this, so I said: "No, major; no brave man would do that. But the doctor will give you his word that he will not carry a cane, for when he is drinking he is too apt to use it. As a friend I should not like to see the doctor play the little-boy act, by carrying these broken pieces of that cane to you. The doctor has made all the amends that I think an honorable man should make under the circumstances."

After thinking awhile the major said he wouldn't shoot the doctor; but his head was too sore to forgive him at the time. He would let the matter drop. And so ended an unpleasantness, which would undoubtedly have culminated in the death of one or both of the parties, had it not been for the interference of friends, who are said to have selected a very appropriate place for the meeting — and it certainly was a grim looking place, with its emblems of death hanging over them and piled all around them, to settle a matter of this kind. N. B. — The doctor stopped carrying a cane.

Chapter Twenty-Eight

The Snake or Bannack War of 1878 I did not take a part in, my attention being wholly occupied at that season of the year in forwarding, and for other reasons to be shown hereafter. But, as I am familiar with many of the incidents of that war, I will give a short sketch of them and as I remember having read or heard them.

It appears that this outbreak occurred on or near the Malheur reservation; those concerned in it were mostly Snake or Bannack Indians (including the renegade bands from which we sixteen miners rescued the beleaguered Rexford families, as told in a previous chapter).

The real cause assigned for the outbreak I am not able to state. The first I learned of it was the news of the killing of some settlers near Malheur in Northeastern Oregon, and the destruction of property. General Howard took the field at once, the Indians retreating westerly across the headwaters of Burnt river and the Blue mountains; thence northerly across the headwaters of the John Days. At the north fork of the John Days river they came upon the first of the numerous flocks of sheep which were being herded on the high hills and mountains during the summer season, killed the herders and mutilated the sheep by cutting off their legs and otherwise maiming them, leaving them to die.

Several others of the first flocks they came to were treated similarly, until they found the sheep too numerous, and the sport became too tame, to satisfy the pampered tastes of the "cultured" red man who had emerged from a hard winter fattened on U. S. grub on a healthy reservation.

Being closely pressed by the troops, the Indians continued northward to Camas prairie (a beautiful valley or basin on the western slope of the Blue mountains near the head of the north fork of John Days river), which had been settled years before by stock-raisers and dairy-men. These having received warning of the approach of the hostiles, had hastily removed their families to places of safety, leaving only a few herders secreted around to look after the stock as much as they could.

At a cheese ranch on this prairie there were a hundred or more cheese in an outbuilding, and quite a number of hogs in a pen, that the owner had not time to turn out. These frisky Snakes coming up, investigated, killed nearly all the hogs, and put cheese under their heads for pillows, thereby furnishing evidence that their favorite food was not pork and cheese, or else were preparing a repast for Uncle Sam's troops who were following them, or probably the Indians' way of telling the troops to "cheese it."

As they moved on through the valley they played many of their clever (?) pranks, such as scattering beans, rice and other provisions, which they had no use for, here and there; ripping open the feather beds and pillows, scattering the down to the four winds of the earth (they left other "downs" to mark their course and progress, for the soldiers following them), taking horses, killing cattle, scattering sheep, killing herders, and similar "innocent pastime."

They had killed several men, and pillaged many houses, burned very few, when, coming to the foot of the western slope of the mountains, their advance came on to a company of forty or fifty stockmen and others who had gathered near Pendleton, on hearing that the Indians might come that way, and were going out to protect their flocks.

This company had stopped to lunch at Willow springs, in a gulch; picketed or tied the most of their horses near some sheds, and, without placing out a guard, were unsuspectingly sitting around a corral eating and resting, when the hostiles came up on the hills surrounding them, and poured a lively fire into them (without first having notified them, officially, that they proposed passing that way that day). Several of the whites were killed, or wounded, before they could get to cover in the sheds, where they were closely beleaguered till dark, when a courier got out, and started for help; and later, the rest of the company came out, bringing their dead and wounded. This is another circumstance which tends to prove that the bravest of men should have with them, and need the advice of some one who knows by experience what might happen in case of negligence, especially in Indian warfare.

The next morning, one Charles Jewel, a prominent stockman of that section, who had also heard of impending danger to his herds of sheep in the mountains, and had started up Butter creek alone, carrying a lot of guns and ammunition to herders, stopped at the house of a friend for breakfast. After breakfast he went out to the stable to resaddle his horses, and his friend went into the garden, when the Indians suddenly fired on them, killing Nelson (the rancher) and wounding Jewel mortally. Supposing they had done their work well, they took the horses and guns, and skipped. Jewel crawled off to the creek and laid in the brush two or three days without food — having crawled to the roadside in the meantime and posted a notice of his condition and whereabouts. A party of settlers finally came along, and seeing the notice, found Jewel, and took him to Pendleton, where he died within a day or two.

The news of the Willow springs fight spread rapidly, and a detachment of soldiers, who were en route to Malheur, were turned off in that direction. They met the hostiles and a lively skirmish took place between them near Willow springs. But the Indians could out-travel the troops over those rough mountains and canyons, so gaining time to form ambuscades for the especial benefit of one and all who followed. After they had given two or three of these free entertainments, they skedaddled, for fresh pastures, leaving the soldiers to bury their dead, and in their haste neglected to leave their addresses for the guidance of those of an inquiring mind, that wished to know where to expect the next bullet (in) bored.

A few renegades from the Ki-use and Umatilla tribes on the Umatilla reservation had joined Chief Eagan's band of hostiles at the first outbreak, and when the advance-guard of the hostiles got so badly split up by the steamboat "Northwest," which General Howard had called into service as a gunboat and blockade-runner on the Columbia and Snake rivers, Eagan changed his course, and went to the Umatilla agency.

About this time some of the marauding squads came on to the main thoroughfare over the Blue mountains, killed some teamsters in the mountains and burned the stage-station at the foot of the mountains; then killed George Coggan, who married a sister of my first wife (Miss Laura Stout) about 1853. Coggan was of English birth. He had not more than a hundred dollars' worth of property when he married, but he soon proved to be a keen trader and, as western men have it, a "rustler," made money fast, and what was better — kept it.

When the mines were discovered in eastern Oregon and Idaho, he came east of the Cascades, bought up some horse-teams at The Dalles and in Walla Walla, and engaged in freighting between Wallula and Walla Walla the first year, and afterward between Umatilla and Boise. While camped near Umatilla on one occasion, the Indians ran off some of his horses. Coggan followed, overtook them and killed one of the thieving red brethren. [The particulars I have forgotten, as they were told to me about the time of the occurrence, but it was freely talked of, and the Indians were very angry about it.] George sold his teams and returned to the Willamette valley, where he wintered with his family.

The next spring he returned east of the mountains, bought up some ox-teams, and commenced freighting from Umatilla to the Boise basin, and continued in this business for several years. In the meantime he removed his family to the Weizer river, near Boise, where he had established a ferry. The family resided there till he sold his ferry and bought a stage-line that ran between Kalama and Olympia. Later he sold this and returned east of the mountains, where he again engaged in staging in the Burnt River country, and in stock-raising. Having some domestic trouble, he separated from his wife, went to Portland, where he became proprietor of the St. Charles Hotel. Here he married an English woman.

In 1878, when the Snakes and Umatillas went on the war-path, Coggan came east of the Cascades to Grand Ronde valley, where he kept his stock (he had some very fine stock — owned the celebrated running horse "Osceola," when he was the fastest horse in the Northwest), returning across the Blue mountains in company with Alf. Bunker, and one or two others. They were attacked by Indians, on the Umatilla reserve. Coggan was killed and Bunker severely wounded. Thus another relative was waylaid, and killed by the Government pets, after amassing a fortune of over $100,000 through his own exertions in the distant West. After toiling for years over rough mountains and alkali plains, through mud, rain and snow, over coming every natural obstacle and amassing a fortune, he is ruthlessly shot down. After the Indians had shot him they piled grass up on his breast and set it on fire, this was probably done while he was dying. Coggan left his English wife a widow in Portland, and his daughter (only child), with his first wife, who had remarried, and resided in eastern Oregon.

Another "rustler" passed over to the majority. His monument stands in Grand Ronde valley, marking the last resting-place of an energetic pioneer cut down in the noon-tide of his success, away from his home and those that he loved; by the hands of — well, I give it up. Can't do the subject justice. I'll leave it, hoping that the great men of State will hear the cry of the widows and orphans of the western pioneers; and grant them a small portion of the annuities and reservations that are so lavishly bestowed upon the murderers of their husbands and fathers, and learn to quote,

"Lo! the poor widows and orphans left homeless behind —
By reservation pets — they in Congress not a friend can find."

A day or two after Coggan was killed, the troops met the Indians just above the Umatilla agency, dislodged them from the brush, and drove them before them on open ground, for nearly a whole day, to the foot of the Blue mountains when the Indians, tired of the amusement, climbed the mountain for a quiet camp. The losses were small.

As before stated, I remained at my warehouses through this last affair, as I was agent for the O. S. N. Co., and many thousand dollars' worth of merchandise belonging to merchants of Dayton, Waitsburg, Pomeroy, and other points, was stored in my warehouse awaiting transportation. Hearing of the movements of the Indians, it was generally believed they would try to cross Snake river, and effect a junction with Moses' tribes of discontented Indians, to the northward, and that they would attempt to cross at my place, at the mouth of Tukanon, that being the crossing of the old Indian trails from Umatilla to the Spokane country. This belief was so strong that the owners of the goods sent me word to bring my family away and let the freight take care of itself. But as I had my wife and an eleven-year-old son besides my tribe (the Palouses) and two cases of needle guns, with plenty of cartridges, I concluded to stay with my warehouses at all hazards.

Big Thunder and others of the Palouse Indians came over and assured me that they would stay with me and help protect my family, in case the hostiles should attack me. Quite a number of the Palouses came and camped near me during the time the hostiles were west of the Blue mountains. Big Thunder kept a large canoe at my place the most of the time. Having told me that if the Bannacks came, he could take my family in his "ca-nim" (canoe), run the rapids below, to the mouth of the Palouse, and hide them in the rocky caverns, where we could whip all that dared attack us.

But General Howard was making it too hot for the hostiles, and finally drove them from place to place till they — like Smelcer's cow, "evaporated," A census of the reservations showed many more lean and lank "wards" than could be found during the "picnic."

And as all could show (?) that they had been out hunting the sportive deer (mow-itch), digging camas, couse, etc., and had met with poor success, they were furnished with a new supply of U. S. blankets, and a few rounds of powder and lead, with which to keep their young men in practice.

I have no evidence that they were furnished with gatling guns. But I have heard the story told, that a certain chief applied to a certain officer, on a certain occasion, for a howitzer. The officer said, "No, can't have it, you want to kill my soldiers with it." "No," said the chief, "No want 'em for soldier. Stick heap good for soldier, want 'em big gun for 'Cow-boy.'"

This outbreak proved most disastrous to the citizens of Umatilla County, Oregon. They were scared away from their homes in the midst of their harvest. Fences were torn down and loose stock destroyed the most of the crops. Much valuable property was stolen or destroyed, and a general stoppage of business for a month or so was the result.

But, unlike Idaho and Washington Territories, Congress granted an appropriation for the benefit of the Oregon sufferers three years ago.

Chapter Twenty-Nine

In 1855, while at The Dalles, in Colonel Kelley's command, I became intimately acquainted with Vic (Victor) Trivett. Vic — as he was known among his friends, and loved to be called — was one of the first printers who came to Oregon. He followed his profession a short time, and then repaired to The Dalles where he located permanently as one of the first settlers in the town; engaged in the liquor trade, or saloon business, and made many warm friends, among whom were Captains Thomas Stump, John Stump, Baughman, Sampson, Gray, McNulty, Wolfe and Van Pelt, of the Columbia river boats; Colonel Wilson, George Allen, Joe Crabb, Jack Vincent, and a host of other early pioneers. I mention the above names because I shall speak of them again in relation to Vic and other matters which came under my personal observation, to illustrate more fully the friendly feeling that existed among the pioneers, no matter what station in life they filled. So deep was this feeling that nothing but death could sever the ties; and after they were, one by one, laid in their graves, their memory remained green in the innermost hearts of the survivors, and their slightest dying requests, though they be ever co odd or whimsical, were carried out or complied with.

I will write, first of Vic, then of the others as I can recall them to memory. Vic was known as the friend of all who needed his aid in poverty or sickness. He was a law-abiding citizen although a saloon-keeper; served in the Oregon legislature through several of its sessions, and filled many other offices of importance and trust, with dignity and honor to himself and his constituents. When he was called on to "pass in his checks" for final adjustment, his great, warm heart, even in this trying moment, could not beat its last throb until he had said to his sorrowing wife and surrounding friends: "Tell Joe Crabb to see that Jack Vincent does not go to the State's prison, and that I am buried on Mima-loose island" (a small island in the Columbia river, a few miles below The Dalles). It is scarcely necessary for me to state that Vic's last wishes were complied with. He died in San Francisco. His remains were brought back to The Dalles, and then by sorrowing friends laid to rest on the island he had selected. A beautiful monument of grey granite, donated by old comrades, was erected to his memory and now stands above his remains in full view of the traveler either by the O. R. & N. Co's railroad or river division, testifying how fully old timers in the West fulfill the dying requests of comrades and friends who have gone before.

Jack Vincent, an old friend of Vic's, had got into trouble and killed a man, which led to one of Vic's requests. Jack was acquitted by a jury of his peers.

Joe Crabb, the other man mentioned, is a sporting-man now residing at Walla Walla. Although a sporting-man, Joe is noted for his gentlemanly comportment, is always ready to assist those who are in need of aid from his friendly purse, and strictly honorable in all his business transactions, a courteous and affable gentleman, a true and warm-hearted friend. His epitaph is yet to be written. May he have an abler pen than mine to record his last wishes.

Captain T. J. Stump, one of the earliest navigators of the Columbia and the rough waters of Snake river, did much toward opening and developing the waters mentioned by causing many improvements to be made on the rapids, and by the cool and daring manner in which he handled his boats while passing through rough rapids and over dangerous falls. He was a man of many attainments. He died while passing through the tortuous channel of dangerous rapids, with his hands firmly grasping the wheel, his long, white beard flowing over his breast, making almost a fitting shroud for the veteran navigator of the difficult waters of the West. But he has left behind him relatives who are worthy of the mantle he left to fall upon their shoulders, who still pilot vessels over the turbulent waters of Oregon and Washington Territory.

Captain John Stump, a brother of Captain T.J. Stump, is a festive youth (?) of some fifty seasons, is a bachelor by trade, and still stands by the wheel — when he is not looking for a young wife; which latter he says he will have if he has to remain in the employ of the O. R. & N. Co. fifty years longer in order to obtain the record necessary in such cases. Captain John is a determined fellow of the good old sort, and I am sure he will "make it."

Captain Van Pelt is yet to be buried on his chosen ground at Celido. I think he will get there in the "sweet bye-and-bye."

Chief Mate Jacob Nalques, the oldest mate on any of the Oregon and Washington waters, and who has devoted forty years of his life to steam-boating on our rivers, says that now, at seventy years of age, he don't think he could carry a 700-pound anchor on board without help. But he is still on deck, and is a good pilot.

Captain Geo. Sampson is the same good fellow that he always was; an able navigator, and a warm-hearted friend. He can tell as good a story as any man in the Northwest. One of his stories I will try to recite here — as it relates to himself and other well-known old timers — as "Samps" tells it:

He, Vic Trivett, French, Stump, Joe ___ and some others had got into the habit of "laying out late o' nights," and (as their wives would have it) indulging in too much "sheep-herders' delight." The ladies finally organized a Good Templars' lodge, and named it "Mt. Hood." This was for the especial benefit of their husbands, and by the blandishments used, they inveigled their unsuspecting better halves into taking the pledge. The captain says all went well for some time; but one evening, on Sampson's returning from a trip up the river, he met Joe on the street, and Joe was "pretty full." On shaking hands, Joe said, "Come, Samps (hic), let's go down to Vic's, and have a drink." "No, Joe," said Samps; "we are Mt. Hooders now." Joe straightened up and asked, "Haven't you taken a drink since then?" "No," said Samps. "Why, you're a (hic) fool," said Joe; "that was (hic) meant for the ladies! Come on!" And "come on" it was. After having "irrigated" "pretty plenty," Joe said, "Come, Samps, let's go to Mt. Hood (hic); it's nomination night!"

"Samps" demurred, as he knew there would be many ladies present, among others their wives; but to Mt. Hood they went. The hall being full, they sat down on the steps in front of the Worthy Chief's station. It was soon declared in order to nominate some one for Worthy Chief. Mrs. F___ received the nomination. Joe started to raise up, but Samps pulled him down. Then Mrs. T___ was nominated for Worthy Vice-Templar. Joe again attempted to get up. Mrs. S___ for Worthy Organist. Again Joe strove to raise, only to be pulled back by Samps. Finally it was declared in order to nominate some one for Worthy Outside Guard. Joe started up again; Samps tried to seat him, but this time it was "no go." He turned to Samps, saying, "Samps (hic), let me alone;" then "Worthy Chief (hic), Brother F___ (hic) has si-faxed around and got his wife nominated for Worthy (hic) Chief. Brother (hic) T___ has fooled around till he got his wife nominated (hic) Worthy Vice-Templar; and here (hic) is Brother Samps, he's si-faxed around till he got his wife in as Wor(hic)thy Organist. I now (hic) nominate my wife Worthy (hic) Outside Guard."

This scene can be better appreciated when I' say that Joe was a fine lawyer, and one of the most wealthy citizens of the city, and that his wife was a most "dressy" and accomplished lady. Samps says this was "their last appearance."

Captain J. W. Troupe who is at this writing, the commodore of the O. R. & N. Co's fleet of magnificent steamboats, which ply the waters of the Columbia and Snake, is a son of one of the first Captains who navigated the rivers of the west. "Captain Jimmie," as his legions of admiring friends designate him, took the wheel at the early age of sixteen; advanced, step by step, as purser, mate and pilot, until at twenty-five he stood in the pilot-house unmatched in his skillful navigation of the turbulent and dangerous waters of the Northwest. His worth has been signally recognized by the companies he has served; not alone because of his brave and careful navigation, but also because of their implicit confidence in his sterling business qualities. He married the eldest daughter of that noble old veteran, Capt. T. J. Stump, mentioned in this chapter, to whom "Capt. Jimmie" attributes much of his success as a navigator. Affable, kind and attentive to those in high and low places alike, Capt. Troupe will never be friendless.

Captain Eph Baughman is another pioneer captain on the waters of the Willamette, Columbia and Snake. He is about fifty-five years old, skillful in his calling, and still has command of the most prominent upper Snake river packet. Captain Baughman is, I am assured, the originator of the style of light draught boats now used on the difficult streams of this coast.

By the way, I must tell one more story of early days. On one occasion I was going to the mines, in company with some other old miners, one of whom was an old sea captain, who is, I believe, still living; so I shall call him Easterbrook for short. He had gained the command of a whaling vessel in his younger days. Leaving his wife and a year-old son at his home away down in Maine, he sailed for the whaling grounds, where he spent two years. He had reached the Sandwich Islands on his return trip, when his owners sold the vessel and cargo, transferring him and his crew to another ship, and ordered him back to the whaling grounds again. He went, and was gone another two years, when, returning with a cargo of bone, ivory and oil, that ship and cargo were sold while he was yet in Pacific waters, and he was ordered home via the isthmus. Arriving at the isthmus, he was ordered to take command of a clipper ship, then lying in port, with a large list of passengers on board, from which the American consul had removed the commander for cruelty to passengers. Captain Easterbrook assumed command, and brought the ship to San Francisco, her destination. This was in 1849. The captain caught the gold fever, and went to the mines, not having seen his family for about five years. "Fickle Fortune" played many pranks with him — as the jade has been prone to do with thousands of other good old timers — yet, from time to time the captain would send sums of money back to his wife and son. The captain was a most jovial comrade, and could tell as good a story as any old salt. He was generous and true, but rather prone to form hasty opinions of those whom chance threw into his company. Withal he was a very sensitive man.

For some unaccountable reason, he took a dislike to me on our first acquaintance, and while he was jovial, free and easy with all the rest of our party, he remained cold and reticent toward me, indicating that he wished no familiarity on my part. As we jogged along day after day, my dislike for him became almost as strong as his was for me. It being spring-time, the small streams were running full, and the roads were muddy. The captain was not the finest equestrian in the world, and some remarks from me about his horsemanship had probably created his coldness on our first acquaintance. So while crossing a swale one day the captain's horse made an awkward flounder and pitched the captain over his head and into the mud. As he was not hurt in the least, all the men except myself were convulsed with laughter. As he scrambled out of the mud I saw him shoot fiery glances at me, but as I was pouty at him, I thought I wouldn't even gratify him by laughing at his mishap. As soon as he saw that I declined to join in the laugh he joined in it himself, and made some droll and quaint remarks about his mud bath.

A day or two afterward I was riding along sidewise with both my feet out of the stirrups. Coming to a muddy slough which was six or eight feet wide, I paid no attention to it or my position in the saddle, because my horse had always waded right through such places; but on this occasion he fooled me some by coming up to the edge of the hole and giving a sudden spring. He cleared the slough all right, but his rider did not — I sat in the middle of the puddle of mud and water, which came up to my neck. Everybody except the captain commenced a roar of laughter. For a moment he looked as solemn as a monk; then he jumped off his horse and came and assisted me out of the mud. Bursting into a hearty laugh, he said: "Buckeye, if you had laughed the other day when I went into the mud, I should have shot you; but as you did not, I resolved not to laugh if you met with a mishap, but this is too rich." And with another hearty outburst he asked, "Why don't you shoot me now to get even?" I said, "Oh, you be ___ blessed."

This tumble and laugh had the effect of reversing matters, and we were soon warm friends. We afterwards met at Shoalwater bay, where the captain had taken a claim and was engaged in oystering. Mischief-makers and tale-tellers had so wrought upon the feelings of his wife in Maine, in the meantime, that she had finally sued for a divorce; but as the captain remitted her money each year, her action wouldn't lie under the laws of that State. The captain having heard of her movement, applied for and obtained a divorce in Washington Territory, and notified her of the fact. Sometime afterwards Mrs. Easterbrook met a gentleman who had been intimately acquainted with the captain, and was conversant with all the circumstances. He told her the whole truth, whereupon she wrote to the captain a very loving explanatory letter, set forth her "bill of particulars," and advised him that if it was his pleasure she would come out to him, as she had plenty of the money that he had sent her, to do so on. A few letters passed between them, when all was made lovely once more, and she started to him, notifying him of the probable date of her arrival at Astoria, so that he might meet her and her son, who was now seventeen years old. The captain told me all about it, and requested me to accompany him. I did so. The first night we stopped with a family that had emigrated from the Isle of Man, consisting of a hale, hearty, gruff old English gentleman, who was considerably given to wit, with his wife and several handsome daughters. The captain had been casting admiring glances at the young ladies, and at the supper table he told the folks that we were on our way to Astoria, where he expected to meet his former wife and marry her over again. The old gentleman exclaimed, "Good idea! Good idea, captain! Heap easier warmin' up cold soup than making new!" This opened merriment for the evening.

We met Mrs. Easterbrook at Astoria, and again, after sixteen eventful years of separation and anxiety, and two divorce suits, the captain had the great, grand, glorious pleasure of again clasping to his manly heart his old, tried and true loving bride, and I am assured that at this writing — a quarter of a century after that second wedding — they are both living happily in their beautiful home on the weather beach, near Shoalwater bay.

This is but one case out of hundreds in which the pioneers of California, Oregon and Washington left loving wives and romping children in happy homes to face the setting sun, toil, privations, danger and bad luck; for years in striving to amass a fortune, cheered only by the hope of again meeting and gladdening the hearts of loved ones left behind, with wealth as well as caresses. Many fell by the wayside, after years of toil, and were laid to rest in unmarked graves, far from the homes they fondly cherished. Some, through adversity, forgot their loved ones far away, and took to drink; some were forgotten by their loved ones; yet others, like the captain, were eventually made happy.

Chapter Thirty

As I said before, I purchased the Grange City warehouse business from the Patrons, or grangers, and pushed the enterprise with the aid of a few friends.

I built six more large warehouses, getting in debt $20,000. A year or so afterward the railroad passed through the property, rendering it entirely worthless as a shipping point; and I have been trying ever since to work myself out of debt. Think I'll do it yet.

I dabbled in politics a little in 1880. I received the Democratic nomination to represent Columbia county in the council of the legislative body of Washington territory, and that fall I was elected to that important position.

I had been nominated years before to represent a county, but I had a great respect for lawmakers then, believed it required a great amount of education, brains, tongue and cheek; and being aware that I possessed only two of these qualifications, (cheek and tongue) at that time, I declined to serve. An old friend — Judge Brisco — urged me to accept the position (or the "chance" to obtain it), saying it would be a good school. He assured me that he thought I would make a good representative, telling me that all I had to do when any one came around me, "log-rolling" or quizzing in regard to any bill, was just to keep my mouth shut and give him a knowing smile, and I would soon be reckoned the smartest man in the legislative body. I told him that the thing I couldn't do was to keep my mouth shut, so I peremptorily refused to represent. As I grew older I presume my cheek became harder, and I had learned to keep my mouth shut sometimes.

So, as before stated, I accepted the nomination, was elected, and subsequently took my seat among the other Honorables.

Nearly all of the other eleven councilmen were learned lawyers, and had represented their constituents and the "dear people" in those legislative halls on previous occasions, and there being only two Democrats besides myself, I didn't expect much help from my fellow-councilmen.

All went well for two weeks, as I remembered Judge Brisco's advice of years before about the smile and shut mouth; and like Senator Nesmith of Oregon, when he first took his seat in Congress, "only wondered how I ever was elected to such a position. After a week or two I commenced wondering how the other fellows got where they were."

When this last thought dawned upon my cloudy brain I had succeeded (by silence) in making a warm friend of the governor of our territory (Newell), who had served as governor of one or more of the older States, and sat in Congress with such men as Clay, Calhoun, Webster, and John Randolph of Roanoke. He was a profound lawyer as well as a skilled physician, so I took advantage of the circumstances and of his ability in several instances. When a prominent bill had been introduced I would converse with him on the subject. Then, when it came before the council for consideration, I would use the knowledge thus gained, *pro* or *con,* to I such good advantage that I was soon dubbed the "war-horse of the council," and was reckoned at least as smart as *any Democrat* on the floor, the governor being the only person who was aware of the source of my "profound legal ability." The governor had told the members of both Houses of the legislative body to walk boldly into his apartments without knocking, whenever they felt inclined to do so (he was a remarkably hospitable gentleman), so, some weeks after I had gained his friendship, I rushed into his office on one occasion with a bill in my hand about which I knew as much as an Indian on the warpath does of charity to those who have fed and clothed him. I was in such haste for fear some other member might drop in and discover the source of my legislative ability, that I had gained the centre of the room before, to my surprise, I saw it was almost full of visitors — both ladies and gentlemen. The governor's two beautiful daughters were acting as his private secretaries. When my buzzard eyes took in the situation I commenced to back out, apologizing at the same time for having made such a rude entrance. But the governor promptly asked, "Colonel, anything I can do for you?" I replied that there was, but I would call at a more seasonable hour when he was less engaged. "Come right in," said he. "These people don't amount to anything, they are only callers." He then introduced me all around, and having ascertained my dilemma, stepped across the room, took down a law volume, opened it, and pointing to a section, said, "That is what you want to look at." I took the volume, and tucking it under my arm in the most learned and approved manner I was capable of assuming, was about to retire from their presence, when the governor asked, "Can't those fellows get along without you for a short time?" "Yes," I replied, "better without than with me!" "Then come here and be seated," said he; "I want to ask you a question or two if you can spare the time to answer them;" "All right," I said, as I seated myself. He then asked, "Colonel, how happened it that you ever got to the capitol as a councilman." I asked if he would keep it a secret if I should tell him. He said he would, and that he would also vouch for all present, *even the ladies;* whereupon I told them that up to the time of the Democrats meeting in convention at Dayton no one had ever thought of such a thing as sending me to the legislature; but just as we had perfected our organization we received a telegram advising us that Judge Hoover, a prominent Democrat and a profound lawyer, had received the Democratic nomination for councilman for Whitman county, which joined Columbia county on the east; and we knew he would be elected. While we were rejoicing over this news, another telegram was received that the Democrats of Walla Walla county (adjoining Columbia on the west) had nominated Judge Sharpstein, one of the foremost and most eloquent lawyers in the territory for their councilman, and we were sure of his election; hence, more rejoicing. Then the question went the round, "What is there left for Columbia county to do? We have wisdom in the east and strength in the west."

Finally, it struck all that there was nothing for us to do but to beautify and adorn the council. I being the only handsome man in the county, every Democratic eye was fixed on me, and I received the unanimous Democratic nomination, in which over two hundred Republican voters concurred on election day. We now stood in the council as the three pillars of Democracy — Wisdom, Strength and Beauty, or Hoover, Sharpstein and Hunter.

The governor then asked how I had maintained my position since my arriving at the capitol. Pointing to his daughters, I said: "Governor, I refer the question." The ladies declared I was the most handsome man who had ever come from the "Bunch-grass country" (east of the Cascade mountains), but would hardly average with the "clam diggers" of the Sound for beauty.

This — coming from the ladies — I was compelled to accept, but I have ever since felt that they were prejudiced in favor of "home production."

On the whole I guess I did very well as a councilman. I could eat as many oysters, clams and scale-fish as any other member; visited all parts of the Sound country (at the expense of the territory); sustained my record for beauty; and, finally, became useful to the other members as a scape-goat; for, on returning home, if any measure had become a law that was unsatisfactory to any of their constituents or others of diversified interests, "It was all Hunter's fault; *I* didn't want it passed!"

So much was said to me and about me, that soon after my return home I was tendered two public receptions, as it was fast becoming patent to the average granger that I must have passed about all of the bills that became laws at that session. Yet, I believe that I am safe in saying that, as a whole, we were an average legislative body. We visited all the places of public resort, such as the penitentiary, insane asylum, Seattle, New Tacoma and Vancouver; in fact, went everywhere we could get a free ride to (most of us were broke).

We found the people affable and kind, as nearly every man we met had "an ax to grind" on our machine.

We made a very pleasant trip down the Sound on the O. R. & N. Co's fine steamer "Geo. B. Starr," commanded by the genial Commodore Wilson. On this trip the chief clerk of the House of Representatives accompanied us. Burk was his name. Among his many other avocations and callings was that of newspaper reporter. He is now acting as my amanuensis, and I must tell the following story mildly, or I fear he will cross it out. Burk was a great hand to be peeking around and sticking his nose into other people's business in search of items. I, knowing Burk's "weakness," and expecting he would soon visit the engine-room, put up a job on him which created some little merriment at the time. Having given the cue to the captain and some of my fellow-members, I slipped away from the rest, and going to the engineer, asked him if he had a man in his crew who could carry his part of a joke without laughing, explaining the prank I wished to play. The engineer referred me to an Irish deck-hand whom I thoroughly posted, and handed him something to treat his mates with, Pat saying, "Bedad, an' it's mesel' that'll fix 'im, shure!" Pat was installed as engineer *pro tem.*, and Burk soon made his appearance, the rest of ns following to take in the fun. True to his instinct Burk picked up a tool and was about to ask some question, when Pat, who seemed busily wiping some part of the machinery, quietly took the tool out of his hand. Burk gave him a peculiar look, but soon had hold of some other article. Pat as quickly took that out of his hand, and received a still more peculiar look. This performance was repeated several times, and until Burk ebulliated, saying, "What do you mean, sir?" "Bedad," says Pat, "it's mesel' that's not loikin' the looks av yes at all, at all; an' yes better be makin' thracks out o' this!" Burk was "all broke up" for a moment, but on looking around he espied me standing behind a screen laughing, and he "came for me." Well, they sold "refreshments" on the upper deck.

* * * * * * * *

[Right here occurred a halt in the writing of this book, as Burk persisted in writing what he thought were some "good yarns" on me, and I persisted in tearing them up.]

Returning from law-making, I resumed my forwarding and storage business. About this time the O. R. & N. Co. built a railroad right through my place (Grange City), and on its completion my property was rendered valueless, and I was left a total wreck financially.

The O. R. & N. Co. made me their agent for Starbuck and Grange City at a salary of one hundred dollars per month, which position I held for two years. Finally I became so rich, and the company so poor, that my services were dispensed with, as they seemed to be able to get men to do the work for nothing and board themselves. My health being good, I didn't begrudge my successor his situation at the salary.

While I was acting as agent at Starbuck, my wife engaged in the chicken business to assist me and the babies in ekeing out an existence. She did well for awhile, but one morning about three o'clock I was suddenly awakened by a shock in the pit of my stomach, which I was soon aware had been caused by a collision with Mrs. H's delicate pedal extremities; and at the same time my ears were saluted with "George, get up, something is catching all my chickens." Jumping out of bed and rushing to the hennery in undress uniform, I saw something bobbing around among the frantic poultry. To grasp a club and make war on the invader was the act of just two seconds. One lusty blow settled it — with me — I reeled toward the house, holding on to the soles of my feet, for my stomach seemed to permeate my lower extremities, and my whole physical system seemed inclined to reverse matters.

Reaching the house, Mrs. H screamed, as she slammed the door in my face, "Don't come in here." She then got a tub of water, a keg of soft soap, a scrubbing brush and a change of such clothing as I generally have on when the educated folks say I am "*en déshabillé*" and set them all out to leeward. Then she went in search of perfumery (carbolic acid, ammonia, chloride of lime and asafoetida. She said our homeophatic family physician had once observed in her hearing that "like cures like, or kills." I answered without any rhetorical effort as I submerged myself in that cold soap and water, that a little more of the "like" I had got in the hen-house would kill anything. The fact is, I had come in contact with the business end of that skunk. After wearing out the soap, water and brush, I took a cologne bath and retired on a lounge that had been prepared for me by loving hands in a remote corner of the wood shed.

The next day, while attending to the business of my office at Starbuck, the train came in and stopped for a few moments. I was out on the platform checking freight, when a very dressy gentleman stepped up to me and asked if I was agent at that place. I answered, "Yes." "What wages do you get?" he asked. "A hundred a month," I replied. "You are very foolish for working so cheap," he observed. I said I couldn't do any better. "Yes, you can," said he, "if you will go with me to Frisco, I will give you $500 a month to work for me."

This sudden proposition checked my work, and I was about to propose the immediate construction of articles of agreement, when I happened to inquire in what way he would expect me to earn such a salary. He smilingly replied that he was a manufacturing chemist, and he wanted me to stand on the sidewalk in front of his warerooms to indicate to the public that perfumery could be purchased within by the cargo. I mentioned a place that he could go to, and went on checking freight.

When the next train arrived, a woman stuck her head out of a car window and remarked, "Whe-e-ew, what smells so?" I said "Mecca is just four miles below here, and you probably smell the dead."

It is perhaps proper to state that there are some wags among the North-western railway conductors, some of that class ran on this particular road, and having heard of my odoriferous adventure among the fowls, they were no doubt whetting their wits at my expense.

When I forfeited my situation as agent (as before stated), I traded for a ho-tel at Riparia. It was soon manifest that I was a "clever fellow," but I couldn't run a hotel worth a cent. So I allowed my wife to landlord it, and I went East with a few car-loads of horses.

While stopping a few days in Dakota I was induced by a few newly made friends to speak a little piece (they called it a lecture) about the resources and advantages of the Northwest corner of the Union. I did the same act in Minnesota afterward, and then — as fortune has for years proved unkind to me — I found myself in a condition to write such a book as this. Now, I fear, I am fitted to go on a lecturing tour. I have all to gain and nothing to lose, for, in the classical words of the poet, "I am busted."

The reader can, perhaps, form a faint idea of the trials, troubles, vexations and "cussativeness" that an unlettered old timer who has picked up all he knows, is compelled to undergo, overcome or wade through in trying to write a book, when he has an educated, red-headed galoot of a newspaper reporter, an ex-clerk of the District Court, ex-clerk of the Probate Court, ex-county auditor, ex-U. S. commissioner, ex-notary public, ex-commissioner of deeds, land agent, broker, collector, conveyancer, insurance agent, auc-tioneer, accountant and commission-man (I got all these big words off one of his old business cards, and put in the "ex's" myself); he is a western-raised nondescript; has been a chief clerk in the legislature, a painter, a carpenter and wood-sawyer; a packer, a stage-driver and a teamster; a merchant, a clerk and a cow-boy; a miner, a vaquero and a school-teacher; can talk a little Latin, Greek, Spanish, Nez Perce, Ki-use and Chinook (and *little* English). He is, or has been, sometimes called a "one-horse lawyer;" has had a "whole pas-sel" of money, lands, mills, horses, town lots, and I don't know what else. But he is now down to my level; he is "busted." He — the fellow above partially described — is now my a — am — well, he spells it a-m-a-n-u-e-n-s-i-s. As I was going to say, the reader will, I hope, sympathize with me, and excuse and exonerate me for anything in these pages that may appear like a strain on the mental faculties; for every time I have left him he has managed to ring some of his big words in on me, and transpose my sentences. When I have demurred, he talked about "grammatical construction," "orthography," and other things which I never saw running wild in the Northwest. Here is an illustration:

"George, let me write up a description of a pack-train, for the benefit of your eastern readers who never saw one."

"Well, go on, Burk; you maybe better at telling my story than I am myself."

* * *

"George, how is this for a starter: 'The pack-trains — of which frequent mention has been made in these pages — were principally composed of mules, bronchos and cayuses, caparisoned with aparajos, hackamores, coronies and cruppers.'"

"Well, I should sneeze; 'how is it?' Because you have served in every capacity in packing — as bell-boy, cook, *savinaro, chinkadero* and *cargadero* — do you suppose those civilized eastern folks can understand all that stuff? Climb down a few stories. Come down! Come down!!"

"Well, how is this, then. 'Gentle reader, I will now endeavor to portray to your mind the muleativeness, trailativeness, and ___'"

"Stop her! Lower your kite. Talk United States."

"Well, I'll try you with another mess. 'As the visitor to these sylvan shores to-day sits in his luxuriant palace car, quaffing the incense ___'"

"That settles it. 'What's a mule got to do with a Pullman car? What 'sylvan visitor' was ever incensed by quaffing at a ten-gallon keg that was lashed on to a mule's back?"

"But, George, you old fossils, when writing, never take into consideration the verbiage, grammatical construction, orthography and punctuation necessary to impart smoothness to your sentences, and ___"

"That's it. When I won't let you write those eleven-dollar words in my book you'll try to knock me out with your mouth. A pack-train was your subject. Go for the mules, and let ___"

"But to the Eastern reader it is necessary to be somewhat explanatory of phrases."

"Well let them come out here and live in a good country once, and they'll 'tumble' to the phrases."

[Tableau].

A Supplemental Chapter

A Few Hints about the Northwest — Its Resources and Attractions

The reader has probably concluded that it would require more and larger reference sheets, to keep me from "scattering," than it used to Artemus Ward — the renowned humorist; and as he lectured on every subject but the one he advertised ("Babes in the Woods"), I maybe accused of writing of everything but the *memories of an old timer,* thereby furnishing additional evidence of the truth of the old adage, "we are all true to our instincts."

Now, I will frankly say that I would destroy and re-write the preceding chapters but for the fear of getting them worse mixed than ever. So I shall trust to luck — an old timer's main-stay — and the charity of the public. In the language of "A. Ward" when he was solicited to visit the towns of Virginia and Nevada, in Montana, at the time the vigilantes were hanging roughs — "I won't; be hanged if I do."

But I must add a brief pen-sketch of the country of which I have necessarily made mention in my stories, commencing with northern California. My description must necessarily be brief, as it would require several volumes of this size to partly describe the country with all its beauties, scenery, wealth and other attractions.

Northern California is bisected longitudinally by two parallel chains of mountains, out of which flow numerous beautiful streams of water, along the most of which have been rich placer and quartz-mines. The broad bottoms or valleys are remarkable for their fertility, and have for years been utilized for gardens, orchards and vineyards. The mountains are covered with valuable timber.

Shasta, the northernmost valley in the State, is perhaps fifty miles long by forty in width; and what was deemed a plain unfit for cultivation at the time of which I wrote in previous chapters, has proved to be the most valuable agricultural land.

That portion of northern California lying east of the Sierra Nevada mountains — which are a continuation of the Cascade range of Oregon — was then considered valueless; but it also has proved to be valuable both for farming and grazing purposes. The climate is mild and health-giving.

Passing northward across the Siskiyou mountains — a spur which runs at right angles with the Cascades and Sierra Nevadas — you find yourself in the beautiful Rogue River valley in Oregon, which nestles among high hills and mountains west of the main Cascade range, and is drained by the beautiful mountain-stream of that name. The mountains and hills are covered with a beautiful growth of pine, fir, laurel and oak timber, while the numerous streams and rivulets flowing out of them are teeming with trout and salmon. A more beautiful and healthful spot than this valley — which is perhaps eighty miles long and from fifteen to forty miles in width — could not be found in any country. All of the mountains named abound in game, such as deer, elk, bear and smaller animals, and were the favorite roving-grounds of the grizzly, who is still often met in his rounds. For a minute description of this lovely and fertile valley, as well as some others I shall mention, I must refer the reader to books especially devoted to them, which are far more descriptive than I could possibly be.

Continuing northward, we cross Jump-off-Jo, Grave creek, Crab creek and Cow creek, with their small valleys and heavily timbered hills; all fertile when cleared; and all of which have been developed more or less since the removal of the Indians. They are fast becoming noted for their beauty, as they always were for healthfulness.

Next we come to the south and north Umpqua's, with their many tributary valleys of beauty and fertility. Then, having crossed the Umpqua or Calipooia mountains, we are in the south or upper end of the far-famed Willamette valley, of which so much has been written by ready writers that I fear any attempt of mine to describe it would be a waste of raw material. Suffice it to say that this whole stretch of country for a distance of five hundred miles, between the Cascade and Coast ranges of mountains, is fast assuming the appearance of the Atlantic and Northern States, in an agricultural and manufacturing sense; though of manufactories a great many more are needed in every section of the Northwest.

By the time this work is published the California & Oregon Railroad will have been completed clear through the stretch of country named, while there are two others funning parallel with it through the Willamette valley; and one transversely from Yaquina Bay easterly across the Cascade mountains, to connect with the Union Pacific, is already completed across the valley, and will, it is expected, reach eastern Oregon during the year. The Willamette valley being the oldest settled portion of the Northwest, the development and improvement is not so rapid just now as in other portions of the country. The many cities and towns, of course, show much progress and substantial growth; while an increased acreage of products, with a corresponding addition to the number of residences, are the most noticeable features in the staid and complacent country surrounding them. The land is very productive, and is held at comparatively low rates.

Crossing the Cascade range of mountains, we enter eastern Oregon, some portions of which I have partially described in this book. It is generally similar to northeastern California, though of course the climate is colder as we go northward. The Blue mountains, with their many spurs, divide eastern Oregon into numerous sections, each comprised of level and rolling prairie of remarkable fertility, skirted and dotted with high hills and timbered mountains which are unsurpassed in the world for grazing purposes. Cool, clear springs and rapidly running trout streams are prominent features, as are also the healthfulness of climate, the mild winters and cool summer nights.

Development has only commenced there. Manufactories of all kinds are needed; and a man can prosper in any vocation he may choose. The price of land is low, and there is much government land still vacant.

What I say of eastern Oregon equally applies to southern and western Idaho, except that the soil is lighter in the valleys, and for the most part requires irrigation to make it produce well.

Crossing the Columbia river, which for three hundred miles forms the boundary line between Oregon and Washington, we find, west of the Cascade mountains, the "Sound country," so called from Puget Sound, the majestic, placid inland sea, whose waters, navigable for all craft, have three thousand miles of shore line in this territory, and abound with fish of every description, both shell and scale, prominent among which are the salmon, rock-cod, smelt, herring, sardine, flounder, oyster and clam. Ships of the deepest draught anchor within fifty feet of any portion of the shore, along which are located the thriving, prosperous and beautiful cities of Seattle, Tacoma, Olympia, Steilacoom, and many smaller towns. The bottoms and valleys along the numerous streams that flow into this many-armed inland sea are mostly "beaver-dam" lands, and are celebrated the world over for producing enormous crops of grain, vegetables, fruit and hops; of the latter the Sound country is becoming the leader of the continent in the amount and excellence of quality of its output. The dense growth of gigantic fir, spruce, cedar, and other fine working and durable timber that covers the millions of acres of hill and mountain land, is being cut and hauled to the water's edge, from which they are floated to numberless mills of immense capacity that dot the shores, where it is made into lumber, which finds a market in every land and clime. It is the grandest lumbering country in the world, and the supply of timber being almost inexhaustable, it will furnish work for multiplied thousands of men for centuries to come, as the manufacturing interests are as yet in their infancy.

These same mountains and hills are underlaid with thousands of veins of the best quality of coal, several of which are being worked, and the output is enormous — iron, lime and building stone also exist there in large, quantities, and are as yet scarcely developed.

A casual consideration of the safe anchorage for all the navies and merchant marine of the world, at one time, in connection with the wonderful productiveness of soil, the everlasting supply of timber, coal, iron, stone and fish, coupled with the beauty and healthfulness of the climate, can but convince any one of the fact that the "Sound country" is soon to outrank in exportation any other section in the world.

The most of the lands contiguous to the shores and larger streams have been entered, and are held at reasonable figures; but there are millions of acres of very valuable timber and coal land still unclaimed and open to settlement.

That portion of Washington Territory which lies east of the Cascade range of mountains, and between the Oregon line and British Columbia, is sometimes designated as the "Columbia basin," or a part of the "Inland Empire," and embraces the Walla Walla, Yakima, Spokane, Palouse, Colville and Okanogan countries or sections, mention of which is made in different chapters of this book; like eastern Oregon, its makeup is of valleys, rolling prairies, hills, mountains and streams. The land as a rule is richer, and affords a greater area for fine easy tillage than does eastern Oregon. Cereals, fruits and vegetables of nearly every kind and description grow to perfection.

In this country we only had a month of severe weather during the past winter, and the thermometer was not as low as zero at any time. Cattle and horses wintered on the range, for the most part without any feed, and the loss was not to exceed five per cent on an average.

Of the Walla Walla section, I have perhaps given an intimation. Of the great Palouse country I might write a whole chapter; but will only say that it is a rolling, alluvial soil, easily worked, well watered, very rich, and sparcely settled.

The Spokane, Colville, and Okanogan sections are more mountainous, and better adapted to stock-raising.

Yakima and Kittitas valleys, on the Yakima river, are proving wonderful producers, though there the soil requires irrigation, which is done at little expense. The hills around these valleys afford range inexhaustible; and there are raised more cattle than in any other section on the North Pacific slope.

What is becoming known as the "Big Bend country," near the geographical centre of eastern Washington, is now attracting the attention of hundreds of settlers, and bids fair to become one of the most prominent sections named.

But there are homes for thousands in each of the sections named. The most valuable lands, near the towns and main thoroughfares, have, of course, been entered, and are held at from $5 to $50 per acre, owing to location and improvements; but in more remote parts the emigrant has no trouble in finding good vacant government and railroad lands at $2.50 to $4 per acre, for, as I have remarked in several chapters, this country is just being developed.

Speaking generally, I will say that the lately organized and planned railroad system is destined within a few years to develop and bring to the notice of the world the country of which I have written, as being a country of grander proportions, more varied scenery, more boundless resources, and affording more rare opportunities to the man who can control a few thousand dollars, than does any other known portion of the globe. Schools and churches flourish in every settlement; academies and colleges are found in all the towns of any considerable size; our laws are just, and are scrupulously executed; our taxes are low; our society compares favorably with that of old states. We are young, vigorous and healthy, with an assured future of wealth and happiness before us.

Three grand transcontinental thoroughfares are open for your travel, ease and comfort, at a trifling expense, by either of which you can in a week's time visit this land of promise. The system of feeders and cross-roads — tapping the grand agricultural, mining and stock-growing sections — which are now being constructed, will afford you an opportunity to see for yourselves. The main lines, as a rule, follow the margins of streams or run through gulches, thereby affording the through tourist a very meagre view of the grand surroundings.

The Northern Pacific and the Union Pacific systems of roads will either of them bring you from the East right into the heart of the country I have mentioned; and once here you will find no difficulty or hardship in visiting any portion of it, or finding good opportunities for any and every vocation you may elect to follow.

In conclusion, I will say that if I have succeeded in this, my effort at bookwriting, in amusing you for a few hours, or imparting any useful information, and have received the price of the book, you may rest assured that I have realized my hopes, and that you have made an old pioneer of this grand Northwest happy; for, remember, that "it takes money to make the mare trot."

In the language of my tribe, "Nika cup-it" — *I have finished.*

www.ingramcontent.com/pod-product-compliance
Lightning Source LLC
La Vergne TN
LVHW091253080426
835510LV00007B/239